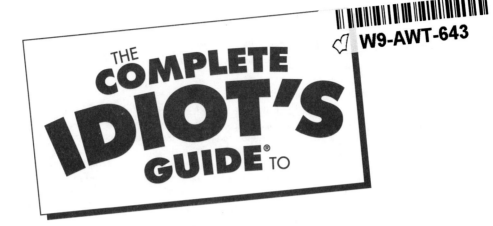

Interpreting Your Dreams

Second Edition

by Marci Pliskin, CSW, ACSW and Shari L. Just, Ph.D.

Revised with Deborah S. Romaine

ALPHA

A member of Penguin Group (USA) Inc.

For Gloria and, as always, for Art.—SJ
For Renee.—MP

Publisher: *Marie Butler-Knight*
Product Manager: *Phil Kitchel*
Senior Managing Editor: *Jennifer Chisholm*
Acquisitions Editor: *Randy Ladenheim-Gil*
Book Producer: *Lee Ann Chearney/Amaranth Illuminare*
Development Editor: *Ginny Bess Munroe*
Production Editor: *Megan Douglass*
Copy Editor: *Keith Cline*
Illustrator: *Chris Eliopoulos*
Cover/Book Designer: *Trina Wurst*
Indexer: *Angie Bess*
Layout/Proofreading: *John Etchison, Rebecca Harmon*

Contents at a Glance

Contents

Foreword

Is there anything more fun than a dream in which you're soaring through the air, arms outspread like the wings of a giant bird, freed at last from the bonds of Earth? On the other hand, what's more frightening than a dream in which you're being pursued by a monster and your feet are stuck in deep, deep muck?

Dreams. They fascinate us with their themes and tantalize us with their mystery. Where do they come from? What do they mean? Are they accurate reflections of our inner world? Do they have special meaning for us, giving us hints as to what action we should take or which path we should follow? Are they a preview of things to come, or glimpses of a life already lived in a distant place and a different time?

Not long ago, I was at a crossroads in my life. I had a successful business giving intuitive readings to people from all walks of life and from all parts of the world. I was writing articles, making speeches, giving interviews, communicating what I knew about the life-enhancing effects of living a consciously spiritual life. People from everywhere were sending me letters, telling me how much they appreciated my message and how I was helping them create better lives.

But I wanted to do more. Though I felt blessed by my ability to touch so many lives in such positive ways, I wanted to extend my reach even further. And so I asked for a dream. I am not a newcomer to seeking solutions in this way. As a young girl, long before I became fully aware of my inherited intuitive gifts, I learned that dreams can provide invaluable support for a healthy "awake" life.

The technique I developed that works best for me is simple. Before going to bed, I write a few paragraphs about whatever it is that concerns me. Then I summarize that concern into a question and imagine that I'm releasing it to a higher power. The question I asked was, "What next step should I take in my work?" In the introduction to my book, *Divine Intuition*, this is how I described the dream I received:

"I am being led down a corridor by two golden angels. I ask them where we are going. They inform me that they are taking me to a class about 'what God wants you to do.' I tell them that I am very excited about this class. I have been praying about this for a long time. I thank them for accompanying me. We reach the classroom door. One angel points to the workshop sign on the door. The title of the class is printed on it. It says, 'Directions From God.' The other angel begins to gently shake me. She says, 'Wake up now and write that down. That's the subject for your next book.'"

And so it was. *Divine Intuition: Your Guide to Creating a Life You Love* was written as a direct result of the information contained in that dream. It's been printed and reprinted in several languages since its publication in 2001, and has confirmed for me in a dramatic way my belief that dreams are a vital component of creating a life you love.

As you can see, dreams can have a powerful and positive influence, and if you're at all interested in accessing that power, you've come to the right place. Authors Marci Pliskin and Shari Just have composed a rich and fascinating book on all aspects of dreams, their meanings, and how they relate to your world. If you haven't been here before, you'll find this second edition of *The Complete Idiot's Guide to Interpreting Your Dreams* a treasure chest of stories, anecdotes, examples, and exercises, carefully crafted to lead you in a fun yet practical way to an understanding of your dreams, and by extension, your life.

A few years ago, the publishers of this series produced a popular book titled *The Complete Idiot's Guide to Psychic Awareness*, now going into its second edition. I was a co-author, and I wrote then that dreams are a gift from your intuition that can lead to important insights about your life. *The Complete Idiot's Guide to Interpreting Your Dreams* will show you how to achieve those insights. As you travel through its pages I wish you a wonderful journey of discovery. Happy reading … and pleasant dreams!

Lynn Robinson, M.Ed., is one of the nation's leading experts on the topic of intuition. Her most recent books include *Compass of the Soul: 52 Ways Intuition Can Guide You to the Life of Your Dreams* (Andrews McMeel, 2003), *Divine Intuition: Your Guide to Creating a Life You Love* (DK Books, 2001), and *The Complete Idiot's Guide to Psychic Awareness, Second Edition* (Alpha Books, 2003). Lynn is a popular and widely recognized author and motivational speaker, as well as a columnist and the Intuition-At-Work Expert for iVillage.com. Her free monthly "Intuition Newsletter" is available at her website, www.LynnRobinson.com.

Introduction

We can be certain of very few things in life. Aside from death and taxes, it seems one of the only things we can bank on is that we have dreams. The sleeping kind.

Some of us remember them; some of us don't. But if you're looking at this book, we bet you want to remember and understand what your dreams tell you about *you*.

As we wrote this book, we found that our interest in and understanding of dreams deepened. As practicing psychotherapists with many years of experience between us, we came to this project with the idea that dreams express our wishes, thoughts, fears, and desires—but often in unusual or unexpected ways!

In our work as therapists, we continually learn that each one of us comes to understand ourselves in our own way and according to our own timetable. This is true for accessing and deciphering our dreams, too. You might find that you remember many dreams each night and can easily see what issues they contain. Or you might warm up to your own dreams slowly. You might decide to skip the chapter on nightmares for a while. Then again, that might be the first page you flip to!

There's no right or wrong way to explore your dreams. They are your creation and only you can know what pace and direction feels right. That's why we've presented a real soup-to-nuts look at dreaming. We wanted to include a varied look at how different people think about this biological, spiritual, and/or emotional activity.

We had fun discovering how other cultures look at dreams, and how some folks imagine that their dreams take them on out-of-body journeys. Our friends and family provided us with many interesting opinions and dreams. We were constantly amazed at the high level of interest virtually everyone expressed in this project. News that we were working on this book was almost always met with, "Gee, that's great. I had the most bizarre dream last night. It went like this …."

But perhaps the most rewarding thing about writing this book was knowing that we'd be providing people with information and tools that could help them understand themselves better and grow from that knowledge.

What You Will Learn in This Book

We've divided *The Complete Idiot's Guide to Interpreting Your Dreams, Second Edition*, into six sections, each of which explores a different aspect of dreams. At the center of each chapter, however, is the basic message that your dreams are your creation, and you are in charge of exploring them or not. Here's what you'll find:

Part 1, "What Are Dreams?" explores some important basics: your awareness of when you dream, how other peoples and cultures have viewed dreams throughout the ages, and what scientists have discovered about the biology of sleep. Throughout this part, we use self-tests and suggestions to help you identify what might be inhibiting you from remembering your dreams or clouding your sleep.

Part 2, "What Are You Dreaming About?" helps you classify your dream images and dream themes. We take a close look at some common dream experiences such as falling, flying, losing money, being chased, having sex with a stranger or famous person, and showing up for a big exam unprepared. We provide exercises and dream worksheets to help you clarify what you're dreaming about.

Part 3, "Decoding Your Dreams," takes a long, hard look at nightmares and how we can reduce the fear factor in them. We also try to understand the puns, jokes, colors, and images in our dreams. Dream exercises will help you begin to figure out such things as what common colors pop up in your dreams, what they tend to signify, and why.

Part 4, "Dreaming Through the Life Cycle," takes a look at what we might be dreaming about—and how well we may or may not be sleeping—at different points in our lives. Have you ever wondered what your baby is dreaming about or how to get your little one through his nightmares? Why is it that Grandpa is nodding off at 6 P.M. but wide awake at 4 A.M.? This section looks at human development from a biological and emotional perspective and how this convergence might express itself in our dreams.

Part 5, "Dreams and Clairvoyance," takes a walk on the wild side. ESP, out-of-body experiences, clairvoyance, reincarnation, and dreaming of our departed loved ones occupy our attention. We also explain how you can program your dreams, how you can "be awake" while dreaming. This is called lucid dreaming, and we give you tips on how to begin to do this.

Part 6, "Recalling and Recording Your Dreams," puts everything you've learned into action. We teach you how to keep your own dream journal and how to use it. You will learn how to get your dreams to help you. This is your chance to find the transforming power of your own dreams! We also take a look at the creativity in dreams and help you access your own.

Extras

In addition to these six sections, you'll find that every chapter contains margin note and sidebar boxes designed to broaden and deepen your understanding of dreams and sleep. These boxes contain interesting tidbits that are sure to catch your eye. Here's what you'll see:

Life Is But a Dream

In these boxes, we provide you with fun and unusual facts about sleep and dreams.

Dreamy

In these boxes, we tell you about famous dreams or dream studies.

Dream Dictionary

Whenever we introduce an interesting or obscure term, we define it in one of these boxes.

Wake Up!

The information in these boxes alerts you to pitfalls you might encounter as you learn about your dreams.

Dreamwork

These boxes contain interesting tips that relate to helping you understand your dreams.

Acknowledgments

There are many people we would like to thank for helping us with this book.

Shari sends a special thank you to people she has worked with over the years who shared their dreams with her and taught her as much or more than she taught them, friends and family who are supportive and most tolerant of her writing efforts. She is grateful for the unfailing support of her children and their spouses: Robin and Mike, Tom and Leslie, and Chris and Jamie. Special thanks go to Dr. Sam Roll for his belief in her when she was negotiating deserts of darkness, and to Dr. Marya Barey for her singular love and inspiration. And most of all, she thanks her husband, Art, who continues to make all her dreams come true.

Marci would like to thank her family and friends, whose support of and patience with her writing endeavors have been key to her perseverance. Most of all, Marci would like to thank Renee Russak, whose love, guidance, and sense of fun makes everything, including the writing of this book, a joy.

We owe our gratitude to Lee Ann Chearney, creative director of Amaranth Illumi-nare. Her deep interest in and commitment to this subject and the process has been impressive. We appreciate her willingness to share her considerable insights and give us the opportunity to share ours. Thanks also to senior project editor Deborah S. Romaine for her assistance with the preparation of this revised edition.

We also thank the many talented staff members at Alpha Books who work so hard to make the *Complete Idiot's Guides* the must-have general reference series available to readers today. Thanks to publisher Marie Butler-Knight for her professionalism and vision; senior acquisitions editor Randy Ladenheim-Gil for her grace, talent, and edi-torial skill; managing editor Jen Chisholm for her patience and diplomacy; produc-tion editor Megan Douglass; and copy editor Keith Cline. Sweet dreams!

Special Thanks to the Technical Reviewer

The Complete Idiot's Guide to Interpreting Your Dreams, Second Edition, was reviewed by an expert who double-checked the accuracy of what you'll learn here, to help us ensure that this book gives you everything you need to know about understanding your dreams and using your own unique dream power. Special thanks are extended to Marya M. Barey, Ph.D., for her expert technical review of this book.

A practicing psychotherapist with over 20 years of experience, Dr. Barey is the branch director and supervising therapist of the Family Services center in Seattle, Washington. She is a member of the Washington Psychological Association. Dr. Barey incorporates dreamwork as an integral tool in therapeutic work with clients.

Trademarks

All terms mentioned in this book that are known to be or are suspected of being trademarks or service marks have been appropriately capitalized. Alpha Books and Penguin Group (USA) Inc. cannot attest to the accuracy of this information. Use of a term in this book should not be regarded as affecting the validity of any trademark or service mark.

Part 1

What Are Dreams?

Are you curious about your dreams—about why you remember them or not, about what they mean or don't mean? If so, join the club. For thousands of years dreams have been a source of wonder, fear, and speculation. From philosophers to psychologists, many through the ages have studied dreams and their meanings.

Before you can begin to decipher your dreams, it's important to understand the very basics about your dreaming life, learn how different cultures throughout history have regarded dreaming, and discover how well you're sleeping (or not!) and when during your sleep cycle you're most likely to dream.

1

Are You Dreaming?

In This Chapter

- ◆ The many definitions of dreams
- ◆ Tonight's dream presentation is ...
- ◆ Play it again
- ◆ What do you want to learn from your dreams?

So what are dreams? Such a simple question to ask, but so hard to answer ... and a question with different answers through the ages. In biblical times, human beings regarded dreams as divine prophecies. During the Middle Ages, dreams threatened people as possible messages from Satan, and rather than get caught red-handed entertaining the devil after-hours, most dreamers kept their dreams to themselves.

Dreams have been viewed as portals to the other side, messages from the departed, catalysts for creative inspirations, or messages from parts of ourselves that we tune out during our waking hours. The ancient Greek philosopher Aristotle (384–322 B.C.E.) believed dreams were part of the body's system of calming the perception of outside experiences so that the inside, the emotions, could become more clear to the dreamer.

Dreaming: What's It to You?

Some researchers see dreams as the mind's way of clearing out the vast amount of information that is collected during the course of the day, making space for tomorrow's data storage. Others, such as dream researcher Jeremy Taylor, believe that dreams bring us lessons and insights.

In a recent highly unscientific poll, we asked a select group of people how they defined dreams:

◆ "Dreams are the movies I see when I go to bed."

◆ "They're obviously messages, but usually I can't decipher them."

◆ "Dreams are my deepest thoughts, surfacing under cover of night, whether I like it or not."

◆ "Dreams are infomercials and I'm the host."

◆ "Dreams? What dreams?"

It's hard to pinpoint exactly what dreams are. The age-old search for a precise definition will probably continue for as long as the question "Who am I?" remains a viable topic for philosophers, theologians, psychologists, biologists, and the rest of us curious yet ordinary dreamers. Can we simply decide that dreams serve an important function in our lives? It's safe to say, yes. Like breathing, eating, and making love, dreaming is part of human nature. It *must* be important!

From Socrates to Descartes to Jung to contemporary New Age thinkers such as Deepak Chopra or sleep researchers such as Harvard's Dr. Martin Moore-Ede and Stanford's Dr. William Dement, humankind has explored the nature and significance of dreams and sleep. This book helps you explore various dream theories and dream types, so that you can make your own decision and develop your own set of tools for better understanding your dreams—and yourself.

How Often Do You Dream?

Everyone dreams. (In fact, new research shows that people who really *don't* dream have lesions in the brain sleep and dream centers and that they also have corresponding brain dysfunction in real life.) Sleep experts tell us that we all have several dreams each night. We spend about one third of our lives sleeping, so we have plenty of time to dream. According to Robert L. Van de Castle, Ph.D., a prominent dream expert, scientists have suggested that we'll each have 100,000 dreams over the course of our lives. That's about 1,300 dreams per year, or 3½ dreams every night!

So you might ask, "Why can't I remember a single one?" Alcohol consumption, certain antibiotics, fever, lack of sleep, and unconscious fears about the content of your dreams all affect dream recall, and perhaps dream content. Scientist Francis Crick, who pioneered research on the structure of DNA, takes the position that maybe we're supposed to forget our dreams—that dreams are a way of cleansing the brain of extraneous information. Perhaps you remember only the dreams that are really scary or upsetting or, if you're lucky, fantastically wonderful.

Dreamy

In the Old Testament, Pharaoh freed Joseph from his prison dungeon to interpret two of Pharaoh's dreams. In the first, seven cows, gaunt and lean, ate seven sleek and fat cows. In the second dream, seven ripe ears of corn swallowed up seven shriveled ears of corn. Joseph divined God's plan of seven years of blight and famine for Egypt. Pharaoh shrewdly stocked up on the ancient version of canned goods.

We tend to dream more toward the end of a sleep period. We're also more likely to remember those dreams we had closest to awakening, or at least remember those dreams most easily. Makes sense, doesn't it? That is when our brain is most rested and more likely to give us the most complete and coherent dreams. There are some physiological reasons for this, which we discuss in Chapter 3. But with a little effort, you can boost your dream recall, and we show you how to do it, too.

In Black and White or in Living Color?

The one thing dreams have in common is that you're asleep when you have them. Aside from that, there are endless variations. Do you dream in black and white? In color? Shared anecdotes of dream therapists and research tell us that most people dream in color, some in black and white. No one is sure why this occurs—one theory is that when the visual center in the brain is damaged or one is color blind then the dream visions will be just like the waking vision—just as no one is sure why a certain percentage of the population is left-handed.

In our experience, we've found that most people report dreaming in color except when they are very depressed. Then they tend to recall fewer dreams, and those dreams have little

Life Is But a Dream

One of psychoanalyst Sigmund Freud's most famous lines is, "Dreams are the guardians of sleep." On the other hand, the renowned writer A. Alvarez says, "Sleep is the guardian of dreams." It's hard to know who's right—maybe both!

color (except for nightmares, which can be vividly colorful). Some people report dreaming exclusively in black and white when they first begin paying attention to their dreams, either in therapy or in individual dreamwork. As they continue to concentrate on remembering dreams, many often report that they begin to dream in color.

Daydreamers

What's the difference between dreaming at night and our daydreams? Certainly it feels that we have more control over the story lines of our daydreams. Remember the last place your mind escaped to during that boring status meeting at the office? Did you ski down a mountainside of fresh powder, yours the first tracks through the snow? Practice your Academy Award or Pulitzer Prize acceptance speech? Relax on a tropical beach? Relive the greatest weekend of your life?

There seems to be a big difference between day and night dreams, even though the physical state we enter when we daydream has much in common with a hypnotic state, which, in turn, possesses certain similarities to a sleep state. However, different parts of the brain are activated in sleep than in waking life. And when you get right down to it, when we're daydreaming we're not physiologically sleeping.

When we're asleep, we're psychologically more vulnerable than when we daydream. In sleep, our *defense mechanisms* are down. We shed the masks we wear in public. Perhaps what is expressed in night dreaming is a better representation of who we are in total, not just our waking wishes and fears. Feelings and thoughts we may not be so eager to take credit for in waking life often surface boldly in the landscape of our dreams.

Dream Dictionary

Defense mechanism, a psychological term coined by Sigmund Freud and amplified by his daughter Anna Freud, describes ways in which we protect ourselves from anxiety by keeping intolerable or unacceptable impulses from conscious awareness. In other words, we don't know we're employing them. Some examples of defense mechanisms are denial, suppression, intellectualization, sublimation, and projection.

Another thing to consider is the language of daydreams versus night dreams. Night dreams speak to us in the language of symbol and metaphor. Words just don't suffice to convey the countless powerful feelings that symbols do. These symbols often are chosen from something that's caught our attention during the day and that triggers a memory, conflict, or concern in us that resonates both in the present and in the past. The language of daydreams, in contrast, tends to be tangible, reflecting events that have clear reality or possibility to them (even if not your personal reality).

Going Back for a Subconscious Replay

Many researchers believe that dreams are a way of revisiting the events—and the emotions associated with them—of our daily lives. Often we simply don't have the time to process the stimuli around us. Nor could we possibly have the energy or ability to digest everything that comes at us during the day. (The old defense mechanism comes into play here, protecting us from emotional overload.) And so, it's at night in our dreams that we rehash thoughts and feelings we've placed on hold.

Say, for example, you had a really stressful day at work. Several co-workers called in sick, e-mail went down, and when the company president stopped in to see how the new campaign was going, you were eating a sandwich at your desk. In your dreams that night, you might replay the day. Only this time when the company president stops by your desk, her briefcase bursts into flames and you quickly dowse them. "What's your name?" she asks. "We're looking for someone like you at headquarters."

Your dream time has been spent recasting your bad day into a story that highlights your coping skills rather than your mistakes and misfortunes.

Going Back for a Conscious Replay

When you replay your dream in your conscious mind, what happens to the dream? Is there a difference between the dream itself and your waking analysis of it? Montague Ullman, a renowned dream expert, tells us that "Dreaming is an intrinsic part of the sleep cycle that recurs every 90 minutes during sleep and is associated with distinct psychological changes that signify a state of arousal. The dream is a remembrance in the waking state of whatever we can bring back from the previous night's [dream] episodes. The two are not the same."

To what extent do we "fill in the blanks" of our dreams when we wake up, and is that a good thing or a bad thing? Why do we do that? We believe that what we choose to add to our dreams is very interesting and potentially useful because it gives us clues about how we wish things to be. Or because by embellishing or continuing our dreams consciously, we can resolve issues provoked by the dream that allow us to become more comfortable with their messages. With dreamwork practice, we can begin to separate what the true dream is from what we add in later to round the dream out, process it, and understand it.

Are Dreams Real? Through the Looking Glass

In Lewis Carroll's *Through the Looking Glass*, Alice is driven to a state of near distraction by Tweedledee and Tweedledum, who each insists that Alice is not real, that she's merely a piece of the Red King's dream. While in this case the blurring of boundaries may have been caused by ingested mind-altering substances, Alice's struggle raises an important question: What is real? Can we prove that our dreams are any more real than our waking lives?

Throughout history, people have struggled with the notion of which is real. An ancient Chinese philosopher, Chuang-tzu, dreamed he was a butterfly. He awoke suddenly and pondered whether he was a man who dreamed of being a butterfly—or whether he was a butterfly dreaming he was a man. The paradox reflects the Taoist belief in the balance and play of yin and yang, the union of opposites.

The ancient Greeks, chief among them Socrates, struggled with proving the existence of a "waking" versus a "dreaming" reality at any given moment. This question—Are dreams real? (and its corollary, Is waking life real?)—is about as difficult to answer as "What is the sound of one hand clapping?" Fortunately, we're not going to try to resolve that thorny issue. Despite all of our high-tech advances in studying how the brain works and how and why we sleep and dream, the more *metaphysical* questions of sleeping and waking reality remain the territory of philosophers—and dreamers.

At some point or other, we've all been spooked by the "realness" of our dreams. Think back to when you were a kid. Didn't you have dreams—both good ones and bad ones—that felt utterly real? And didn't it take some time and some persuasion from your folks to convince you that what you dreamed wasn't real? In our culture, as we grow up we learn to differentiate between inner and outer reality, mostly at the expense of the former. The truth is, don't you still have the occasional dream where you wake up and wonder if the dream was indeed real?

Dream Dictionary

Metaphysics is the philosophical exploration of the nature of reality and being.

Misconceptions and Superstitions About Dreams

Since paying attention to our dreams often has been relegated to the back burner in recent times, it makes sense that over the years various peculiarities have surfaced regarding this potent expression of feelings. Haven't you been warned that if you dream of falling and you hit the ground, that means you'll die? Or if you dream of someone else dying, it means that person will die?

The language of dreams is the language of metaphor. The people and events that populate your dreams represent your worries, concerns, and fears about circumstances and changes in your life. Fortunately they also represent some of the best events of our lives past, present, and possibly future. They appear real, perhaps because this puts them in a context your conscious mind can begin to understand; some appear real because the same regions of the brain are activated as would be if the events were happening in real life. As much as dreams of death might seem frightening omens, death is a powerful and classic metaphor for transition.

Dreamy

Legend has it that Abraham Lincoln, a few weeks before his assassination, dreamed he saw someone lying in a coffin in the White House. He asked a person in his dream who was in the coffin and that person answered, "The president." Whether or not this is true, little historical documentation survives to tell us. What history does document is that threats against the sixteenth president's life were frequent, and at times his guards changed his travel plans to whisk him from the prospect of harm. No doubt Lincoln did dream of being assassinated, in the same way that personal fears and worries may show up in the dreams of all of us.

Whose Dream Is It, Anyway?

How often do you awaken from a vivid dream to wonder, "Wow, where did *that* come from?" Unless we consider the possibility that some dream messages could involve the paranormal, including (but not limited to) visitations from deceased loved ones, angels, or the God of your understanding, then we can acknowledge that we are the creators of our own dreams. (We'll talk about dreams that are messages in later chapters.) In most dreams the imagery arises from within us to express something about us. The symbols, puns, scenery, characters, and actions within a dream are products of our own hopes, fears, memories, and experiences.

Wake Up!

Can't recall your dreams? Maybe you don't want to! If you're feeling anxious or frightened, you might not be ready to face the emotions encoded in your dreams. Think about what may be scaring you. Be patient. Just as you're in charge of creating your dreams, you're also in charge of how you remember them. Sometimes your inner self, or psyche, needs to feel 'safe'—that you are emotionally ready to handle the feelings that will accompany the dream—for you to remember a disturbing dream.

Exploring Your Dream Landscape

Are your dreams straightforward representations of what happens to you during a given day? Or are they long, bizarre odysseys in which characters, places, and time frames *morph* into each other? Are your dreams primarily about people, or do you find there are mostly inanimate objects in your dreams? Do you tend to dream about people you know, about strangers, or about famous people? Do you talk in your sleep or wake up laughing? Do you often watch the action from the sidelines or are you a main participant in your dreams?

Dream Dictionary

In Greek mythology, **Morpheus** is the god of dreams. He's the son of Hypnos, god of sleep. Morpheus formed the dreams that came to those asleep. He also represented human beings in dreams. The name Morpheus is derived from the Greek word for "shape" or "form." Our colloquial use of *morph* comes from this word.

Perhaps there are many animals in your dreams. Animals are especially prevalent in children's dreams. Some researchers have suggested that a high percentage of animals in our adult dreams is a leftover tie to our primitive, cave-dwelling past and expresses some of the basic concerns about our survival.

A lot of dreams seem perfectly reasonable during the dream … and totally fantastical when we wake up and think about them. You may find that as you think more about your dreams and their basic themes, the ways your dreams make you feel and your questions about them will multiply rapidly.

Do you look forward to going to sleep and dreaming? Perhaps anticipating an entertaining internal double feature? Do you try to dream … or try not to? Here's a short self-exploration to help you investigate what you expect, and what you might like to learn, from your dreams.

1. I want to know what my dreams mean because …

    a) I've always been curious about my dreams.

    b) I feel there are special meanings to some of the images that appear regularly in my dreams, but I don't know how to figure out the connections.

    c) I feel there are dreams that do have meanings, but my dreams make no sense.

    d) Perhaps my dreams can help me to understand my unconscious, touch my innermost soul, or, if it is possible, even try to go beyond the limits of my physical body.

2. I remember my dreams ...

   a) Several times a week.

   b) Several times a month.

   c) Seldom or never.

   d) Only when the dream is especially vivid or repeats.

3. I think exploring my dreams could help me ...

   a) Face and overcome my worries and fears so both my sleeping and my waking lives are more peaceful and in both I feel more content.

   b) Find answers to questions I have about issues surrounding a current life situation (such as looking for a new job, or my relationship with my life partner or family member).

   c) Come to terms with experiences from my past that may be blocking progress toward my happiness and success in waking life.

   d) Have some fun getting to know more about who I am and what is important to me—both awake and asleep!

4. My dreams seem more vivid ...

   a) When my daily life is most intense.

   b) When my daily life is more relaxed and I can sleep in.

   c) Whenever I have a lot on my mind when I go to bed.

   d) When I make a conscious effort on waking to remember my dreams.

5. I seem to dream less when ...

   a) I'm extraordinarily tired.

   b) I've eaten within two hours of going to bed.

   c) I've taken a certain medication or had alcohol within two hours of going to bed.

   d) I don't know why sometimes I seem to dream less than other times.

In the coming chapters, you'll find more targeted self-explorations to help you figure out how you feel about your dreams, how to understand what they might mean, and how to use your dreams to empower your waking life. Whether you are plagued by nightmares (which, by the way, can be powerful positive messages for you—yes, that's true!), intrigued by a puzzling or repeating dream, or just plain curious about what your dreams have to say about who you are, we'll help you develop your own, personalized method for encouraging, understanding, and directing your dreams.

Your Dream Journal

Throughout this book, we ask you to record your dreams and give you guidelines for interpreting them. Each chapter offers you a unique dream exercise. We suggest that you keep a loose-leaf notebook handy, one you find appealing. You can use a bound journal, if you like, such as the dream journals you can buy at bookstores. But we prefer loose-leaf over hard-bound notebooks because you have the option of adding pages and rearranging their order.

Additionally, it's a good idea to have a pocket in the notebook. Once you get started on the process of examining your dreams (and yourself!), we think you'll find bits and pieces of dreams and insights occurring to you at all times of the day or night. So if you jot down a note on a napkin, for instance, you can store it in the notebook's pocket until you find time to transcribe it into your notebook. Some people simply would take that napkin and glue it into the notebook. That's fine! Others find it helpful to carry a small notebook and pen or a mini-cassette recorder at all times, so they can record their insights and thoughts. Choose whatever feels right to you. Ready? Let's become dream catchers! Here's a short exercise to get you started.

Choose one recent dream and record it in your dream journal. Then, find three adjectives for how the dream made you feel. Here are a few ideas: joyful, vibrant, agitated, ashamed, restless, surprised, optimistic, sexy, distracted, petulant, enraged, curious, concerned, powerful, reluctant, shrewd. The adjectives you choose may not seem to go together, but that's fine—part of your task in exploring your dreams is to resolve seemingly incongruous dream events, images, and emotions.

The Least You Need to Know

♦ Dreams are part of the human experience, and fascinate us today as much as they intrigued our ancestors.

♦ Aside from the possibility of the paranormal or precognitive dream, we're the creators of our individual dreams. Our dreams might express our inner wishes, desires, fears, and conflicts that have arisen during the day or over the course of our lifetimes (or both).

♦ Many factors affect our ability to recall our dreams, including how well we sleep, illness, medications, alcohol, defense mechanisms, and age-old misconceptions and superstitions that can make delving into our dreams seem formidable or scary.

♦ Dreams that occur while we sleep are different from daydreams. Sleeping dreams usually express more truthfully an inner struggle because our defensive guard is lowered while we sleep.

♦ Night dreams have a language all their own, one that is most often metaphorical and symbolic.

Dream Weavers: Dreams and Vision Quests of the Past

In This Chapter

◆ Dreams and mythology

◆ Dreams as prophecy

◆ Dreams and the body/mind

◆ Dreams for the twenty-first century

For as long as the human race has had oral traditions and written words, we've known of dreams. Did dreams happen before we had words with which to speak them or symbols with which to write them? We can't answer that for certain, but what we do know is that the earliest recordings of human-kind gave us dreaming images in and for every aspect of life: remembrances of creation, guides for living our spiritual lives, guides for living with others, and guides for taking care of the planet. Let's take a look at the dreams and vision quests of dream weavers throughout human experience.

Dreams as the Source for Creation

The mythology of the aboriginal people of Australia relates that 'in the beginning there was Dreamtime'. The seeds of the spirits, which had long lain dormant in the womb of the Earth, emerged to take shapes that were part human, part animal, part plant. As they wandered the fields and forests, they encountered mounds of earth and sticks; these were human beings waiting for the spirits to sculpt them into life, which the spirits did, carefully crafting arms and legs and faces, then turning their handiwork free to become the fathers and mothers, brothers and sisters, caretakers of the Earth and all of its elements. The spirits of Dreamtime—ancestral figures such as Rainbow Snake, Lightning Brothers, and Cloudbeings—remain part of contemporary aboriginal belief.

Their dreams bond the aboriginal people to the land that supports them in integral and inseparable ways. This same connection joins the worlds of waking and dreaming, as the tradition of the *walkabout* demonstrates. In indigenous tribes, walkabouts are journeys that follow a ritual path of songlines along the tracks of ancestral travels to relive the creation myth. The modern walkabout involves using trains or the family truck, but still includes sacred ceremonies closed to outsiders.

> **Dream Dictionary**
>
> **Walkabouts** are the waking and dreaming journeys aboriginal peoples embark upon, retracing familial ancestral paths by following songlines, the trail of words and music scattered along with the ancestor's footprints.

The mythologies of other indigenous cultures similarly blend creation and dreams. The Uitoto, indigenous people of southern Colombia, for example, have the Father, Who-Has-An-Illusion. This divine entity touched a mystery and an image and he began to dream and think. As he dreamed and thought, he brought into being all that is a part of the Uitoto's world.

Who's Dreaming Who?

In her book *A History of God* (Knopf, 1993), theologian Karen Armstrong suggests that humans create conceptions of God that have to be of use to them in cultural life, and that when one religious system ceases to work, another is brought into being. If we conceptualize gods who dreamed us into being, it's no wonder that dreams continue to be a source of fascination across time and culture.

Take the biblical book of Genesis, which is filled with dreams, or visions, in which God makes frequent appearances. God does everything from commanding Abraham to hit the road, to requiring Noah to pack up and hop aboard. God even appears to a

Philistine king in a dream to tell him to quit dating Sarah, whom the king mistakenly believes is Abraham's *sister* but is in fact Abraham's *wife*. It's a divine dream visit with benefits for Abraham, in the end, as the king quickly ends this taboo romance and gives Abraham gifts of silver and cattle—providing God's chosen people with some much needed supplies for the long haul.

Many ancient texts record dream interpretations and discuss the relevance of dreams in the scheme of human existence. The Indian Upanishads, a collection of over 100 philosophical texts scholars believe were written between 1000 and 300 B.C.E. to codify the foundations of ancient Brahman Hinduism, present the waking state as the venue of physical existence and the dream state as that of mental existence. One's dreams provide the opportunity to gain insight and enlightenment, according to the Upanishads, free from the constraints and structures of the material world. The Babylonian Talmud, written between 200 B.C.E and 200 C.E., similarly codifies Judaism and stresses the importance of interpreting dreams within their context to the dreamer.

"Seeing" Things

Visions and prophecies, both waking and dreaming, fascinated the ancient Celts. Archeologists have discovered caves with drawings that depict ravens speaking—giving guidance and foretelling the future. But if a raven showed up in a dream, the ancient Celt didn't jump for joy. Dreams of ravens in this culture foretold of carnage and death. Talk about a nightmare!

In Celtic lore, one inherited, in a mystical rather than genetic sense, the gift of *augury*, or second sight. Augury ceremonies began with fasting and asking God for images that would explain the future. When the augurs opened their eyes, whatever they saw became the basis for interpretation. As in the case of many ancient traditions, the visions and dream lore of the Celts were closely tied to the seasons of the planet, and in the role this natural timetable plays in human survival.

Dream Dictionary

An **augur** is a person who interprets omens, signs that seem to portend future events. The word retains its original Latin spelling and means, literally, "to augment," with the implication of prosperity.

Here are some famous augurs, both real and mythological:

◆ In Greek myth, *Cassandra* was doomed to be an unheeded prophet. Although born a princess with the gift of prophecy, Apollo decreed that no one would ever believe Cassandra's dreams.

- A twelfth-century mystic and Benedictine nun, *Hildegard of Bingen* (1098–1179) called herself "God's trumpet" and became renowned for her visions. Even Pope Eugenius III affirmed her visions—no small feat for a woman in those days … or in any days for that matter.

- French warrior *St. Joan of Arc* (1412–1431) was burned at the stake when she refused to deny that divine inspiration was the source of her prophetic visions and dreams.

- Visionary English poet and painter *William Blake* (1757–1827) created illustrated manuscripts of his prophetic dream visions on innocence and experience. One of the most famous, *The Marriage of Heaven and Hell*, written in 1792, reflects a strong biblical influence.

- Today, *Shakti Gawain* is well known for her method of creative visualization in which people adapt the dreaming process to waking life—creating visualizations of the life they want. A contemporary form of prophecy!

In ancient Egypt, the gods gifted important community members with dream visitations if they provided adequate preparation. The chosen ones used sacred place and sacred ritual to create the right atmosphere for the appropriate god, and prayed for a fruitful night of dreaming. Sometimes dreams and visions came to the average person, who might not know that he or she was special until the dream or vision was received, but usually the gods passed over the typical Egyptian in favor of the VIPs in the community.

Researchers have found dream interpretations dating from about 2000 B.C.E. written on Egyptian papyri. Mantic dreams, or personal prophetic dreams, held odd clues that, when unraveled, gave the dreamer insight into his or her personal destiny.

Life Is But a Dream

Fasting or eating of the proper foods is often seen as one way to gain spiritual power and access to dreams or visions. It's all a part of getting the right amount and quality of sleep. From British royalty in the Middle Ages to the pioneers of the American West, herbal aids, such as pillows stuffed with hop flowers, have been used to induce sleep.

Egyptians sought clues to their mantic dreams in animate and inanimate objects. Called *omina* (omens), these signs could include just about anything from a cloud shape to a cat's eye, to the pattern of blood vessels in a lamb's organs. Eventually, written texts, some of which survive today, codified the list of omina. In some respects, these were the earliest examples of modern-day dream dictionaries: lists of what various signs mean. Ancient omen texts were extremely literal; they clearly spelled out what would happen if, for example, you dreamed of seven thin cows devouring seven healthy ones. If the omen was bad, there were rituals the individual or community could engage in to ward off the evil foretold in the dream.

Dreamy

Egyptian pharaoh Thutmose IV, who ruled Egypt from 1425 to 1417 B.C.E., learned in a dream that he would ascend to the throne. The god Horus appeared in a dream to tell Thutmose IV that he would become king if he cleared away the sand that was covering the great Sphinx that honored Horus. The young prince obliged and, when his older brother died in battle, Thutmose IV became king. Thutmose IV ended years of strife and established a reign of peaceful prosperity by negotiating diplomatic relationships with neighboring countries.

More Myth: The Greeks, the Gods, and the Body/Mind

References to prophetic dreams abound in Homer's epics, the *Iliad* and the *Odyssey* (ninth century B.C.E.). But as the Greeks became renowned for progress in medical knowledge about the human body and how it worked, the emphasis on dreams as a prophetic instrument changed.

Hippocrates (460–377 B.C.E.), often called the Father of Medicine, wrote 70 or so books on health and established the basic rules of a physician's conduct in what became known as the Hippocratic Oath, which graduates from medical schools pledge to uphold even now. He believed that while the body stopped to rest during sleep, the mind did not. Hence, dreams. Plato (427–347 B.C.E.) continued the argument that dreams came from inside the human body, were psychological and physiological, and had nothing to do with external mystical visitations.

The Greek physician Galen (131–200 C.E.) postulated that dreams held clues to the dreamer's possible future physical illnesses. Artemidorus, Galen's contemporary, wrote an encyclopedic work divided into five books called *Oneirocritica (The Interpretation of Dreams)*. Artemidorus collected dreams of citizens of Greece and traveled throughout Asia Minor categorizing and analyzing dreams. His book is another forerunner to our modern dream dictionaries. But, as contemporary dream researcher Robert Van de Castle points out, because Artemidorus urged that interpretations take into account the particulars of the individual dreamer, dream scholars remain impressed with the depth and scope of Artemidorus's work. Post-Artemidorus, dream research or interpretation remained dormant until its major emergence in the psychoanalytic theories of Sigmund Freud in the nineteenth century. We'll discuss psychology and dreams in Chapter 4.

Dream Dictionary

Oneirocritica comes from the Greek words *oneiros*, meaning "dream," and *kritikos*, meaning "critical." The interpretation of dreams is establishing a name for itself!

For the Greeks, the mystical connection to the gods began to coexist with medical knowledge and a curiosity about the human body and mind. Several shrines to Aesculapius, a real-life healer who lived during the twelfth century B.C.E. and was later deified, were built with the express purpose of receiving a dream visitation from this Greek deity. The dreams revealed cures for illness. *Dream incubation* (which other ancient cultures such as the Egyptians and the Chinese also practiced) became exceedingly ritualized. People flocked to the temple of the desired Greek deity and indulged elaborate preparations to invoke divine visitations in their dreams.

Dream Dictionary

Dream incubation is the practice of seeking out dreams to answer specific and general questions. Ancients believed the closer you were to a deity, the easier to "catch" the dream sent. So sleeping in the temple was the surest way to produce a divine dream. The Greeks used dream incubation for healing; the Egyptians, mainly for prophecy.

Twentieth-century American scholar and writer Joseph Campbell (1904–1987), author of *The Masks of God*, a four-volume series on comparative mythology, and *Myths to Live By*, embarked on a lifelong study of folklore, dreams, and myth. Campbell believed that everything—heaven, hell, all of the worlds, and all of the gods—exists within us. The different energies in our bodies take on images and conflict with each other. This is what gives rise in our dreams to all sorts of mythical figures common to all cultures. He likened our human dream life to a fishing expedition into the vast ocean of mythology.

Dream Travel: The Astral Body

Numerous ancient cultures believed that the spirit wandered free from the body during dreams. But what if we have *another* body—one that becomes dominant when we sleep? In 1927, A. E. Powell wrote a book on the *astral body* that remains a resource today. In *The Astral Body and Other Astral Phenomena*, Powell writes that not only do we all have an astral body, but that we retreat into our astral bodies when we sleep and, upon awakening, tend to have little recollection of this time beyond what we might attribute to memories of dreams.

Powell states that we can train ourselves to consciously control the astral self and use it to obtain a conscious existence, 24 hours a day, 7 days a week. In this process, we alternate between the physical world and the astral plane, and we're aware of where we are all of the time. (Fascinating idea, but kind of exhausting to think about.)

One of the first learned, and perhaps most interesting, uses of this capability is travel in our astral state. In this state we can move both quickly and over a great distance. This would seem to account for the many stories that people tell of having great knowledge of a place where they've never been.

Dream Dictionary

The **astral body** is believed to be a second, diffuse body, an aspect of the self surrounded by an aura, a light radiating from the human body of flashing colors, and composed of matter finer than that of physical matter. A shimmering silver cord connects the astral body to the physical body. The astral body expresses feelings, passions, desires, and emotions, and acts as a bridge between the physical body and the mind.

The word astral comes from the ancient alchemist term for starry, or luminous, the way astral matter was perceived to look. The luminous aura is the portion of the astral body that extends beyond the physical body. The greater one's feeling state, the brighter the aura. The aura of the Buddha is said to have radiated 3 miles from his physical body!

In this view, dreams are the work of the astral body/mind during sleep. To get the most out of your dreams, those believing in astral projection say you should concentrate on noble thoughts as you're drifting off to sleep. (So plotting vengeful acts against your annoying co-worker is a definite no-no.) If you *do* concentrate on noble thoughts, you'll be more likely to experience dreams from the astral plane, and they will be useful to you.

James R. Lewis, Ph.D., author of *The Dream Encyclopedia* (Visible Ink, 1995), points out that astral projection is one means of explaining dreams about flying and psychic dreams. Flying dreams, common to most everyone, even appeared in Artemidorus's book, *Oneirocritica*, written centuries before the Wright Brothers invented the airplane and humans experienced the thrill of flight without the fall. Additionally, it's been suggested that when you dream of an event and wake up to find that the event really did occur, then what happened was that your astral body went on a journey you decided was only a dream.

Wake Up!

Some people feel they can easily and often without their control go "out of body." They feel like they're watching themselves from a distance. This can indicate many things, among them a way of coping with stress or trauma. If this happens to you frequently, you may wish to discuss it with a therapist.

We don't have definitive proof that the astral body exists, at least not as of this writing. But the grand link of the human body and the human mind is one that scientists, philosophers, poets, and ordinary dream enthusiasts like us are continuing to explore with great curiosity. Religion and science still vie for the explanation of why we dream, what it means, and whether our dreaming minds have the ability to go beyond our physical bodies.

Just a Dream

Modern interest in dreams and dream interpretation encompasses the full spectrum, from scientific evidence to metaphysical experience. Why do we dream, and what do our dreams *really* mean? In many respects, we are no closer to definitive answers to such questions than were the ancient philosophers and their texts. What does seem unequivocally true is that dreams can have multiple layers of meaning and that they are contextual to the dreamer.

As we begin to explore our own dreams and discover what truths they hold, we'll assign to dreams their unique place of importance in our current Information Age—a time when the Internet makes communication seem instantaneous and the world's peoples are linked more closely in a global awareness. As we move forward humanity will unearth, for our own time, the spiritual, emotional, social, and political contexts of our dreams.

We need to look deeply into our dreams to understand the fears and potentials of manifesting humanity's—and our own—brightest present and future reality. As we work through, for example, our emotional responses to our dreams in the wake of 9/11 and other troubling world or national events, we should focus on using the power of those dreams to learn, to release fear and anger, and to direct our waking efforts toward creating increased peace and understanding in our world.

A Dream Labyrinth

Labyrinths are paths that follow intricate, symmetrical patterns from an outer entry point to the center. Following a labyrinth—whether you walk it or trace it with your finger—can be a journey to personal enlightenment. Labyrinths come in all sizes and patterns, made of all sorts of materials from cultivated hedges to lines on paper (like the one here), yet have in common that there is only one way to follow the path to its conclusion. One of the most famous labyrinths is on the floor of the Chartres Cathedral in Paris, which is an inlaid pattern of stone tiles.

A labyrinth may help you understand a dream, or set the stage for a night of restful sleep and (hopefully) productive, insightful dreaming at times when you feel the need to turn to your dreams for guidance or insight. Like the ancient Egyptians journeyed to the temples to incubate dreams of healing, you can travel the path of the labyrinth to encourage healing dreams of your own. All you need for your labyrinth dream journey is this book (or a photocopy of the labyrinth figure), a quiet place where you can travel the labyrinth without distractions or interruptions, a cushion or blanket to sit on, and some candles.

Chapter **3**

To Sleep, Perchance to Dream

In This Chapter

- Circadian rhythms set your sleep cycle
- dREaM: REM sleep, NREM sleep, and dreams
- Getting enough, and getting good, sleep
- The healing ability of dreams

Before we go any further in our exploration of dreams, we need to consider a related, all-important subject: sleep. We have to be asleep to dream. And in our 24-hour society, practically a world that never sleeps, getting a good night's sleep can become a true challenge. But if you're interested in boosting your dream life and simply living healthier, paying attention to how much—and what quality—sleep you get is a very good idea.

Sleep deprivation is a chronic problem that's embedding itself in our very way of life. When we don't get enough sleep, we lose the ability to concentrate, and our motor skills aren't as sharp. Recent studies suggest that drowsy drivers are as or more dangerous than drunk drivers. In one study, participants who stayed awake for 17 to 19 hours did worse in driving-performance tests than people who had blood alcohol levels of 0.05 percent, the standard of intoxication in many countries. Other studies show that brain activity dramatically changes with sleep deprivation.

Moving to the Rhythm

And what happens to dreams when we're sleep deprived? Most people who are forced to stay awake will begin to experience visual misperceptions, sometimes including illusions and hallucinations. Do we need our sleep? You bet. Do we need our dreams as well? Let's take a look at the way our bodies sleep and dream. Consider the following list:

♦ The ripple of a pebble dropped into a pond

♦ A C-major piano chord

♦ Ocean waves

♦ A beating heart

♦ The germination, maturation, and death of a flower

♦ A battery's current

♦ Electrons dancing in their orbital shells

So which of these do not belong? If you say they all belong, you're right. Each item in this list embodies its own cyclical rhythm. There's one more important item to add to this list: your body.

Setting Your Body Clock

Virtually all species of life have internal clocks that regulate their waking and sleeping in a daily pattern, consisting of approximately 24 hours, called *circadian rhythms*. The human body clock is controlled by a small group of neurons in the brain's hypothalamus, called the suprachiasmatic nuclei, which receive information from the eye's retina using the nervous system as a pathway. So our body clocks are influenced by the presence or absence of light. A pretty good system for humankind—pre-electricity, that is: to sleep when it's dark and wake when it's light. The circadian clock is a part of the body's general system of *homeostasis*.

Our circadian body clock continues to tick regardless of external stimuli, helping to keep us awake or encouraging us to fall asleep as evolution has programmed us to do. Ever pulled an all-nighter and gotten your second wind right about breakfast time? That's your circadian clock at work. Even if you felt wide awake then, though, you weren't as fresh as if you'd had a full night's sleep!

Dream Dictionary

Circadian rhythm is the synchronized action of the body's impulse to stay awake or fall asleep. Without it, we wouldn't be able to establish patterns of order or behavior in our day. Circadian comes from the Latin *circa* meaning "approximately" and *dies* meaning "day." Circadian rhythm helps preserve the body's homeostasis, or its ability to maintain an internal stability.

Chronobiology, the study of the daily rhythms of living organisms, seeks to explain phenomena such as why human body temperature reaches a low point in the morning and why blood pressure peaks in the afternoon. When we ignore our internal clocks, hormonal secretions—released on the circadian rhythm pattern—suddenly don't match our activities, and we're thrown out of balance.

Dream Dictionary

Homeostasis is the body's tendency to adapt internally to external conditions or situations that try to disturb its equilibrium, such as changes in light or temperature.

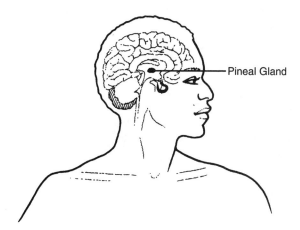

- Pineal Gland

The pineal gland helps regulate the body's internal clock.

The pineal gland, located deep inside the brain, secretes the hormone melatonin into the bloodstream. For centuries, scientists couldn't figure out its function. In the seventeenth century, French mathematician and philosopher René Descartes (1596–1650) thought the pineal gland released "spirits" into the blood. Today, it's thought that the pineal gland participates in the regulation of the internal human body clock. It secretes more melatonin in darkness (say, on a dark night or in a basement apartment!) and decreases output of the hormone as light levels increase (say, during bright daylight or at night in Hong Kong or Las Vegas!).

So if you take melatonin supplements, will you have more intense dreams? Maybe. Melatonin creates longer REM phases of sleep (more about REM sleep coming up), which means more opportunity to dream.

Wake Up!

Though melatonin is a popular supplement sold in health food stores, it is a hormone and should be treated with the same consideration as any over-the-counter or prescription drug. Ask your physician before you begin to take melatonin or any kind of vitamin, hormone, or herbal supplement.

The Science of Sleep

Popular notion once held that when humans slept, the goal was to restore the body's energy reserves. That is, our neurons, by day a fired-up network, gradually dimmed at night, turning off one by one, like the lights in a big-city skyscraper. As we finally fell asleep, scientists believed the neurons went dark and slept themselves. Dreams, then, functioned as "guardians of sleep" that occurred during periods of light sleep or in the morning to make sure the brain woke slowly enough to reactivate its neurons.

If our daily rhythm was that we "shut off" when we flicked off the lamp switch by our bed, then who could blame the soul (as ancient Indians, Chinese, and Greeks believed), itching for night life, for taking leave of the body to go traveling around town looking for action?

dREaM Sleep: The Dream State

In the early 1950s, the biggest breakthrough in the scientific study of dreams came about quite inadvertently in the research by a professor at the University of Chicago. Nathaniel Kleitman was curious about studying whether the cycle of motor activity—including eye movements—in infants would somehow reveal a predictable pattern of awakening, cueing the baby to nurse at the mother's breast. Eugene Aserinsky, a young medical student, observed the infants using an electrooculogram (EOG), a machine that records eye movements.

Kleitman and Aserinsky noticed that sleeping infant and adult subjects exhibited rapid eye movement (REM) several times during the course of a night's sleep. Each REM cycle lasted from 3 to as long as 55 minutes in some individuals (scientists have since confirmed the general length of REM sleep to be anywhere from 5 to 30 minutes). They wondered what the subjects could be "seeing." Maybe an internal image ... a dream?

Continuing their work throughout the 1950s, the researchers, aided by colleague William Dement, proceeded to wake subjects during REM cycles and ask for dream recall. The results proved their hypothesis that REM sleep and dreaming were closely related. Repeating the experiment 343 times, they discovered that when sleepers woke during a REM cycle, between 80 and 95 percent reported dreaming.

Ongoing research studied the varying waves that an electroencephalograph (EEG), an instrument for measuring and recording the electrical activity of the brain, registered during sleep and compared these to REM cycles. The relationship suggested something diametrically opposed to the prevailing belief of sleep as a slowed-down, uniform state of rest for the brain and body. Not only was the EEG measuring periods of unexpected brain activity, but during the REM cycle respiration and heart rates were slightly elevated.

By the time John F. Kennedy was inaugurated as president of the United States in 1961, the scientific community had come to the stunning conclusion that sleep consists of two separate states, REM and NREM (nonrapid eye movement). Sleep could no longer be thought of as "brain dead" or dreams as an inducement to the sleep state. Indeed, during REM (about a total of 90 to 120 minutes of our total sleep each night), the human brain is hopping, working as intensely as at our top waking speed!

So how come our bodies aren't hopping, too? That's because a nerve center in the brain holds the body in near paralysis during REM sleep. Scientists today also call REM sleep "paradoxical" sleep, for this reason. So while our bodies slumber motionless, our minds busily engage in the activities of a dreaming world.

Sleep: A Cycle in Four Stages, Plus REM

Most of a night's sleep, about 80 percent (more or less), occurs in the 4 stages of non-REM (NREM) sleep. While recent research indicates that we dream during NREM sleep, too, NREM dreams seem to be less specific in recall and less vivid or intense. We experience about four or five cycles of sleep every night, each consisting of a flow through the NREM stages to reach a burst of dreaming REM.

One complete sleep cycle lasts an average of 90 minutes, and this amount of time varies through the life span. (For more on sleep/dream patterns at different ages of life, see Part 4.) Figuring on this, we can assume it takes a bit more than a solid hour of sleep before we can launch into the REM dream state. As we sleep through the night, our REM bursts increase in duration, with the longest one occurring before waking. That's why morning dreams are often more involved, vivid, and easier for dreamers to recall. The sleep cycle is called an *ultradian rhythm.*

Dream Dictionary

Unlike circadian rhythms, which take about a day to go full cycle, **ultradian rhythms,** such as the human sleep cycle, are biological rhythms that occur more than once during a 24-hour period. The ultradian rhythm of the sleep cycle is repeated four or five times during each full night's sleep.

NREM Sleep Stages, Plus REM

Stage	EEG/Brain Activity	What You Experience
1	Beta waves of the waking state.	Temperature and blood pressure drop; shift to alpha waves; some theta slightly; muscles relax; hypnagogic waves are possible; images occur; you're easily awakened.
2	EEG shows sleep spindles alternating with K-complexes.	Slower eye movements; what wakes you up in Stage 1 produces only a distinctive episodic waveform K-complex; but if you're roused, you'll say, "Who me? Asleep?"
3	EEG shows larger, slower delta waves.	Temperature drops; no eye movements; breathing and heart rate slow down; you enter deep sleep.
4	Percentage of delta waves on EEG increases to 50% or more.	All body functions slow down; no eye movements; human growth hormone is released; muscles relax; it's hard to wake you up.
REM	EEG resembles a waking state.	Blood pressure rises; heart and respiratory rates go up; the nervous system's normal regulation of body temperature disappears; rapid eye movements occur.

The Science of Dreaming

Why do REM sleep and dreaming exist? Scientists are still working to figure that one out. Some researchers believe REM's function is to jump-start the brain out of its deep NREM slowdown, and it's well known that it's easier to wake someone up out of REM than NREM sleep. But even with the intense burst of neuronal stimulation during REM, experiments show that some neurons actually shut off. Serotonin, histamine, and norepinephrine, neurotransmitters hard at work during waking hours, decrease output during NREM sleep, and stop altogether in REM sleep.

Another idea about REM sleep holds that the dream state facilitates the brain's ability to incorporate memories, and in so doing, increases the brain's capacity to learn. This is based on sleep-deprivation studies that show subjects performing poorly in tests of learning skills. Other researchers view dreams as "brainstorms," neurological events meant to process and purge unnecessary information from the day now ending, clearing and organizing for the next day's brainwork.

In the late 1970s, two neurobiologists at Harvard, Drs. J. Allan Hobson and Robert McCarley, came up with a hypothesis about REM called activation-synthesis. This idea does a pretty good job of explaining how dream sensations may occur, but falls short when it comes to the complexity—to the often fully plotted and developed stories—our dreams can tell.

Dream Dictionary

Hypnagogic hallucinations are images, usually characterized by vivid, psychedelic colors, that come as we lose conscious control of our minds and we slip into NREM Stage 1 sleep. They may have much to do with whatever thoughts from the day are stirring about in our minds, but possess no real structure at all—although this doesn't mean they're unimportant. Often they are accompanied by involuntary jerks of the limbs.

During REM, researchers say, electrical activity begins in a part of the brain that has no ability of higher consciousness and singles out areas in the forebrain that do, areas that are responsible for senses and feelings. As electrical impulses reach it, the forebrain responds by painting a picture: the dream. In this view, dreams are seemingly random physiological events—not highly articulate, psychological manifestations chosen by the dreamer's mind because they hold meaning for unconscious awareness, acting to mask unconscious wishes and desires. Or to use a famous Freudism, these scientists might say, "Sometimes a cigar is just a cigar," meaning it's not a symbol endowed with deeper, hidden, and often profound meanings.

We're currently witnessing an explosion of data about the human body and how it functions in health and illness, including insights into the intimate connections between our bodies and our minds.

Dreamwork

The activation-synthesis idea is reminiscent of a seventeenth-century emphasis on empirical data, occurring during a historical time of similar rapid advances in scientific methods of study. At that time, British philosopher John Locke (1632–1704) postulated that dreams resulted from the measurable exposure of study subjects to external stimuli before they fell asleep that then became incorporated into their dreams in some way. In contemporary times, this might be a television commercial that is playing as you drift into sleep.

Should You Remember Your Dreams or Forget Them?

Have you ever been awakened by a particularly vivid dream? We'd bet that more often than not, you later had difficulty remembering it. Maybe what you could remember is the feeling that you dreamed about something weird or awful or funny. But not the dream itself. Perhaps as the day wore on only fragments stuck with you. In Chapter 1, we mentioned that the unconscious might repress dream recall to spare us undue anxiety and discomfort. But there are differing opinions in the scientific and therapeutic community about the importance of remembering our dreams.

If dreams are just the brain's way of efficiently processing excess images and sensations, then why would we want to remember them? We certainly wouldn't need to, or so it would seem. Researchers know that dream recall is greater when accompanied by higher cortical activation during a REM sleep period. This happens most frequently in the late morning hours and may be a reason why many people experience and recall vivid dreams after sleeping in on weekends. To further facilitate recall, a calm and quiet environment upon waking can help the dreamer consolidate the contents of a dream into waking memory.

Dreamy

"Kubla Khan: Or, a Vision in a Dream," Samuel Taylor Coleridge's (1772–1834) famous poem, begins with a preface by Coleridge where he recounts dreaming the entire 200 lines of the poem ("if that indeed can be called composition in which all the images rose up before him as things, with a parallel production of the correspondent expressions, without any sensation or consciousness of effort"). Upon waking, he remembered it whole and began to write it out. But, after being detained for an hour by an associate, Coleridge could summon only a "vague and dim recollection of the general import of the vision," and lost the last 10 lines altogether.

We think it's helpful to remember your dreams because the feelings you wake up with (both emotional and even physical) and how you proceed through the day may be influenced by what you dreamed the night before. Remembering your dreams allows you to ascribe appropriate feelings to your waking state—and your dream residue.

How Much Sleep Is Enough for Dreaming?

If we sleep the recommended seven to eight hours a night, half our dream time comes during the last two hours. So the eighth hour will consist heavily of dreaming. But about four million people in this country suffer from insomnia. Without the proper amount of sleep, our brain functions, muscles, and organs are not restored and we feel groggy. We might fall asleep at inappropriate or even dangerous times during the day. We feel irritable and can't concentrate. We get less REM sleep. We feel depressed. Recent research shows that we may suffer certain illnesses because our bodies do not get enough of the right kind of sleep. We need some shut-eye!

While the amount of sleep needed for healthy functioning differs from person to person, it is commonly accepted that in times of illness or stress your body requires more sleep. Many people feel the need for less sleep in spring and summer, when the days are longer. (Remember those circadian rhythms …!)

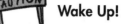

Wake Up!

Ongoing difficulty sleeping might indicate a medical or psychological problem. Repeated difficulty getting to sleep or persistent difficulty staying asleep (early morning awakening) might indicate depression, anxiety, or a physical illness. If your sleep is seriously out of whack, it's wise to consult with your doctor or mental health professional.

How Are You Sleeping?

Have you thought recently about how much sleep you get each night, and of what quality? Consider the following quiz:

1. On average I sleep _____ hours per night.

    a) 15 or more

    b) 4

    c) 7 or 8

2. I usually wake up _____ time(s) per night.

    a) I need a calculator to compute that.

    b) I can't even wake up in the morning.

    c) Maybe one

3. If I do wake up during the night, it's because

    a) I can't stop thinking about Chicken Little—if what he said about the sky falling in is true—or, I never fell asleep in the first place.

    b) I'm so worried I won't feel rested in the morning.

    c) I have to go to the bathroom.

4. When I wake up in the morning, I feel

   a) Like I've been in a war zone.

   b) Asleep.

   c) Reasonably well rested.

5. The best way to get me out of bed in the morning is to

   a) Whisper that I only have five hours before my morning meeting.

   b) Toss cold water on me.

   c) Slowly raise the shades.

6. The best way to describe my relationship to sleep is to say

   a) It eludes me.

   b) It consumes me.

   c) It's a nice place to visit.

We hope you were able to answer C to most questions. We all have some not-so-great sleep habits, but they're not problems unless they're persistent and interfere with our ability to sleep as much as we need to—or to stay awake the next day.

Healthy Sleep ... Good Dreams

Experts tell us that we shouldn't exercise vigorously less than three hours before bedtime because exercise stimulates the release of adrenaline. Exercise raises core body temperature, which drops five to six hours later. Drowsiness and a deeper sleep are both associated with the drop in core temperature. So the optimal time to exercise is late afternoon or very early evening, or five to six hours before bedtime.

Thinking about a nightcap? Well, if you want a good night's sleep, think about passing it up: Studies show that drinking alcohol three hours before you go to bed suppresses both REM and the deeper sleep cycles. Although there hasn't been much research into how alcohol affects dreaming, we know it alters sleep patterns and diminishes REM sleep—which means less time dreaming. And while you may have an easier time of falling asleep, you'll be up with the rooster's crow; alcohol consumption close to bedtime is associated with early morning awakening, a phrase scientists and mental health professionals use to describe an abnormally early cessation of sleep.

REM sleep decreases with the usage of barbiturates (drugs that mellow us out and help us fall asleep), unless we use them regularly. But since barbiturates are addictive, withdrawal from their use can stimulate nightmares. Other medications such as some antidepressants can inhibit or enhance your ability to fall and stay asleep. Check with your physician if you think your medications could be affecting your sleep patterns.

Scientists have found that caffeine should be avoided six hours before you turn in for the night. Stimulants delay the onset of sleep and disturb REM cycles. Nicotine is an even more powerful stimulant than caffeine. It raises blood pressure and heart rate, and stimulates brain wave activity—all of which get in the way of falling asleep. Studies have shown that heavy smokers take far longer to fall asleep, spend less time in REM and non-REM sleep, and wake up more often than nonsmokers.

Strategies for Sweet Dreams

Can you eat your way to a good night's sleep? Perhaps! A heavy meal before bed might make you feel sluggish and tired but keep you tossing and turning. A light snack before bedtime, however, especially one that contains tryptophan (an amino acid that induces sleep-promoting properties), can be relaxing and help you get to sleep. Some foods containing tryptophan are milk, cheese, bananas, and turkey. The herb chamomile is noted for its sleep-inducing properties. A lovely cup of warm chamomile tea—herbal, which has no caffeine—could be just what you need to nudge you over the edge into blissful sleep.

Meditation is a simple and effective way to relax both your body and your mind in preparation for restful sleep. Here's a meditation exercise you can follow or adapt:

1. First, prepare your sleeping environment. A room that is cool, dark, and quiet is generally the most supportive for sleep. You might enjoy calming music to help your transition.

2. Next, take care of your "personal" environment. Brush your teeth, go to the bathroom, do whatever you do to get yourself ready for bed.

3. We suggest you turn off the light and get into bed before you start, so if you fall asleep during your meditation you can stay put for a restful night. Lie on your back with your arms at your sides and your legs outstretched, and close your eyes. Make sure you're warm and comfortable.

4. This meditation starts with five deep, cleansing breaths. Breathe each one in over a count of five, hold the breath for a count of five, and let it out over a count of five.

5. As you breathe in, envision that you're drawing each breath into your body from your toes, and that it travels all the way through your body to the top of your head as you count to five. When you exhale, envision the reverse—that the breath travels from your head through your body to exit through your toes. With each breath, allow thoughts and tensions to flow from your mind and body.

6. Continue to breathe in a calm, measured pattern. Beginning with your toes, focus on relaxing your muscles. Let your mind shift its entire attention to the muscles in your toes. See and feel the muscles loosen until all your toes can do is lie there.

7. Gradually move up your body—your feet, your legs, your hips, your pelvis, your abdomen, your chest, your arms, your neck, and your head. Keep your mind's focus on the muscles—how tense and tight they are, still in their positions of action from a day of supporting you and your activities.

With luck, by the time you get to the end of Step 7 it will be all you can do to stay awake. Don't fight it! Let yourself fall asleep. If restful sleep has been a challenge for you, perhaps this meditation will lead you to an amazingly restful night's sleep. Place a sleep sachet filled with herbs such as lavender and chamomile under your pillow for sweet dreams!

The Bedroom Is for ... Sleeping

One challenge many of us face is being able to leave the day behind when we turn in for the night. Do you use your bedroom for family meetings, doing your taxes, or finishing up work you brought home from the office? Are you one who reads, eats, or watches TV in bed?

These are habits that allow your mind (and body) to remain alert and busy in bed ... not exactly conducive to falling asleep. Training your mind to view the bedroom as a place for no activities other than sleeping and sex will help you get over the periodic pitfalls of sleep disturbance more quickly.

CAUTION Wake Up!

A nice, hot bath before bed? Physiologically, blood rushes away from the brain to skin surfaces. So when you hop in a (relatively) cool bed, your temperature drops, leaving you very sleepy. But if you're pregnant, have a heart condition, experience dizziness, or have high blood pressure, check with your physician before taking the plunge.

Sex? Did we say sex? We did! Sexual stimulation and orgasm release endorphins, which are hormones that relax you, making it easier for you to get to sleep.

One thing is for sure: No matter what your sleep habits are, the more comfortable you can make yourself, the better you'll sleep and the more time you'll spend dreaming.

Dreams May Be the Body's Natural Healer

Dreams may be seen as healing in different ways. From a psychological perspective, dreams are often viewed as lost parts of ourselves that can be reclaimed, making us whole. As we said in Chapter 2, dreams have often been seen as conduits to healing— remember Aesculapius, the legendary healer in classical Greece? Additionally, many people find that creative visualization, even lucid dreaming—the practice of becoming conscious of one's dreams and directing them—are healing on many different levels.

Certainly, whatever meaning you personally ascribe to the function of REM sleep and dreaming, it's clear that a good, healthful night's sleep gives your body—and your dreaming mind—a great environment for promoting your physical and mental health!

> **Dreamwork**
>
> Wide awake in the middle of the night? The best thing to do is … get up! Experts discourage lying in bed for more than 15 minutes waiting for sleep to return. The bed is for sleeping, not *worrying* about *not* sleeping! So go to another room and read, knit, or listen to Mozart until you feel yourself becoming drowsy. Then go back to bed.

Your Sleep Worksheet

For the next seven nights, record your sleep habits. You can copy this form and fill it out, so you can add it to your sleep journal. Tracking your sleep habits helps you to see what patterns you've developed that either support or challenge your ability to fall asleep and stay asleep.

Sleep Worksheet

	Before bed activities	Time to bed	Time to fall asleep	Did you wake at night?	Did you dream?	How did you feel in the morning?
Day 1						
Day 2						
Day 3						
Day 4						
Day 5						
Day 6						
Day 7						

Observations and comments:

After you understand what your usual sleep patterns are, you can identify ways to make changes that are more supportive of a good night's sleep—and more conducive to a night of dreams!

The Least You Need to Know

- ◆ Circadian rhythms are internal clocks that govern all living organisms.

- ◆ Our sleep cycle occurs in a distinct pattern, and dreaming takes place in the REM period.

- ◆ Good bedtime and bedroom habits can improve sleep and time spent dreaming.

- ◆ Meditation offers a peaceful transition from the hectic waking world to relaxation in preparation for restful sleep.

- ◆ Dreams can be healing.

4

What Psychology Teaches Us About Dreams

In This Chapter

- ◆ Exploring beneath "see" level
- ◆ Psychoanalytic dream theorists: Freud, Jung, and Perls
- ◆ Being conscious about your unconscious
- ◆ How important are dreams to *you?*

"For the waking there is one common world only," wrote Heraclitus, a sixth-century B.C.E. Greek philosopher. "But when asleep, each man turns to his own private world."

Since the beginning of history, humans have suspected that dreams were "different," that they came from a place other than the everyday here and now. Traditional cultures thought that dreams were messages from God, or the medium through which special powers were passed from the supernatural to the human. Dreams were used by writers to move their plots along—the first significant poem ever written, *The Epic of Gilgamesh* of the third century B.C.E., is punctuated by meaningful dreams that help plot movement—and some great artists used dreams to inspire their flights of fancy. "I've always had access to other worlds," wrote Leonora Carrington, a twentieth-century surrealist painter. "We all do because we all dream."

In Western culture it wasn't until the late nineteenth century that the study of dreams returned to Heraclitus's idea of dreams as a person's "own private world." As psychology and psychoanalysis developed, so too did the interpretation of dreams as they related to each individual's own personal situation and consciousness. Three twentieth-century psychoanalysts—Sigmund Freud, Carl Jung, and Frederick "Fritz" Perls—were primarily responsible for this new vision of dreams and their meanings, with Sigmund Freud leading the way.

Freud's Dream Theories

What do the human psyche and an iceberg have in common?

Give up? Okay, we'll tell you. Each has a hidden area below the surface that is far larger than what's visible. In humans, the part of the iceberg that's below sea (or "see") level is the subconscious or *unconscious.* The part that's visible is what we're aware of, our conscious thoughts. While philosophers, writers, and thinkers throughout history have hinted at the notion of an unconscious, it was Sigmund Freud (1856–1939) who conceptualized the layout of the psyche and coined the term "unconscious."

Dream Dictionary

According to psychoanalytic theory, the **unconscious** is the sum of all thoughts, memories, impulses, desires, and feelings of which you're not aware but which influence your emotions and behavior.

Freud believed that nothing we did occurred by chance. Unconscious conflicts centering on aggression, sexual impulse, and the unrelenting desire for pleasure motivated every action and thought we had. The way he saw it, in order to fit into civilized society, we buried our primitive appetites. But since we couldn't eradicate our impulses entirely, we had to make do with shoving them deep down into the messy interior of our psyches.

Freud thought that the trouble with burying something as potent as the id (the pleasure-seeking, sexual, aggressive core of our being) is that it pops up every now and then in disguised configurations. It refuses to be denied. It's gotta have a release, one way or another. Sometimes this comes out in Freudian slips—verbal mistakes that tell us something about our unconscious wishes. These slips can occur in waking life, but also in our dreams. They convey something we weren't aware that we felt or desired. Here's an example: You dream about a third-grade teacher who made your life seem like hell. In the dream you say, "Hello, Mrs. Pernokas, I thought you were dead." What you'd meant to say was "retired." Oops. For a second the censoring aspect of the self was on the fritz, and you expressed what you really felt—hostility.

But how do you know what your unconscious is all about (and thus how you really feel and what you really want) if, by its very nature, it's hidden? A good place to start is an examination of your dreams, at least according to Freud. He referred to dreams as the "royal road to the unconscious" and believed that you act out in your dreams the *id* desires that you can't admit or act on in your waking life. The other parts of your psyche as defined by Freud—the *ego* and the *superego*—are less vigilant when you sleep. In other words, your guard is down during sleep, giving your unconscious wishes a chance to escape, to rise to the surface for expression in your dreams.

But wait. If that's true, if you get the chance to act out all your hidden desires in your dreams, then why on earth do you sometimes have silly, incoherent, scary, or tragic dreams? Well, now here's where things get *really* interesting.

Although your guard might be down while you sleep, according to Freud, it isn't absent altogether. Even while dreaming you might feel upset and anxious about the powerful desires or emotions your dreams are expressing. To preserve sleep (remember, Freud once said that the purpose of dreams was to guard sleep), your mind does a little after-hours censoring. In this way, you get the best of both worlds: Your dreams are a compromise because they express your wishes in a disguised, and therefore nonthreatening, way at the same time you're enjoying some undisturbed shut-eye.

> **Dream Dictionary**
>
> The **ego** is that part of the psyche that acts as the gatekeeper between instinctual (**id**) feelings and the sense of propriety and conscience (**superego**).

Dreamwork à la Freud

Freud breaks down this censoring process, which he called "dreamwork," into several steps: secondary process, condensation, displacement, and projection. By uncovering how and what you censor during your dreams, you can discover a great deal about your true feelings and motives (or so the theory goes). Let's take a look at what each type of dreamwork really means:

- ◆ **Secondary process.** This is the way we manage to make a whole story from the content of dream, however disjointed or bizarre that content may be. Think of it this way: Suppose you were responsible for an episode of *Seinfeld* and you were told it had to have these things in it: Elaine on a unicycle with a kitten in her hair, a pagoda, your humanities professor in the form of Kramer, Jerry giving birth in the Library of Congress, and George having a cupcake with Janet Reno. Your attempt to make sense of this is just like what the secondary process does by coming up with some kind of story that includes all these parts. But in so doing, it actually disguises whatever the dream was originally about. The sense it makes of the parts, the dream it presents us with, is its *manifest content*. Freud was convinced that you had to decode the manifest content and find the hidden meaning, or *latent content* of the dream.

> **Dream Dictionary**
>
> **Manifest content** refers to the literal story and symbols of the dream. **Latent content** refers to what true meaning lies behind the dream symbols. Another way to think about it is manifest content is the wrapped package while latent content is the hidden contents. Freud believed the "gift" was far more important than the "wrapping."

- **Condensation.** Condensation refers to the tendency to combine a number of latent dream thoughts into a more succinct element. Eminent psychoanalyst and writer Charles Rycroft states that in condensation single details of our dreams may stand for several topics; two or more images fuse to form a composite image, the meaning of which has something to do with each image. For example, if you dream of cookies about to burn in the oven from your childhood home, the condensed image of the oven may indicate that you are both wishing for the comforts of the past *and* feeling that your current situation is "too hot to handle."

- **Displacement.** Displacement refers to the way we can reduce our anxieties by dreaming about them in a safe way. You express an urge but you redirect it onto another person or object. For instance, suppose you're not aware of how angry you are at your teenage son. In the world of id instincts, you might even feel your rage is murderous. But instead of having a dream in which you kill your own kid (now *that* would produce anxiety and wake you up), you dream that Beavis and Butthead (his favorite TV characters) die in a skiing accident. In short, when we displace, we use a symbol as a stand-in for meaning. Hence, the well-known Freudian sexual symbolism: Anything remotely phallic shaped is a symbol for a penis (guns, sticks, Eiffel Tower …) and anything remotely resembling a receptacle is a vagina (cup, cave, box …).

- **Projection.** Projection is similar to displacement, but reduces the process a step. In your dreams when you project your repressed fantasies onto someone or something else, you're still getting to dream about that thing, but you don't have to take responsibility for that upsetting wish. Using the last example of the murderous parent, with projection your teenage son would actually get the ax, but someone other than you would be wielding it. Gruesome example, right? Just remember: These are just feelings that everyone experiences from time to time. Certainly you should never act on them!

To help him figure out what his patients' dreams truly represented, Freud encouraged them to free-associate, to simply say what first came to mind about each image or action in the dream. With free association to help analyze the manifest dream, it becomes possible to understand the dream as an attempt at wish fulfillment.

Clearly, interpreting your dreams according to Freudian precepts is not an easy process; in fact, Freudian analysts go through years of training before they're ready to do so. But even simply reading about the methods of interpretation can help you explore the meaning of your dreams.

> **CAUTION**
>
> ## Wake Up! _____
>
> There's a world of difference between thought and action. There are no wrong or bad thoughts, feelings, or dreams. As writer Carson McCullers once said, "Nothing human is alien to me." But how you *act* on your feelings can be good, bad, wrong, or right. If uncovering feelings in disturbing dreams puts you in danger of acting on them, *stop.* Seek help from a mental health professional.

But What About Anxiety?

Freud's take on dreams and his assertion that they are of central importance was brilliant and remarkable. But that's not to say he was 100 percent right. The idea that dreams were a "safe" form of wish fulfillment has many, many critics. You might be surprised to hear that the list of skeptics includes even Freud. He became less wedded to that idea later in his life.

> ## Dreamwork _____
>
> A dreamer dreams of running through a meadow of wildflowers; wind streaming through the dreamer's hair and clothes; and flowers, trees, and grasses waving. Laughing, the dreamer stops and stoops to sample the aroma of a bright red flower, but is startled to see the image of the dreamer's mother's face at the center of the flower— and the strong reaction jolts the dreamer awake. Free association of the manifest content of this dream reveals what Freud believes is the true hidden meaning—for example, the mother may be holding the dreamer back from blossoming fully as an individual.

And what about those anxious dreams; is that wish fulfillment? Freud might argue that it's disguised wish fulfillment, but he also said that anxiety dreams are the result of failing to achieve a good enough disguise so that the underlying wish came too near the surface, and *presto*—you found yourself in that dream where you are once again taking a test for which you are unprepared, or naked in front of the PTA.

Freud also said that anxiety dreams were a function of repressed sexual impulses. This brings us to the second big criticism of Freud's take on dreams: the idea that everything from cigars to toothpicks represents the phallus; and that caves, jars, pits, and other passive receptacles stand for the female genitals. Freud was a product of his gender, race, class, and generation. His preoccupation with sexual imagery may have a lot to do with the sexual repression of the Victorian era and/or his own relationship with sex. Clearly, the meaning he assigns symbols may say more about his culture than about any fixed reality. His assertion that women are marred versions of men and his ignorance of many of the dynamics between mother and daughter certainly call into question some of his conclusions.

> ### Life Is But a Dream
>
> Because Freud began his study of dreams with his own, many of his critics—and there are lots of them!—say that the preoccupation with sex that forms the core of his dreamwork theory reflects only his own conflicts and shouldn't be applied to everyone.

Again, many of Freud's theories, including those that relate to dreams, have come under much disfavor of late, perhaps because of his insistence that all roads lead to repressed feelings of sexuality and other hidden desires. When it comes to interpreting dreams, many people look rather to one of his disciples, Carl Jung, for inspiration.

Carl Jung: Archetypes and the Collective Unconscious

Carl Jung (1875–1961), 19 years Freud's junior, corresponded with Freud from 1906 until 1913. Freud even considered Jung his heir apparent. But they broke off their relationship over their differing views of—you guessed it—dreams. Both men believed in the existence of the unconscious and in the importance of dreams, and delighted in each other's intelligence and curiosity.

But there were differences, and these differences eventually led Freud to feel betrayed by Jung, on whom he had lavished attention, while Jung came to feel like the paternalistic Freud would go so far as to stifle his voice in order to preserve Freud's own theory regarding dreams.

Jung had a, well, *nicer* view of the unconscious than Freud. Instead of regarding it as that wild animal part of our psyche we fight against, Jung saw the unconscious as a collection of many sorts of spiritual aims to welcome and explore. He firmly believed that our dreams weren't disguised attempts to hide true feelings from the waking mind. Rather, they were clear attempts to guide the waking self. The goal of living (and of our dreams), as he saw it, was to accept and integrate all parts of ourselves. So naturally, he considered dreams as expressions from one part of the self trying to communicate with the conscious part, striving toward wholeness: Dreams didn't disguise the unconscious, they revealed it. Jung once said, "It is on the whole probable that we continually dream, but that consciousness makes such a noise that we do not hear it."

As James R. Lewis in *The Dream Encyclopedia* points out, Jung thought of ego as the individual's self-image (so the sentence "You have an ego the size of Rhode Island" makes sense in this context), and the image we project to the world he called the "persona." But in order to get along in society, Jung believed we jettisoned certain aspects of ourselves, which he referred to as the "non-self." These rejected pieces congeal into an unconscious structure which he coined the "shadow."

Additionally, there are feminine traits (anima) that are repressed in the male psyche, and there are masculine traits (animus) repressed in the female psyche. The anima, animus, and the shadow should be integrated into the ego. Jung thought that we fall in love with our opposites as a way to become whole. If we have lots of anima but no animus, for instance, we might find ourselves head over heels with someone chock-full of animus. This view of finding in your partner what you lack in yourself is accepted in many schools of couples' therapy. Harville Hendrix talks about this—using different lingo—in *Getting the Love You Want* (HarperPerennial, 1990). This is not to say that Jung believed we're always aware of what we lack and what we need, so it's very likely that we could be drawn to someone and not understand why.

In dreams, all these separate aspects of the self appear. Here's what we mean:

- **The persona.** As discussed, this is the image we present to the world and not our "real self." In dreams, the persona appears as a person of some kind, either ourselves or someone else. Being naked in a dream can symbolize the loss of persona.

- **The shadow.** The shadow is the instinctive or weaker side of our nature, and provokes negative reactions such as fear and anger. Its appearance in dreams can suggest we need to exercise more control over our weaknesses.

- **The anima and animus.** The anima is the feminine side in a man's personality, often represented in dreams by a beautiful or goddesslike figure. The animus is the masculine side in a woman's personality, represented in dreams by a godlike, heroic, or powerful man.

- **The divine child.** Jung defined the divine child as the symbol of the true self. The appearance of a baby or child in a dream suggests vulnerability, but also freshness, spontaneity, and potential.

- **The wise old man.** Symbolized by a father, priest, or other figure of authority, the appearance of the wise old man in a dream can represent the self or a powerful figure.

◆ **The great mother.** The great mother is a symbol not only of growth, nurturing, and fertility, but also of seduction, possession, and dominance. The great mother appears in many forms: mother, princess, or witch.

Because Jung believed that there's no latent content to dreams, the manifest dream supplies the dreamer with all the knowledge she or he needs. He advocated dream amplification to explore a dream's meaning. This is a way to try to see what words, images, and beliefs arise when we think about our dreams. He was hoping to find a broad understanding of the images that extended beyond the bounds of the dreamer's culture. Jung asked that patients describe to him a dream as if he were totally ignorant of the objects, people, and setting in the dream. That way, the patients could voice the totality of the dream experience, without self-judgment or explanation.

Jung thought that dreams followed a dramatic sequence, like a play in four acts. The first acts would introduce the characters, the conflict, and then there would be some sort of resolution to the drama. Similarly, the end of the dream-drama would pose the solution to the problem facing the dreamer.

Dreamy

Toward the end of Jung's and Freud's friendship, Jung had a dream of exploring a house, descending its many levels until he reached rooms he hadn't realized existed, finally arriving at a cave containing two skulls. Jung believed the dream was a metaphor for his exploration of his soul, down to the level of the collective unconscious. Freud, on the other hand, thought the two skulls (representing Jung's wife and sister-in-law) indicated the dream's expression of hidden wishes.

Jung also believed there were different kinds of dreams: insignificant or objective dreams about everyday life events, significant dreams or dreams about inner life, and great dreams, dreams in which the *collective unconscious* came into play. While our own lives mold the personal unconscious, the collective unconscious represents the broad human memory that exists within each of us and takes the form of *archetypes*—mythical images that occur in every culture throughout time. These archetypes can appear in dreams—the same images that appeared to our ancestors and speak to us today.

Examples of archetypal images are the wise old man, the earth mother, and the "mandala" (sacred wheel) found in art, science, and religions throughout the world. Jung discovered many archetypal dream images because his patients' dreams contained symbols that were strange to them but that held significance as mythic world images.

Near the end of his career, Jung explored mysticism and related his dream theories to the paranormal. Many people have been inspired by his work, among them psycho-analyst and writer James Hall and mythologist Joseph Campbell.

Freud and Jung are not the only psychoanalysts who developed theories about dreams and dreaming. Fritz Perls is the founder of Gestalt psychology, a type of therapy that focuses on integrating emotions and feelings into harmony in the here and now. He also had a theory about what dreams reveal about the unconscious.

> **Dream Dictionary**
>
> According to Jung, the **collective unconscious** is an innate tendency to organize and interpret our experiences in similar ways to each other. As a species, then, humankind possesses a group awareness that functions below the surface of conscious understanding. The content of the collective unconscious is expressed primarily in symbols Jung called **archetypes**.

Fritz Perls: The Gestalt of Becoming Your Dreams

Frederick "Fritz" Perls (1893–1970), the founder of Gestalt therapy, is the third pillar in the triumvirate of dream-meisters we'll talk about. *Gestalt* is a German word meaning "shape" or "form." Gestalt therapy studies our perceptions and behaviors with respect to the wholeness of our responses. In other words, Perls's goal was to help people discover the emotional holes in themselves that were unconsciously disowned, refill them, and become a unified being once again.

Perls believed that our dreams contain disowned parts of the self. How he sought to reintroduce these denied aspects of our personality into conscious awareness is where his original approach comes into play.

Everyone and *everything* in the dream represent part of the dreamer's psyche in the here and now. We are the creators of and actors in our dreams. So in order to find out what we've disowned (or where our emotional holes are), it was important to retell the dream in the present tense and tell the dream from the perspective of each character and object. One way he teased out various elements of the dream (and the self) was by using the "two-chair" or "empty-chair" technique. The dreamer sits on one chair and takes on the characteristics of an object or character in the dream. Then the dreamer changes seats and directly addresses the first character or object in the voice of the second, and so on. By repeatedly shifting chairs and characters, the parts of the dream (of the person) come into focus in terms of content, posture, tone, and emotion.

Here's an example of how Gestalt therapy works: Suppose you had a dream that you were running through a field of yellow flowers very quickly. The Gestalt therapist might ask you to act out your role in the dream as well as the role of the flowers. The therapist might also ask you to verbalize how each "character" felt. Remember, Gestalt therapists, in an effort to be in the "here and now" insist that you enact the dream from every angle in the present tense and from each object's point of view.

> **Dream Dictionary**
>
> In Gestalt psychology, **gestalt** refers to any of the patterns that make up all experience.

> **Dreamwork**
>
> For some people, it may be uncomfortable to look at a dream from a Gestalt view. Just the same way some people are uncomfortable with the notion of actors bursting out in song in Broadway musicals, you may find it difficult or uncomfortable to "become" the images of your dreams. But you can learn much from trying out a new way of perceiving dreams. So open yourself to experimenting with Freudian, Jungian, and Gestalt vantage points and see how you like the view revealed from those perspectives.

Taking on the role of the running person, you might say to the flowers, "Your existence matters because you are beautiful and graceful and truly alive." At this point a Gestalt therapist would actually ask you to switch chairs and speak to the now empty chair in the voice of the flower! You, as the flower, might have this to say to the empty chair (representing the running dreamer): "You just keep running by me. Ignoring me. You are in such a rush that I get afraid you'll step on me and crush me."

At this point, the dreamer might realize that she doesn't feel that she possesses in her waking life the qualities that the flowers do. She doesn't feel graceful or beautiful in any meaningful way. As she realizes that she's missing these feelings in herself, she may begin to realize that the flowers in her dream are her creation—so this must mean that somewhere inside her reside the attributes of beauty, grace, and vitality! Once she recognizes this, a Gestalt therapist might say she now can reclaim these buried aspects of her personality.

Many people have found this approach useful. Dream expert Robert Van de Castle thinks this approach works well with recurrent dreams and especially nightmares. The dreamer can reduce the potency of the fear by having a confrontational "conversation" with the part of the dream that is so tyrannical. However, critics also point out that Perls's approach can feel too confrontational and aggressive. But the Gestalt way of looking at dreams can supply us with an immediate understanding of our dreams and what jigsaw pieces of the self have been missing.

Now You Be the Therapist!

Each of the three approaches to dream interpretation that we've discussed in this chapter—Freudian, Jungian, and Gestalt—offers a different window on your dreams and their meanings. You may find that you naturally gravitate toward one or another of these approaches. Or you might wonder which to use for your dreams.

Let's put one of your dreams to the test. Get a pen or pencil (and a watch or timer for the Freudian exercise), and make yourself comfortable in a place where you can avoid distractions and interruptions for about an hour.

First, write down a dream that you've had. If you can't think of a recent dream, you can use a dream from your dream journal.

Next, use the dream you recorded to complete each of the three exercises in the following sections.

Your Freudian Dream

The Freudian approach attempts to uncover what you censor during your dreams, and how to reveal your hidden desires and motivations.

1. Read your dream as you recorded it.

2. Set a 10-minute timer (or note the time on your watch to mark off 10 minutes).

3. Write down any and every word, term, memory, or image that comes to mind as you think about the dream. Keep writing for 10 minutes. This is an example of free association that we mentioned earlier.

4. When your time is up, look at what you wrote. Do any patterns or themes emerge? What do your thoughts tell you about the dream and why you dreamed it?

Your Jungian Dream

The Jungian approach holds that the dream contains all the information you need to understand its archetypal message.

1. Read your dream again as you originally recorded it in your dream journal.

2. List the main characters (or objects) and events in the dream. Take as long as you like, and go back to your dream as often as you wish.

3. Explore your dream's cast and plot. How do the characters or objects relate to you and to each other? Are there characters unlike you or unknown to you? How do you think these characters feel in your dream? How might their qualities fit into your life? What might the unknown symbols or people signify in your life?

4. Looking back at Jung's classification of dream types, would you classify your dream as insignificant, significant, or great (archetypal)?

Your Gestalt Dream

Perls's Gestalt approach looks to dreams as the discarded or disowned aspects of the self that you need to recover and restore.

1. Read your dream once more as you recorded it.

2. Identify the dream's key elements, how that element feels, and what it envisions its role in the dream to be. Use your five senses to explore and express the dream's elements, to "be" the element. (If you're "being" a rock, you might feel you are important because you are steady and solid.) Fill in the following table:

Element	How It Feels	Object's Role

3. What is your relationship to each element? Does the element represent something that is "missing" in you?

How Important Do *You* Think Dreams Are?

How is the meaning of the dream you explored in the previous exercise deepened or influenced by each method of interpretation: Freudian, Jungian, and Gestalt? As you get more adept at using these ways of looking at dream meanings, you might discover that one approach resonates more powerfully for you. You also may discover that different kinds of dreams lend themselves to different ways of interpretation. And, of course, as you make your way through this book you'll be able to mix and match techniques that give you a personalized theory of your dreams. These exercises may produce deep material that should be processed slowly. You might want to do each method on a different day or at least take a break between them. If this type of work consistently upsets you, consult a therapist.

As you consider dreams and dreaming, where do *you* think dreams originate? Are dreams neurological firings of synapses designed to purge and cleanse our brains of information overload? Or are they profound psychological windows to our most inner feelings, thoughts, and desires? Could both be true?

A medical doctor we know once told us she felt there was a reason why the unconscious was *un*conscious: Otherwise, we'd know all that stuff below the surface. But perhaps our unconscious *is* a way of knowing for all of us—representing that "gut" feeling or intuitive knowledge we all possess but often don't access or trust with much confidence. Exploring our dreams is a rich tool for honing self-knowledge, that intuitive self-awareness that resonates with honesty and integrity in both our waking and sleeping lives when we are connected to it with conscious intent.

The Least You Need to Know

- Everyone has an unconscious, and it contains the hopes, dreams, and desires that we repress to feel comfortable with others and with ourselves.

- Freud thought that the content of our unconscious had to do with aggression and sex. The latent content of our dreams acts out these drives in a disguised way.

- Jung believed that our dreams contain messages from our individual self and from our collective, societal self. We need to evaluate each kind of dream in both broad and intimate terms to further our quest for spiritual and emotional wholeness.

- Perls developed the Gestalt approach to dream interpretation, in which each aspect of the dream represents a piece of the self. The goal is to reintroduce all the pieces of the dream to the dreamer, allowing the dreamer to "fill the emotional holes."

5

Waking Up to Dream Messages

In This Chapter

- ◆ Keeping an open mind
- ◆ Between sleep and wakefulness: hallucinatory images
- ◆ The dream scale of relativity
- ◆ Dream themes and symbols

Remember when you were a kid and your parents told you that you might find the answer to what was bugging you if you "slept on it"? You know, like where you put your homework or your dental retainer? And do you remember that sometimes their suggestion actually worked?

We think there's a lot to "sleeping on it." While we sleep we give our waking minds a rest and give our unconscious a chance to speak. One of the aims of this book is to get you in touch with the messages your intuition sends to your conscious mind. In our fast-paced world, taking time to slow down and even get *enough* sleep—much less to consider the meaning of our dreams—can be a challenge. We feel it a worthy challenge; one that may change your life and infuse it, perhaps not with more time in your busy schedule, but with a greater calm and directed approach to making your way through your waking day.

Know Thy Dreams, Know Thyself

In the previous chapter, we gave you a crash course in psychoanalytic dream theory. Hopefully you tried out the dream exercises and got a taste of how Freudian, Jungian, and Gestalt dream theories work. Maybe you even felt inspired to learn more about one or more of these methods. (Appendix B can direct you to other resources.) But if you've noticed yourself scouring your dreams for archetypal images at the expense of personal associations, it's time to loosen your grip on Chapter 4. It's important to be open to the messages your intuitive heart sends to your rational head, so you can begin to know yourself by knowing your dreams.

Not every old man in your dreams is a Jungian archetype; sometimes an old man is just an old man—your grandfather, your next-door neighbor, a former teacher. Most Jungian therapists do caution against attributing all our dreams to the collective unconscious, saying instead we should focus on the individual meanings they have for the dreamer. It's a better idea to search for the cultural significance of a certain symbol after searching for the more intimate significance of your dreams. Search for the archetypal symbol only if you're stumped as to what your dream means. This way, you can work backward from a societal to a personal perspective.

Likewise, not every snake in your dream is a Freudian phallic symbol. You are not forever dreaming of killing one parent and sleeping with the other. Sometimes, as Freud himself acknowledged, a cigar is just a cigar. In the same vein, if talking to an empty chair upon awakening to clarify your dream feels like you're, well, talking to an empty chair, then forget the chair Gestalt, at least for a while.

One reason people have difficulty remembering their dreams is that they are oversubscribing to one brand of dream theory or another. Think about it. You feel you just can't connect that blue shoe that dances across your Aunt Fannie's face with any archetypal or sexual symbol. Pretty soon you get frustrated with your failure to interpret the "right" way, and you stop dreaming a lot, then you feel you stop dreaming altogether.

Life Is But a Dream

According to Ann Faraday, Ph.D., dream researcher and author of *The Dream Game* (Harper Paperbacks, 1990), the best indicator of remembering dreams is degree of interest. Engineers usually recall fewer dreams than artists. In modern Western society, women normally recall more dreams than men. Faraday says this is because men are trained to direct their energies toward world affairs, while women are allowed a more "feeling" approach to life.

Your dreams are about you. Not about Fritz or Carl or Sigmund. As long as you are truly interested in recalling your dreams, chances are you can learn how to do so. The more you allow yourself to be the expert, the more of an expert you become.

The other important aspect to recalling dreams is to be sure to welcome (and even invite) a wide variety of dreams. People who are only interested in certain types of dreams choke off the many messages available in favor of the few. So don't just look for dreams about George Clooney, Julia Roberts, your past lives, or which numbers to pick the next time you play the lottery. Be open to all sorts of messages.

Hypnagogic and Hypnopompic Experiences

The hypnagogic images are due to the hypnagogic state (that drowsy feeling that overcomes you as you drift off to sleep). The complement to this is the hypnopompic state, which describes the state you pass through from sleeping to wakefulness. In both, it's common to experience vivid auditory and visual hallucinations.

Can you think of times when you were floating off to dreamland but you felt suspended between wakefulness and sleep? Maybe thoughts left over from the day flitted through your mind—only they had this odd, hallucinatory quality to them. Or completely different material may enter your mind. Some people report hearing music during this pre-sleep time. It's also not uncommon in this state to think you're really experiencing what's in your mind—telling your significant other to move the clothes from the washer to the dryer, for example, or your boss that you want a raise. Or perhaps you are taking a dip into the collective unconscious. In this entryway to sleep, called the hypnagogic state, it's nearly impossible to separate reality from fantasy. You experience a similar state on the other end of sleep, the hypnopompic state. When you awaken, you might vaguely remember your hypnagogic and hypnopompic experiences and believe (or wonder if) they were real.

These dreamlike experiences aren't exactly dreams because you're not exactly asleep. And they aren't really happening, at least externally. Rather, they're hallucinatory events—visual, auditory, and, in the hypnopompic state, olfactory. (This adds a surreal twist to the adage, "Wake up and smell the coffee.") As you're drifting off to or out of sleep, your brain is producing alpha waves. Some sleep theorists postulate that these experiences occur as the waking part of us struggles to retain or regain control from sleep.

Stephen LaBerge, Ph.D., of Stanford University and co-author of *Lucid Dreaming* (Ballantine, 1990), thinks that by making suggestions to ourselves during the hypnagogic state we can influence the content of our dreams. We'll look at this subject, called *lucid dreaming*, in Chapter 21.

> **Dream Dictionary**
>
> **Lucid dreaming** is the name given to the technique developed by Stephen LaBerge, Ph.D., who scientifically demonstrated the dreamer's ability to consciously alter the content of dreams. Sleep researchers use his findings to treat nightmares. Many lay people use his work to solve their problems in dreams.

Some people believe that hypnagogic and hypnopompic images are really flashes of past-life experiences. Some dream researchers theorize that hypnagogic and hypnopompic hallucinations account for perceptions of intruders or alien abductions.

Sleep Paralysis

For some people (about 6 percent of the population, according to recent studies), the transition from sleep to wakefulness literally entraps them. They experience what sleep experts call sleep paralysis. During REM sleep when dream activity is most active, the brain inhibits physical movement (see Chapter 3). This helps to protect the body by preventing it from acting out dream events. In people with sleep paralysis, the part of the brain that controls this inhibition is slow to release the body.

"There would be nights when I would be so afraid to go to sleep," musician Sheryl Crow told *Rolling Stone* magazine of her experiences with sleep paralysis in a 1996 interview. "It's a bizarre and twisted feeling where you feel completely paralyzed. And then the fear that comes along makes your heart race; it makes you sweat."

Although sleep paralysis can be terrifying and feels endless to the person experiencing it, episodes seldom last more than a minute or two—the time it ordinarily takes to wake up. But the memories of sleep paralysis episodes can stay with the dreamer for days, months, and even years. Some people who regularly experience sleep paralysis learn to recognize the state, which helps take the edge from the fear. Scientists do not know for sure what causes sleep paralysis, although it seems to run in families (Sheryl Crow's mother also experiences sleep paralysis) and seems more prevalent in people who also have narcolepsy, a sleep disorder in which a person experiences episodes of involuntary sleep.

A Picture's Worth a Thousand Words

If words are the foundation of written and spoken human language, why aren't your dreams depicted in words? Here are some speculations:

- ◆ I read all day, why would I want to read at night, too?

- ◆ I'm a rotten speller.

- ◆ My eyes are *closed*. Duh.

- ◆ Words alone can't convey all the things that happen in my dreams.

Chances are you guessed the last option. And you're right. Have you ever wondered why your dreams aren't a stream of words running across the dream screen? Granted, those who can't read would be pretty bored at night, and okay, this would also nix the experience of dreams for all prehistoric peoples, but is that it? Is there some other reason you dream about the *image* of a suitcase and not the *word* "suitcase"?

Pictorial language is the most economical, jam-packed way to express our thoughts and feelings. The symbols in our dreams present condensed versions of our hopes, wishes, and fears. Symbols and pictures predate language. (There is no evidence that cavemen and women wrote "Kilroy was here" on cave walls; instead they drew pictures of male, female, and animal figures.) Perhaps these folks' dreams, before language developed, were akin to silent movies.

We now have a soundtrack for our dreams, but it can't express so exactly the message of a dream in which, for example, you are riding the crest of a wave and you're not sure if it will bring you to shore or out to sea where sharks await you. In that single snapshot, you may ascertain that you feel you are not in control of your destiny and that the paths that await you are as different as life and death. Further, because you are smiling, this image expresses a certain confidence that you can "ride this one out" to a positive outcome.

> **Dreamy**
>
> Jean Paul Richter, a popular German novelist at the turn of the nineteenth century, once said, "Dreams are an involuntary kind of poetry." What a beautiful way to express how each and every one of us becomes a poet when we use symbols in our dreams!

The usage of images in poetry comes close to mimicking a dream experience. Poetry uses metaphor—a kind of displacement (remember Freud's inclusion of this in his dream theory?) in that it borrows attributes from one object and ascribes them to another (as in "your lips are sweeter than wine").

Poetry doesn't follow a linear, sensible pattern; it contains its own messages coded into its symbols. Interestingly enough, Samuel Coleridge, author of the evocative poem "Kubla Khan," insisted that he dreamed this poem during a three-hour nap. Hundreds of poets attribute their inspiration, if not the poem itself, to their dreams.

Drop That Dream Dictionary!

Dream dictionaries fill shelves in the bookstores. Each one will tell you what the symbols in your dreams say about you. There are two problems with this. First, the books themselves contradict each other, and second, most likely they contradict you.

The language of dreams is, above all, a personal language. You can't learn it the way you learned Spanish. Sure, to a certain extent, humans are all in the same boat; we all laugh, cry, need food, shelter, and sleep. And sure, this results in some common experiences and symbols, but that doesn't mean you're the same person as your best friend or sibling—no matter how closely your life experiences have dovetailed.

From a historical standpoint it might be fun to page through a dream dictionary. Dream dictionaries can reveal the predilections of a certain decade or culture. You'd expect to find a dictionary compiled in 1960s West Germany to differ from one compiled from people's dreams who live in Los Angeles in the twenty-first century. By the same token, a dream dictionary written from a clinical psychological perspective most likely will differ radically from one written by a student of New Age philosophy.

If leafing through a dream dictionary sparks your imagination and gives you inspiration to tackle the meaning of your own dreams, then go ahead and look up the meaning for "rat," for example. One dictionary will tell you it indicates you need to take time out from the "rat race," another will suggest it alludes to thoughts of death (as in the plague). Maybe this applies to you. Or maybe you had a pet rat, so you associate many loving qualities to it.

Common Dream Themes

Because we are all from planet Earth, there are some general dream themes that depict common life concerns such as being unprepared for a test, forgetting things, falling, flying, appearing naked in public, being chased, meeting someone famous, and having sex. But a word of caution: Even though these are general kinds of themes, the specific meaning of each does differ from person to person. A dream of standing at the Academy Awards podium likely has a very different context for you than for Nicole Kidman!

Your Dream Symbols

Do you find that the same elements keep coming up in your dreams? Maybe your sister, in your dreams, always wears blue and carries a pencil in her right hand. Or whenever you've had a particularly stressful day, there are clocks in your dreams. Repeating elements likely are symbols for you, images intended to convey certain messages.

Personal dream symbols often have personal meanings that go beyond universal meanings. A clock, of course, is a common image to represent time. But perhaps for you, it also signals that time is running out to make key decisions in your life. Or maybe it represents keeping things in order (à la your grandfather, who used to start each morning by making sure the time on every clock in the house was precisely the same). The context of symbols in your dreams helps you to interpret their meanings.

Not every object, person, or event that appears in your dreams is necessarily a symbol. But images that appear frequently bear further investigation. You can identify the dream images that are metaphoric messages for you by creating your *personal* dream dictionary. You can use your dream journal for this, or use a separate notebook. Here are some guidelines:

- ◆ For two weeks, write down as many images as you can recall from your dreams. Use single words—dog, fire, highway, sailboat, flying. Do this when you first wake up, while dream images are still fresh in your mind. List the words down the left side of your paper, leaving plenty of room to go back to add comments later.

- ◆ If there is a clear context for the symbol, write it to the right of the word.

- ◆ Each time an image repeats, make a tally mark to the right of the original word. If there is a different context for the image, make a note of it.

- ◆ At the end of two weeks, review your list. You might want to organize it in some way—perhaps alphabetically or thematically. What images appear most frequently? What images strike you as unusual?

- ◆ Add to your dream dictionary as new images become apparent.

Dreamwork

It's a good idea to include in your dictionary other aspects of your dreams: *actions* (running, soaring, dancing); *feelings* (abandonment, joy, fear, nostalgia); and *colors*. Do you hear certain sounds or experience certain smells? Include these, too. And take note of key events that seem to repeat in your dreams; these often have symbolic meanings apart from your literal interpretations. Make note of the feelings that these symbols engender, both during the dream and upon waking.

Dream symbols change as you do, and may acquire additional or new meanings as you become more adept at identifying them and using them to decipher the messages of your dreams. You're likely to find your symbolic "vocabulary" is quite extensive.

All Dreams Are Not Created Equal

There are times in your life that are turning points: graduation from high school, marriage, divorce, career changes, the birth of a child, and a serious medical diagnosis are just a few. At these times, your dreams are apt to both reflect the struggle you're in and express some fears, hopes, and wishes that, if understood, may aid you through the turbulent times.

Back in Balance

It also appears that dreaming helps us regain our sense of balance. Feeling out of control in our waking lives can trigger our dreaming mind to pitch in by supplying us with more images that we can use to help us master the challenges before us. Sometimes, by paying particular attention to dreams during times of upheaval, we can realize new, creative ways to respond to the problems at hand or that we have resources to help us that we had not considered.

CAUTION | **Wake Up!**

If you're going through a particularly stressful time, you may decide that, for the moment, deciphering your dreams is simply too much. Maybe what you need is to read a good book, go to the movies, or take the dog for a walk. That's fine. Sometimes when we are particularly emotional and vulnerable, the best way to care for ourselves is to take a break from our problems.

Consider the example of a young man who recently received a promotion at his law firm. You might think his dreams would express feelings of triumph or delight. But no. Instead, his dreams were filled with images of quicksand that kept sucking him down. As he began to take these recurring dreams more to heart, he was able to get in touch with a part of him that was fearful that his increased professional responsibilities would eclipse his desire to continue studying jazz piano.

Dreamwork

What are your personal dream themes? You've probably begun to notice that certain elements, symbols, and feelings crop up in your dreams. One way to begin to name your dream themes is by titling your dreams. Leave a blank space at the top of your nightly dream journal. Immediately *after* jotting down your dream, create a one- or two-line title for it. The title may reflect a feeling, thought, idea, or a dream you have at particular times—such as "my test-stress dream."

All Dreams Have Meaning—But Do I Have to Know *All* My Dreams?

You can recognize important dreams by their power and by the feelings with which they leave you. Did you ever have one of those dreams you just couldn't "shake"? Maybe it was so vivid that it felt real. Maybe you dreamed of people who meant so much to you at one time, but you hadn't thought of them in years. Or maybe you had a dream in which you felt euphoric, as if some secret about your life had been revealed to you. These dreams are marked by their intensity.

But we have several dreams each night, right? And maybe we remember one or two, or just fragments. Some dreams seem pretty straightforward, commenting on our present lives, perhaps even what we did that day. Some dreams feel like warnings (like the jazz piano player/lawyer's dream). Still others feel like gifts, they are that wonderful and seem to point to hidden reserves of joy, talent, and creativity.

You may decide to look at some or many of these dreams. Some you'll want to explore by yourself, with a therapist, in a dream group, or with your partner or best friend. Some you may want to ignore for a bit. Since your dreams are messages of yourself *to* yourself, it's up to you to decide who else gets to be let in on the message.

How many messages are too many? If you remember lots of dreams, you might find yourself inundated with messages. It's important to not go off the deep end in this journey. Remember to challenge yourself at work, go for walks with friends, play darts, play with your kids. Dream exploration shouldn't take you away from your life, it should enrich it. We suggest you record all your dreams—especially at first—but only focus on one or two a week.

We think you'll find plenty of material in one or two dreams. Don't worry about which dreams to choose; the central concerns we have tend to repeat themselves in our dreams until we acknowledge them.

Cracking the Code

So you say you're ready to wake up to your dream messages? But wait, are you also saying your messages are in a code you don't understand? This might be because you haven't used the right tools to crack the code. Patience, they say, is a virtue. We also believe that there are times when, despite our enthusiasm, we're simply not ready to understand what our dreams convey. The material may be too threatening for our current level of emotional development.

It's also a good idea to make sure you aren't sticking too close to one mode of dream interpretation. Are you trying to see your sexual urges in every dream? Are you dismissing dreams that don't seem to be about your desire to become president of the United States?

There are as many messages in our dreams as there are emotions in our hearts. But there are some kinds of dreams that seem to focus on certain kinds of messages. For instance, there are creative dreams, dreams in which the power of the symbols is so dazzlingly evocative that when you wake up, you may feel a need to paint, or sing, or write.

Other types of dreams seem to point out the obvious. Well, this makes sense if you remember that dreams are always focused on our own personal issues, not on global economic concerns. Sure, we can have dreams that apply to society as a whole, but they always apply to us first and foremost. We tend to dream about our relationships, jobs, hobbies, and day-to-day concerns, along with all the hopes and fears that each contains.

> **Dreamy**
>
> Mary Shelley was inspired to write *Frankenstein* after sitting around one night telling ghost stories with her relatives and friends. Before going to bed, she was encouraged to write a horror story. That night she had a nightmare that became the basis for her book.

Have you ever had a dream in which the answer to a particularly annoying or difficult problem was revealed to you? A problem that you'd been wrestling with for a while? It's not uncommon for solutions to come to us in dreams.

Take, for example, a woman who had written a short story. She labored over every character, every word, every plot twist. But no matter what she did, there was something "off" about it. Not being easily dissuaded, she worked even harder at it and gave it to her editor to critique. But it still didn't quite gel. One night, she dreamed that the main character in her story paid her a visit and told her that the problem was that she was writing the story from the point of view of the wrong character and she should actually choose another character's point of view to tell the story most effectively. The next day, the writer took her character's wise advice and the story came together.

Sometimes, we are able to alter the plot or outcome of our dream stories by training ourselves to become consciously aware that we're dreaming. We're having lucid dreams. Check out Chapter 21 for more on this subject.

The messages that riddle your dreams are created by you and they are for you. You can observe them, explore them, illuminate them—all at your own pace.

The Least You Need to Know

♦ The more interested you are in recalling your dreams, the more of your dreams you're likely to remember.

♦ Dreams come to us in symbols that have many layers and meanings. Above all, the meanings are individual and personal.

♦ Like other life events, many dreams are ordinary and some are significant. You can choose which dreams to explore.

♦ Our dreams can help us unlock our creativity or show us a solution to a problem.

Part 2

What Are You Dreaming About?

Let's get down to brass tacks. Do you dream about falling? Flying? Being chased? Having a sexual encounter with a famous person (or a stranger)? Losing money, teeth, or the address where the exam is taking place? Finding riches?

These are all very common dream themes that often have both literal and symbolic meanings. The meaning that matters most, however, is the one that is unique to *you*. These are *your* dreams, and only you can know what they're all about. Read on for some guidelines to lead you along your path of self-discovery.

Chapter 6

Up in the Air: Dreams About Flying ... and Falling

In This Chapter

- ◆ No ticket needed for this flight
- ◆ Who's in control?
- ◆ Crash landing ahead!
- ◆ What your dream flights and falls tell you

Do you fly in your dreams? People who do often report that the experience is one of exhilaration and freedom. The constraints of real life disappear, and even the sky itself is an invitation, not a limit. Many dream interpreters view flying free and unfettered under your own power in your dreams (Remember Superman and Lois Lane: "You've got me? Who's got *you?*") as an advanced dream skill.

What about falling? Chances are you're like the rest of us and have occasionally taken off on spectacular night flights or stumbled, tumbling down, down, down. Remember, we don't always *hurt* ourselves when we fall, and falling can often be interpreted as the need to pay attention to overcoming a stumbling block or as the prelude to a leap into flight.

Ancient cultures often viewed dream flights as spirit journeys. While the body slept, the soul traveled, visiting loved ones near and far—and even those who had passed from this life. Although clearly the physical body had limits, the intangible soul did not and was free to wander and explore. A luminescent silver cord tethered the soul to the body so as the body awakened, it drew the soul back.

The traditional psychoanalytical party line (courtesy of Dr. Freud) on flying dreams is that they refer to sex. And only sex. Certainly this can be one association to flying, but there are many others. Dream expert Dr. Gayle Delaney notes that Freud, departing from his sexualized view on flying dreams, later suggested that childhood experiences such as being tossed into the air or playing on a seesaw might account for flying dreams.

Today, we tend to take a broad and general view of flying dreams, associating them with feeling on "top of the world," an attempt to rise above problems, or the attainment of personal or spiritual understanding (rising to a "higher ground"). It all depends on how you feel as you fly, the particulars of your journey, and what happened in your waking life before you took off.

Dreamy
The dreamlike imagery of surrealist artists such as Salvador Dali, Max Ernst, and René Magritte, among others, captured the fancy of a public already intrigued with the dream imagery of Freud's *The Interpretation of Dreams* and other writings. Dali's painting *Dream Caused by the Flight of a Bee* portrays a woman peacefully sleeping, her own body suspended above the ground, while a flying elephant dangles from the sky (and two snarling tigers leap from a pomegranate!).

Modes of Transportation

Dream flights seldom require waiting in line, photo ID, or seat assignments. You might fly through the air in a car, boat, or train. You might hang from the cross frame of a giant kite or ride the back of a soaring hawk. In dreams, nothing is too weird, extraordinary, or illogical. Maybe you're 10 miles above the earth in an Otis elevator; maybe you're on a magic carpet, on a Frisbee, or in a bathtub. As often as not, dream flight doesn't even require a vehicle of any sort. You might "swim" into the sky or just float through the air.

How do you get up in the air? We know people who flap their arms like birds, find wings sprouting from their heels, dash down a runway, or sit in a train that speeds up until it flies off the track and into the air. Are you in charge of getting off the ground or is someone or something else responsible for propelling you airborne? Common flying aids in dreams include:

◆ Elevators

◆ Amusement park rides

◆ Rockets, guns, or cannons

◆ Slingshots and catapults

◆ Coats, capes, hats, shoes

◆ Our limbs or other parts of the body

One woman had a recurring dream that she was piloting an array of brightly colored ribbons that formed a firm platform beneath her and then trailed into streamers behind her. Each time she tried to take off, the loose ribbons became entangled and knotted. She then spent the rest of the dream untying and releasing them. We might surmise that the brightly colored ribbons symbolize the pleasing parts of her aspirations but there were factors in this woman's life that grounded her, perhaps keeping her from pursuing her goals.

Taking Flight

When you take off in your dreams, do you enjoy a smooth departure that launches you right into flight? Or are there challenges and difficulties? Generally, the easier it is to get off the ground and stay off the ground, the freer and more in control a person feels in the dream—and perhaps in life.

Who's in Charge?

Who is the pilot of your vehicle of flight? Are you in the front, the back, or clinging precariously to parts not intended to hold passengers? Are you comfortable or scared witless?

Riding as a passenger, especially in a back seat, might remind you of being a kid, having Mom and Dad chauffeur you around. Ah, those were the days, no real worries. Such a dream might indicate a wish to have others take care of you. Are there people in your life who could be more nurturing? Can you think of a way to ask that of them?

Then again, riding in the back seat of the flying car might feel like you're really not in charge of your life—and you don't like that feeling one bit. You feel just as powerless and bossed around as when you were a kid and had to do everything your parents told you.

Or maybe you're in the driver's seat and your family or co-workers are sitting in the back seat. How does it feel to be at the helm? Do you feel trusted, confident, or proud? Or maybe you feel overly responsible for everyone's lives. Have you been concerned about providing for your family either emotionally or economically lately? In other words, why are you having this dream now?

Spreading Your Wings

Sometimes our flying dreams are so glorious we don't want to come back down to earth. We've sprouted wings and we want to keep on flying. This tends to happen more often in dreams where we're flying without benefit of a plane, train, or automobile; it's just us and the wide-open sky. We're free of all pedestrian responsibilities.

Dreamy

In Greek mythology, imprisoned Icarus attempts to escape from King Minos using a pair of wax-and-feather wings his inventor father crafted for him. But he flies too close to the sun, melting the wax holding his wings together, and falls to the earth. Contemporary author Milan Kundera wrote in his novel *The Unbearable Lightness of Being,* "The heavier the burden, the closer our lives come to the earth, the closer our lives come to the earth, the more real and truthful they become."

At a certain point in your flight of fancy you may become aware of someone beckoning to you from the ground. Or maybe in your dream you're flying to school and you hear the bell, but you just don't want to come in for a landing. This might indicate a desire for more freedom and less responsibility in your life. It also might tell you that you're resistant to taking on a responsibility that you should; maybe you should swoop down and see what that person beckoning you wants. Maybe it's time for you to buckle down—just for a little while, and with the hope of making your wildest dreams more of a reality.

Flying High

In most flying dreams, we're aiming to experience a feeling of freedom and joy. One dreamer performs gymnastic feats, another counts the rings on Saturn as she charges into outer space, still another floats gently on a falling leaf. Often these feelings stay with us for hours or days. Clearly, flying is an expression of unrestrained movement, a breaking free of the constraints that keep us tied to the earth. Consider this *dreamlet:*

I dream I am sitting behind my desk at work and I've just cleared off the last paper in the "To Do" pile. I rise, like a helium-filled balloon, and pass through the window. I float out of the city, over the lake, and to a castle where I take a seat at the head of a banquet table and enjoy a sumptuous feast!

Do you fly a few inches from the ground or are you off in outer space? Flying high above the earth, looking down on your town, may connote a successful effort at getting a "different perspective" on things. It may be, for you, the ultimate indication that you're free of old constrictions, internal or external. If you're just skimming the sidewalk, this might indicate that you're not yet comfortable enough to really let fly; but it also may tell you that you're well-balanced, able to fly while remaining well-grounded.

Dream Dictionary

A **dreamlet**, a term coined by dream researcher and interpreter Ann Faraday, is a dream fragment, a piece of dream belonging to a larger dream.

How does it feel to fly in your dreams? Are you ...

♦ Scared that you'll fly too high?

___ Always ___ Often ___ Never

♦ Frustrated that you can't go higher?

___ Always ___ Often ___ Never

♦ Elated that you defied gravity?

___ Always ___ Often ___ Never

♦ Exhilarated by the speed of flight?

___ Always ___ Often ___ Never

♦ Alone, or is there someone with you?

___ Always ___ Often ___ Never

Scary flying dreams leave us feeling out of control. We might find ourselves hanging from the edge of a cliff, or even falling. This can tell us something about what's going on in our lives. Are we overburdened at work and at home? Do we feel powerless? Sometimes the anxiety associated with flying too high can reflect a fear of success or a fear of a new challenge.

Is there something—a tree, telephone wires, a force field, a wall—that prevents you from going higher or farther? This just might indicate barriers in your life that get in the way of your growth. Or maybe your flight is dragged down by extra burdens that you carry. Are you having trouble letting go of old issues? Is there someone in your life with whom you have a limiting relationship? Recognizing the messages in dreams such as these can give you the clarity you need to talk to this friend, relative, co-worker, or partner.

Other flying dreams can speak to the insecure and/or aggressive parts of us. Are you always flying the friendly skies alone, looking down on the rest of us, feeling ever so slightly superior? Maybe this expresses a wish that you be above others and above the nagging insecurity that, deep down, you fear you're not quite as good as the next guy. Maybe you have a strong need to be first, to be the best, and this is symbolized in your dreams by flying the fastest or the highest.

Or perhaps your solo flights mean that you like to show off for your friends on the ground. Maybe you're reveling in your hard-won attempts to grow in some aspect of your life. It's natural to want validation.

Flying solo also can indicate a feeling of loneliness and isolation. Maybe there's no one watching you swoop and soar. Or it could indicate a wonderful, healthy feeling of individuality and freedom from others' expectations! Again, what flying means for you depends on how you feel in your dream and on how you feel about what's happening in your waking life.

Life Is But a Dream

As we mentioned earlier, during the REM sleep state the body lies motionless in a sort of paralysis while the brain is intensely active. One theory is that signals intended for the body to move are often incorporated instead into the story of the dream and manifest as images of flying, jumping, or running. So flying dreams may have a basis in physiology as well as psychology!

Are You There Yet?

Are you flying to a destination? To the launderette? To Disneyland? Are you enjoying the ride, or does it feel that you'll just never get there no matter how far you fly? The sensation can be one of pleasant, lazy exploration or it can be frustrating and unfulfilling. Depending, of course, on you.

In waking life, are you forever working, and never getting much of anywhere? Does it feel like you don't know where you're going? Or you know where you want to go, but life's thwarting you by throwing up obstacle after obstacle, making it impossible to reach your goals? Your flying attempts could tell you something about your direction (or lack of) in life. Perhaps your dreams aren't like your life; perhaps you fly straight from point A to point B without any difficulty at all. Or your dreams might closely mirror your waking frustrations; you may find that your flying feels labored and aimless.

The Great Chase

Have you ever had a dream in which something big, scary, and totally awful was chasing you? Did you ever run away from it so fast that you actually began flying away from it? This dreamer's experience is fairly common:

> *I was walking down a dark corridor and I felt someone behind me. I felt his breath on my neck. I flew, swam the breaststroke actually, into the open sky. He was still behind me. I was afraid to look at him. I swam through the air as fast as I could. I got away.*

In the previous dream, the dreamer is running (swimming) away from something frightening. In as much as dreams reflect all aspects of ourselves, the dreamer just might be running away from some part of himself that he's not quite comfortable with. Knowing this, the dreamer can wonder if there's something about himself that's hard to accept. If so, is that really the best way to handle things? Or maybe running away is, for now, the best way he can cope with a tough situation.

> **CAUTION**
>
> **Wake Up!**
>
> If "chase" dreams occur frequently and are disturbing or nightmarish, seek the support of a loved one and/or a mental health professional to help you get at the underlying causes of the dreams. Maybe it's better to stop running!

Crashing, Wiping Out, Falling Down

As we go to sleep, we often experience the sensation of falling. We're "falling asleep." This occurs in the hypnagogic phase we mentioned in Chapter 5—the conscious mind recognizes its entrance into the sleep state. But this is very different from falling dreams.

How did your last falling dream happen? Did you fall down a well? Did you trip? Did you go sailing off the edge of a cliff? Were you pushed? Did you take a big swan dive off a tall building? Did you fly off into an exhilarating dream flight, then realize the only way back was a crash landing? When did you last have a falling dream? And how did you feel?

"Falling" has a lot of metaphorical meanings. In our dreams, falling is usually associated with fear and unpleasantness. We might fear falling from a loved one's good graces or falling from a position of power, wealth, or happiness. Sometimes we fall in our dreams just as someone in our waking life is rising in some way: getting a promotion, getting married, winning the Ironman triathlon. Falling dreams in response to these events might be letting us know we feel inferior in comparison or that we feel we can't keep up with our more successful friends.

Ann Faraday, dream expert and author, cautions us to first consider a falling dream (and any sort of common dream theme) to be a warning dream. On a literal level, falling dreams can alert us to a danger our unconscious (but not conscious) mind might have registered. If you dream you're falling down your front stairs, it's a good idea to check them and make sure they're secure.

Losing Control

Maybe your falling dreams have a lot to do with sex and romance. Could tumbling down a mountain indicate that you are "falling" for someone? In less modern times, when a woman dreamed of falling, it represented her wish to yield sexually. She was, as they say, a "fallen woman." This can be true today, too, but the interpretation is no longer restricted to women.

Generally, falling dreams are associated with loss of control and a feeling of helplessness. It's possible that our first steps as toddlers—and the many falls we took—are being touched upon in our falling dreams. It has also been suggested that falling dreams hearken back to primitive humans' very real fears about falling out of trees.

We know someone whose father, when she was a toddler, used to lift her up over his head, rocking chair and all, when he arrived home from work every day. For this now-grown woman, flying and falling dreams have a continual sense of thrilling and frightening precariousness, of steepness and terrible wonder. Her father safely settled her back to ground when she was a child. What (or who) is going to keep her from falling as an adult?

> **Life Is But a Dream**
>
> Dreams of falling and flying are common in almost every culture—though their meanings will differ depending on that culture's particular beliefs and customs.

Are your falling experiences like landslides? Can you anticipate the fall or does it happen suddenly? Do you begin falling by crashing through a ceiling, tripping, flying through a plate glass window? Or do you simply find yourself hurtling through space?

Letting Go

Hold on a minute. Sometimes falling dreams aren't terrifying at all. Sometimes they're kind of ... nice.

> *I was teetering on the edge of a cliff. Rocks were falling out from under me. My heart was racing. Then I fell. I landed on my feet, balanced on a surfboard, riding an awesome wave! I rode safely in to shore.*

A falling dream, one where you land safely, can leave a dreamer with a sense of relief. Maybe in your waking life you're trying to keep too many balls in the air. Such a dream might indicate that you need to relax and let one or two balls drop. And if you do, you won't die. Quite the opposite. That's why it's important to think about what waking event or feeling may have triggered this dream.

Booking Passage on the *Titanic*

In your falling dream are you careening through space all alone? With others? Are you wearing a life vest? Are you in a boat? Are you on the starship *Enterprise* (and which crew members are with you?) about to crash-land on a planet in a galaxy light-years from Earth?

The distance you travel as you fall might clue you in to how out of control you feel, as will the contraption you're strapped into. A short fall out of a ground-floor window is different from an endless free fall through the sky. Generally, a falling dream in which you're not the skipper or pilot or driver indicates that you feel out of control *and* that you've given the control over to someone else. A dream in which you're the captain of the *Titanic* and not a mere passenger might mean you feel responsible for and guilty about some action of yours that has gone terribly wrong.

To the Rescue

So you're falling, faster and faster toward the ground. You're scared you're going to crash. Do you?

Who Saves You?

Most of us wake up before hitting bottom—sometimes with heart pounding and breath rasping, just as if we were really *that* close to a crash! Every now and then, a crash landing seems inevitable. Do you crash ... or are you rescued? Most often, someone or something comes to the rescue. Because this is a dream, who or what doesn't always make sense. It could be your cat, a mysterious stranger, a teacher from grade school. It's worth exploring the meaning of your rescuer. Although on the one hand you crafted the rescue (after all, it's your dream), on the other you've chosen a rescuer that has certain representations for you. Animals are known for their keen sensitivity to all sorts of events we humans are slow to recognize, like severe weather (tornadoes) and earthquakes, or other critical events like fires and floods. Perhaps you're feeling the need to be rescued, but don't know who to turn to for help … hence the stranger who materializes in the knick of time. Sometimes figures from the past—like that grade school teacher—represent a time of familiarity and safety that you'd like to return to.

When there's no one to save you, you have to save yourself. This scenario might be a metaphor for situations in your waking life. Perhaps you're in a relationship you know is unhealthy, or it's time to leave your current job for better opportunities elsewhere. Or maybe you're in a circumstance over which you have little or no control—your company is downsizing or your landlord sold the house you rent. Some people have falling dreams in which they can decelerate their fall so that they land gently. This may represent a triumph over feeling so out of control.

What Happens If You Fall and Hit the Ground?

A common superstition holds that if you hit the ground in a falling dream, you'll die. In our experience and in many dream studies, no evidence of this can be found—even in a metaphysical context. So why does this myth persist?

What may happen when we're falling is that we wake ourselves up because we've been taught that it's too dangerous to stay with the descent. Researchers know that falling dreams occur most often during the REM stage of the first sleep cycle—a little more than an hour after you start falling asleep. Falling dreamers sometimes jerk or twitch their legs or arms and end up waking themselves up. We don't know why this happens, but these movements, called myclonic jerks, may occur as an instinctive response to what the brain perceives as a potentially threatening environment. After all, the brain cannot distinguish between a dream event and a waking event.

Your Dream Worksheet

Think about a flying dream and a falling dream you've had. If you're drawing a blank, here's a tip: As you're falling asleep, suggest to yourself that you'd really like to have a flying or falling dream. Picture it. Feel the sensations. This works more often than you might expect! When you wake up, record your impressions and feelings. Use the following questions to record your impressions and feelings about flying:

1. Describe how you took off and stayed airborne.

2. What was your body telling you as you flew?

    a) That you are lighter than air

    b) That you'd better be careful dodging the thunderclouds and lightning bolts

    c) That you are powerful and capable

    d) That you were running out of gas

    e) Other:

3. Did you experience bodily sensations and feelings?

    a) A tightening of the chest

    b) Tears in your eyes

    c) Butterflies in your stomach

    d) Other:

4. Are these feelings and sensations familiar to you either in the past or currently?

Use the following questions to analyze your impressions and feelings about falling:

1. Describe how you fell. What are you falling from?

    a) A cliff

    b) Down an elevator shaft

    c) Off the wing of an airplane

    d) Other:

2. Are you pushed, do you trip, or does no one seem to be responsible?

    a) Who is piloting the airplane you are falling from?

    b) Who owns the building that has the open elevator shaft?

    c) Whose land is the cliff on?

    d) Other:

3. What is your emotional reaction to the fall?

   a) Fear or terror

   b) Confusion

   c) Apathy

   d) Release

   e) Anger

   f) Other:

4. What is your physical reaction to the fall? Do you

   a) Claw and scrape at the air?

   b) Roll yourself up into a ball?

   c) Spread your wings and try to stay airborne?

   d) Relax your muscles and trust you'll land softly?

   e) Other:

5. Which, if any, of the feelings or bodily sensations are familiar? What do they remind you of either currently or in the past?

Do *You* Want to Fall, or Fly?

In our flying and falling dreams we can travel the distance between heaven and hell and all points in between. More to the point, we can run the gamut of emotions that can fill such a vast space. So start taking a look at these "ups" and "downs" for what they might be telling you about your excursions in reality. Maybe you'll feel more comfortable in your falling and flying dreams so that you can free fall with confidence, fly with exuberance—and know what your particular falls and flights say about your waking life and experiences.

There is a Zen story about a man who continually walks into the same pothole when crossing the street. At first he forgets the hole is there and walks into it. Later, he plots other routes to avoid the hole. Weary of this tactic, he defiantly steps purposefully into the hole. In your dream journal, highlight or take special note of several dreams in which you stumble or fall. Like the man in the Zen story who must develop elaborate strategies in his struggle with the stubborn pothole before he can be at peace with its presence in his path, look at your falling dreams to see how you can turn your falls into flight.

Gently encourage flight in your dreams by placing an object or photograph that you find comforting and reassuring under your pillow before sleep—anything from a feather to an angel card to the boarding pass stub from your last terrific vacation flight to a picture of a height you'd like to reach, such as the sacred Incan Machu Picchu. Be patient and tenacious and look carefully at how your dreams and waking experiences evolve as you work with the metaphor of flight.

The Least You Need to Know

+ Flying and falling dreams are quite common.

+ Flying dreams tend to be enjoyable and come to us when we feel we're making some sort of breakthrough.

+ Sometimes attempts to fly in dreams can indicate that we're trying to escape internal or external conflict.

+ Falling dreams often cue us into the fact that we feel out of control or that we're not living up to expectations—either internal or external.

+ Learning to fly can empower both your sleeping and waking awareness!

Chapter 7

Weighing Worth: Dreams About Money and Value

In This Chapter

◆ What do your dreams about money reveal about you?

◆ For richer or poorer

◆ When you have it, what do you do with it?

◆ From dream to reality … manifesting abundance

When did you last dream of winning the lottery or learning that the peculiar figurine you've had on the coffee table all these years is really an antique worth enough to send a child to college? Were you sure that this meant you were going to come into a small (or major) fortune? Did you call in sick to work that day, just to be ready for your big payout? Or maybe you dreamed the stock market took a dive or your bank discovered that your deposits for the past 10 years had been counterfeit. You might awaken from this kind of dream in a cold sweat!

Many people believe that money dreams are prophetic. Fortunately or unfortunately, depending on whether you're making it or losing it, these dreams rarely have anything to do with literal wealth. Yet money in your dreams can be a powerful metaphor. Money itself is neither good nor bad;

however the way we feel when we have it, want it, need it, lose it … well, that sure can make us *feel* good or bad. Dream dollars are about more than money. In our culture, money represents values, power, and status. So when it shows up in our dreams, it can reveal a lot about how we feel about ourselves.

Staying Current

What do we mean by "rarely have anything to do with literal wealth"? Maybe you left your purse at the dry cleaner's, but you haven't quite "noticed" yet. That might prompt dreaming of a torrent of bills as big as Niagara Falls burying you. You might dream of all the diamonds in your wedding ring falling down the drain. On the other hand, maybe you dream that you're playing fetch with your dog and he brings you a wad of bills. Did you recently misplace your rent check? This could be an unconscious indicator that leads you to the real-life missing moolah. Having money when you need it is all about staying current in your life. After all, money is currency. When you're current you are up-to-date, in circulation, accepted.

A Mark, a Yen, a Buck, or a Pound

Money has different names in different countries of the world—literally a language of currency. Ever dream that rent check for your Paris flat had to be made out in French francs? People who are fluent in more than one language may have bilingual dreams. But for those of us for whom English is the gold standard, dreams about foreign currencies could evoke our fascination for, or fear of, exotic places, customs, and peoples.

And in a world where we're watching the global economy and assessing the stability and growth of currencies all over the world, dreams about the stock market or foreign currencies can signal an internal, unconscious assessment of personal risk and/or a willingness to cooperate—even a desire to travel. Euros, anyone? We wonder how many of the world's many currencies turn up in Warren Buffet's dreams!

In a different way, money represents a universal language—the language of numbers. Concepts can be communicated in mathematical terms. Dreams about specific amounts can have a special meaning for the dreamer. If something costs $62 in your dream, or the numbers in your dreaming checkbook just don't add up, for example, clues to the proper dream interpretation may lie in a look at the numbers themselves. You'll see more on the significance of numbers in dreams in Chapter 14.

Worth and Value: Anxiety About Money

Dreams in which you lose money or valuable objects may be expressions of feeling out of control. More to the point, when we feel out of control, we don't feel safe. In our culture, the common feeling is that the more money you have, the safer you are—from homelessness, hunger, untreated illness—in short, from all the scary stuff. When we lose money in our dreams, we're often expressing symbolically a feeling that we're vulnerable and weak; that we've lost our position of power and safety.

"Self-worth." Interesting how that term uses the language of commerce. Oh, and then there's the term "moral values." And what about those times when you're feeling "emotionally bankrupt," or you decide it's time to "invest in yourself." These common phrases all allude to value and worth, although they have nothing to do with money, per se. Instead, we use these phrases to describe our emotional cores. When money shows up in our dreams, it may be telling us that we need to deal with psychological issues regarding self-esteem, power, ambition, and emotional and moral values.

> **Life Is But a Dream**
>
> These days, dreams involving money can be about a lot more than just the cash in your wallet. Credit cards, loans, mutual funds, cash advances, ATM transactions, and debit cards are a sampling of the many forms dream money might take.

In his waking life, this dreamer is concerned about his adolescent daughter entering high school. He's a protective dad. Of course he can't be positive that she'll be safe from gangs or drugs and alcohol. His worry shows up in his dreams:

> *I get on a bus and I don't know where it's going. I ask the driver, but he just tells me to pay my fare. I make my way toward my seat, even though the bus is lurching from side to side. The bus driver grabs me and tells me I haven't paid the full fare. I'm scared. I reach into my pocket and give him my last dollar. He tells me I have to get off the bus; it's not enough.*

This dreamer is experiencing feelings of "not being in the driver's seat" and of losing precious money, likely a symbol for his daughter, and of losing other "valuables" in his life. He also apparently fears not having enough money (power) to protect all of those "valuables." This dream borrows from his reality to set the stage for the coming events to play out: His daughter will be taking a new bus route to school and he's not familiar with it.

What if we could give this concerned dad a different ending for his dream:

I didn't think I had any more money, but then I saw that my wallet was on the floor of the bus! It was hard to reach, other passengers tried to grab it. But I finally got it. I gave the driver another dollar and took my seat.

This, as the saying goes, changes everything. A dream in which you get back what you misplaced suggests that you're already looking for ways to solve your problem. And that you may have a treasure of unexpected or unconscious coping strategies.

Fears of Poverty

Do you have dreams in which you suddenly find yourself without a cent? Have you gone, in your dreams (or perhaps more appropriately, nightmares!), from queen of the hill to pauper? Do you feel as if you are caught in the Great Depression or a Dickens novel? Look at the following dream example:

In my dream, I received my paycheck—in the amount of $0! Next thing I knew, I was lying down on my office floor and my colleagues didn't see me. They all stepped over me and walked around me, even the ones I considered my friends. It was like I didn't exist.

Very often, dreams in which we suddenly find ourselves with no money reflect fears that we're losing our "place" in the world. Perhaps we're worried about company downsizing, or that we won't get into a graduate program. Or maybe we're realizing on some level that we're about to "lose" something important, that we're about to become "poor" in a personal way. Are kids about ready to leave home? Is a close friend moving away? Are you facing retirement? These normal life changes are losses and can feel like it. They reconfigure the lives we've grown accustomed to, and cause us to reevaluate our priorities. This reevaluation process is certainly food for dream thought.

Wake Up!

If you're having dreams of becoming poor, try to think about what you're afraid of losing in life. Are you sending yourself an alert of an impending loss? Sometimes dreams of losing money or other valuables are messages that you need to take control of circumstances and finances before they *do* become losses.

Dreams of loss and poverty can reveal feelings that you don't deserve what you have. Sometimes coming into significant wealth, even when it comes through your own long, hard work, creates the feeling that your abundance is unearned and maybe unfair to others. You might dream of losing it all and wake up feeling relieved!

Remember when you were a kid and you'd get a great pair of jeans only to find that three months later you couldn't wear them any more? You grew out of them. We also grow emotionally. Sometimes we grow out of our old ways of looking at the world, and it's time to lose those old ways, just like we lost the high-water jeans. What freedom! Your dream may be reinforcing your readiness to grow and change. Dreams of things that are broken, or that break in the dream, often reflect worries or fears about losing material possessions or money. This "dream brokenness" may reflect fears of real brokenness—in your career, in your personal life, or as the family breadwinner. Do you feel out of control, or not in control, when it comes to your earning capacity or job situation? We generally perceive broken things as events that aren't our fault or that have inevitability to them. And to "go for broke" implies you're willing to risk "breaking" everything, inviting poverty and loss for the potential gains that are at stake. To go for broke and win … now there's a success story!

Fears of Success

Sometimes we fear success—even more than we fear failure. We're scared we'll reach for that brass ring and fall flat on our faces in front of everyone. Also, we might be scared that success will take us away from familiar people and places we love. Success, after all, changes people (so goes conventional wisdom). Success fears might manifest through dreams of impoverishment or of losing money, resources, and other valuables, of reaching the top of the money and success mountain only to fall all the way down again. You can't lose what you don't have, right?

Dreamy
Author Franz Kafka (1883–1924) used his writings to explore the often blurry line between dreams and waking. In one of his most famous novellas, *The Metamorphosis*, the main character, Gregor Samsa, awakens to find that he has become in real life the loathsome insect of his nightmarish dream. Kafka's style of writing was itself dreamlike, creating a plausible transition. *The Metamorphosis* explores the responses of Samsa's family and associates to his new physical form, presenting an insightful exploration of values.

Dreams of Abundance

Isn't it wonderful to have dreams of abundance? You want to stay asleep forever, lavishing in such dreams! These dreams often feature a profusion of the material items we associate with wealth and prosperity. Perhaps you're behind the wheel of a fancy sports car or watching the drawbridge go up so you can pass through in your yacht.

You might be wearing elaborate jewelry and fine clothes, or enjoying a cup of tea (or snifter of brandy) in front of one of the seven fireplaces in your mansion.

Do such dreams mean you're about to come into amazing money—write a best-seller, clean up on stock investments, sell that beachfront property to an investor who wants to build a resort? Well, anything's possible, of course. But more likely, dreams of material abundance suggest that you're happy and satisfied with your life. All is well!

Oprah Winfrey said, "Luck is a matter of preparation meeting opportunity." A sudden lucky dream windfall can correspond to a time in your waking life when you're getting ready to try something new. Getting lucky in your dreams reinforces your confidence to pursue your new goals. Your luck could even signal an internal desire to become more generous with others (or even with yourself!).

The Value of Sex

Okay, we've got to say it. Here goes: Sex. Yes, sex. Sometimes (but not always) dreams about losing or finding money or becoming rich or poor are about our sexual selves. Because some theorists went overboard in attributing everything in our dreams to sex, we can tend to under-attribute our dreams to sex. A dream in which you become poor might just be letting you know that you are losing that part of your life, that you're working too many hours, taking on too many responsibilities, so that your sexual self has been depleted. Conversely, a dream about finding or achieving wealth (unexpected or expected!) could signal satisfaction with the rich relationship you are exploring with your sexual partner.

Buried Treasure

If we can look at the loss of money as a loss of power and position (both internally and externally), then we can see finding or winning money as the opposite. Finding buried or hidden treasure might be a metaphor for finding internal riches. The $1000 bills you find in your dreams might refer to the good qualities you see in yourself, qualities you've suppressed because of people or situations in your life.

This sort of dream usually gives us a feeling of excitement—like winning big at blackjack or the lottery. We might also feel a sense of relief that everything will now be fine. We're usually enjoying ourselves in these dreams.

Midas or Scrooge?

But wait a minute … do you spend the money you find in your dreams? Or do you hoard your riches in a shoebox? What we do with the money can be as telling as actually finding it. If we save it, hide it, or hang on to it for dear life, that might indicate that we don't feel secure yet. We fear we'll lose these positive feelings and realizations about ourselves just as magically as we found them. But if we spend it (and on whom?) we can be expressing a feeling of satisfaction, safety, and a desire to share ourselves with others.

Easy Come, Easy Go

Maybe in your dream you had it all and by the end of the dream everything was gone. How did this happen? Did you give it all away? Did it slowly fall through small holes in your pockets? Did you keep a little, just a little, for yourself? Do you feel relieved or despondent that your dream wealth has evaporated? This might tell you that there's part of you that is afraid to acknowledge or rely on the good things in you and in your life. This might be that old "fear of success" issue kicking in. It also might mean that you no longer see the world in black and white, either have lots of money or none, but that you are understanding that life experiences often have gray areas.

Making "Change"

Did you win or find coins? The metaphorical language of dreams is nothing if not clever, and often items that appear in dreams have symbolic meanings that play off their literal meanings. Coins, in waking life, are change. We might even call them "loose" change—implying, perhaps, a diminished value. We also might "change" them in for bills—easier to carry.

Did you find so many coins that they were weighing you down? Did you give them away (or lose them) to free yourself from the weight and responsibility of having to haul them around? Or can you look at the dream through the lens of your waking life and see that there are circumstances (perhaps financial) that you're avoiding or ignoring that really need your attention?

Dreamwork

Ask yourself: What will people think of me if I have more money? Make a list of at least 10 people. Include people who have died, because we have internalized their ideas. Put a star next to any person on your list who shows up regularly in your dreams. Chances are, that person's views strongly influence how you think of yourself and your views on money.

The Big Inheritance

I am sitting in an apartment, one I've never seen before. I look up and see the woman I've been dating sitting in a rocking chair. I realize the chair belonged to my grandfather, but now it's mine. I haven't seen it since I was a kid.

What does it mean to come into an inheritance? By now we're all clear that any dream element usually means something different for everyone. But for this dreamer, it signaled a real turning point in his life. He'd been wondering about his relationship with his girlfriend, where it would go. In his dream he received the gift of his grandfather's rocker. His grandfather was a man of wisdom and authority. In a way, the rocker symbolized a passage into the dreamer's own sense of himself as a mature man. (Talk about an inheritance!) That his girlfriend was in the chair told him that her presence in his life was in some part responsible for this growth.

Generally, an inheritance signifies the acquisition of parts of the self that leave the dreamer feeling empowered. However, it could be that this empowerment is gained at the expense of someone else.

A Thief in the Night

In waking life you're a law-abiding citizen. The mere thought of jaywalking gives you hives. But in your dreams you're a bank robber, an embezzler, a master jewel thief.

Well what are you stealing? What's that you shoved into your pocket? Are you hoping no one will notice the coins you're taking from the till? Could it be that you're ready to reach out toward your goals, financial and otherwise, but there's a part of you that's afraid someone will try to stop you? Or that you might get in your own way by admonishing yourself: "Who do you think you are? You can't possibly try out for the lead in the musical!" But the thing is, you really want to play the role of Maria in *West Side Story*. So in your dreams you're stealing money. The money can be a stand-in for the confidence you need to go after what you want.

Dreamy
Psychotherapist and best-selling author Thomas Moore recounts a dream in which a man holds him up on a dark city street saying, "Give me your change." Moore cleverly gives the robber the small sum in his left pocket and keeps the larger sum in his right. On waking reflection, Moore wonders whether the "change" has anything to do with money at all. Moore wonders if he's secretly hoarding his "soul money," willing to give of himself in small ways, but holding back in larger, more important areas of life.

Are you stealing from a particular someone? Could it be you're angry with this person? Envious? Does he or she have a quality that you wish you had? When we take things in our dreams, it can be a positive indication that we're "reaching out" for the attributes that we associate with things we value. We view these as rightfully ours, although perhaps beyond conventional reach. Exploring the layers of meaning that such dreams hold may lead you to innovative solutions for problems and challenges in your life.

Are you being held up at gunpoint in your dreams? Pickpocketed unaware? Or does a gust of wind whisk away your money? Do you recognize the thief? Do you struggle against the burglar? What does the thief take, exactly?

How do you feel about it?

Generally, being the victim of a crime suggests that you feel like … well, a victim. You feel powerless. What might be going on in your life to give you a dream like this?

Then again, maybe you masterminded the heist so that you could feel relieved of a responsibility. Have you been feeling trapped in a life in which you can't rely on others, but it always seems the world is relying on you?

Family Values Around Money

Our values around money and possessions take root when we're very young. To understand how these early perceptions affect us as adults, we need to trace those roots. Once you see where they go, you can shape and change the "money tree" that grows from them so that you can create the prosperity and abundance you desire. Start thinking about what money means to you.

- Did you get an allowance when you were a child? How much? What did you have to do for it?

- Were there fights about money when you were growing up? Who fought whom? What was the result? How did you feel about the fighting, the results?

- What was the economic standard of living in your house? Who was comfortable/uncomfortable with that standard? What messages did that give you?

- Is yours a family of savers or spenders?

- Do you remember any sayings about money that you heard over and over again growing up? For example: "We don't have money for that today," or, "Better to have 1 nice thing than 10 cheap ones," or, "It's only money!" or the ever-popular, "A penny saved is a penny earned!"

How do these early perceptions affect your current attitudes and feelings about money, values, and worth? Your responses to these statements can help you assess what you think and feel about money values:

- The image that pops into my head when I think about having enough money is:

- That image makes me feel:

- When I think of others having more money than me, the image that pops in my head is:

- That image makes me feel:

- I dislike money because:

- I like money because:

The next time you dream about money, consider its imagery in the context of your answers to these two sets of questions. Your metaphorical riches can lead you to new understandings about what you value in life, and how your beliefs and actions support or don't support your values. Write about your money dream in your dream journal:

- Describe the last dream you had about money.

- What did you find/lose in your dream? What did you do with/without it? What were the circumstances? How did you feel?

- Do these feelings remind you of similar feelings you have regarding other people, situations, and especially how you feel inside? Are these familiar feelings either from the past or are they current?

Dream Incubation to Cultivate Prosperity

In many ancient cultures, as we mentioned in earlier chapters, people traveled to the temples of their deities to sleep in the shadows of holy powers and abilities. Through their dreams people could obtain healing, wisdom, comfort, prosperity—whatever the deity symbolized.

You need only travel as far as your bedroom to create your dream temple. There you may try to incubate dream prosperity and abundance that leads to waking riches. Choose a small item that represents your perceptions of abundance. This might be a $100 bill, a flower, a drawing from your child, a tool of your trade or of your profession. It might be a shell from the beach where you'd like to live, a photo of the boat you want to own, a blank check. You may also write out what you would like to have.

Carry this item with you on your physical person every day. Each night, meditate on this item as you fall asleep. Open yourself to new possibilities that can help your dreams of prosperity and abundance manifest as your waking reality.

The Least You Need to Know

- People have complicated attitudes toward money in our society.

- Early attitudes about money shape our adult perceptions and behaviors regarding finances, saving, and spending.

- Dreams about money and possessions often reflect perceptions about what we value in life and how we feel about ourselves.

- When we dream we're losing or finding money, often we're struggling with our changing values or with our changing self-concept.

- You can use dreamwork to invite prosperity and abundance (however you define these) into your life.

The Thrill of Success, the Agony of Defeat: Dreams About Making the Grade

In This Chapter

- ◆ Are you prepared?
- ◆ What worries you, failure or success?
- ◆ Modeling your dream influences
- ◆ Lights … camera … action!

You might've expected that when you got out of school, tests and auditions were safely behind you. No more need to worry about making the grade; you've passed. But it sure didn't take long to discover that nothing is farther from reality! With so much of everyday life feeling like competition, from finding a parking space to getting a job or promotion, it's little wonder so many of our dreams put us to the test.

Dreams can give us messages that are sometimes disconcerting, ambiguous, and downright confusing. Frequently we re-experience thoughts and feelings about issues we thought were settled long ago and for good.

What's hard to keep in mind is that dreams are our ticket into the Biggest Show on Earth—our own psyches.

That's why it's sometimes important for us to attend to our dreams as if we're sitting in the audience under the big top. Relax and let the dream images wash over you; pull from them your emotions, thoughts, and understandings. And treat yourself to that second bag of peanuts.

Dream Dictionary

Psyche is Greek for "the breath," literally, and refers to the human soul or spirit.

Certainly the dreams we have about success and defeat often seem Fellini inspired. What does your *psyche* want to teach you about your life goals?

This Is a Test

> *I walk into a meeting with the senior partner at the law firm where I work as an associate attorney. It's 10 A.M. sharp, as scheduled. He says, "You're two hours late. Well, here's the test. We want to see how you're performing." He tosses me the LSAT. I have no idea why I have to take this law school entrance exam again, nor do I remember what I'd studied 10 years ago.*

Dream tests are common. Often, like this one, they take us back to a time when we had to take a real test or exam that was stressful. In your dream you might sit down to take the test, confident of your ability to excel—then discover it's in a foreign language, one you don't understand. Or maybe you forget in which room the exam is being given, so you dash from room to room, flinging doors open, never finding the right place. Wait ... finally you do find the room, but then realize you forgot your pen. Or your pencil breaks. Or the professor tells you, in front of your classmates, that the test was yesterday.

Wake Up!

Have you been ignoring assignments, worrying about that presentation at work, or putting off dealing with your taxes? Are you up for a promotion, or are you thinking of changing jobs or careers? Sometimes "examination" dreams can alert us to the fact that we are unprepared—and serve as a wake-up call to get motivated.

Sometimes we have these kinds of "examination" dreams when we're actually facing a major test of skill, endurance, or ability in real life. Perhaps you've made it to the final round of interviews for a job or promotion, or the marathon you've spent eight months training for is just a week away. Most of the time, we're more than ready for, and capable of meeting, these challenges. So why aren't our dreams giving us clear signals that we're brilliant and assured of success? Because usually there's a part of us that's nervous, insecure, and afraid, and sometimes the only time that part can express itself is when we're dreaming.

Can You Make the Grade?

That little voice inside us that crops up in our dreams letting us know that we're going to screw up the speech, exam, recital, presentation, or _____ (fill in the blank!) is not easily silenced. And it's often not plain speaking either; your angry mother won't stand in front of you and tell you you're clumsy and accident prone; perhaps instead you'll dream of a big black truck bearing down on a child in the road.

The hang-ups that keep us from succeeding (or at least give us anxious dreams about failing) and make us afraid of both success and failure are usually deeply rooted inside. They're those negative experiences we've had that we tend to believe say something true about who we are. But they don't speak the truth. No one is born to be a failure. Everyone has the capacity to succeed.

What about this dream test scenario: You arrive at the test two hours late, without a pen, and when you look at the questions you realize you don't understand them at all. Yet you decide to go ahead anyway. You borrow a pen and magically tap into some hidden reservoir of knowledge. How does that feel? Pretty great? You bet! This type of dream is a nice editorial about your coping skills and your inner resources.

Smart or Stupid: When You Have to Know Your Stuff

The exams we take in our dreams come in a wide variety. Not surprising when you think about how competitive we are. Why, three-year-olds compete for spots in preschools! (Sure, it's the parents who are trying to edge each other out, but think about what the children learn from this!) When was the last time you took part in an exam or a competition? How about this morning, when you took the back roads instead of the thruway that you knew would be crowded? And hey, you did get to work before your boss! Or maybe you ran in a Fun Run last Sunday. A nice 6K jog, benefiting a worthy cause. Did you find yourself sprinting toward the finish, trying to smoke the front-runners?

Dreamy

Remember the first scene in Tom Cruise's breakthrough movie, *Risky Business?* In the dream, he rides his bike to a friend's house and goes inside to discover a sexy blonde in the shower. She wants him to join her. As he walks toward the shower, the distance seems to increase and the bathroom fills with steam. When Tom gets to the shower door and steps in, he's suddenly in a classroom—a bit of a shock for him—and he's got only a few minutes to complete an entire standardized exam.

Unfortunately, in our examination dreams, more often than not, we don't smoke the competition. We fail. We arrive unprepared, if at all. We're simply not making the grade. Perhaps these dreams mirror a situation in our lives where we feel we're being scrutinized, examined, or tested.

Often dreams of this sort suggest we feel unprepared for a challenge that may be personal, that may relate to our life's goals. That's why the dream is accompanied by frustration and distress. It's rarely about the content of the test; it's about how we feel anticipating our failure. We rarely sweat it when we don't know the answers on *Jeopardy*, but if knowing those answers meant something deeper, something about how we're measuring up, then you bet we'd be upset if we missed, for example, "Historical Speeches for $100."

Turning the Tables

> *I looked at the test, and I realized I'd studied the wrong subject. My heart started to race. But then I decided I'd just try to answer the questions anyway. Even though it seems ridiculous now that I'm awake, it was reasonable in my dream that although I'm an accountant I'd be able to answer questions about … bricklaying!*

Dreams are often the perfect forum for experimenting with courageous acts and impulses. Eventually, your dream courage becomes waking courage as you take on the inner and outer negative influences in your life and work to overcome them. Where does this burst of confident knowledge come from? We often surprise ourselves, in dreams and in waking life, with facts or abilities we forgot we had. How about that last time you played Trivial Pursuit and you found yourself blurting out an answer to an unlikely question?

Life Is But a Dream

Scientists have observed that during REM sleep the hippocampus, the brain center thought to involve learning and memory, exhibits a steady electrical rhythm. Some researchers believe that this activity shows the brain's incorporation or strengthening of memories during dreaming sleep.

Have you ever noticed that the best way to study for an exam is to do it over several days so that as you sleep each night your brain organizes the material and stores it for your use? With the right amount of sleep, stimulation, and preparation, the brain usually comes to our rescue in our dreams and waking life … if we let it. If we are open to our deepest thoughts, if we dare to risk opening our mouths, picking up that pen, or raising our hands, we often find that we knew more than we thought we did.

Fear of Succeeding

> *I am running a long race. I'm nearing the finish line and I'm winning. Suddenly I become frightened that they will shoot the first one to cross, so I slow down and let the guy in back of me pass. Then I wake up—I have no idea if he got shot.*

You'd think that getting a promotion, having a baby, or buying your first house would be cause for celebration. Well, it is and it isn't. Each success involves change—and loss. When you get your own office on the mezzanine, you no longer have the camaraderie of your co-workers on the main floor. Or when you buy your first house, you have to say good-bye to the apartment you've lived in since college!

Perhaps you feel guilty that one of your co-workers didn't get the promotion. After all, why you? She's worked there longer. Maybe you feel guilty that you got pregnant easily, unlike your best friend who has been trying to conceive for years. Or you feel that your studious brother should have been the one to get accepted to Yale, not party-hearty you.

It's common for these issues to show up in our dreams. Generally dreams in which we fail an exam, botch a presentation, or retreat from a challenge in some way tell us that we're scared to succeed ... not that we can't succeed. It could be we're not sure we're ready to leave our familiar comfort zone, that we're feeling guilty because someone we care for isn't having the same good fortune as we are, or that we just can't seem to get it through our heads that we deserve success.

Take a moment to think about a recent triumph in your life. What did you gain from it? Money? Respect? Power? Happiness? Now think about this: What did you have to give up? And how did you feel about that?

Dreamwork

Many of the world's most successful people take advantage of the restorative tonic of power-napping. Margaret Thatcher, the former British prime minister, is a well-known power-napper. These short 10- to 20-minute interludes of NREM Stage 1 or 2 sleep aren't enough to get to dreaming REM, but they are enough to fuel the body and mind and increase productivity. Try it.

Fear of Failing

When our dreams tell us we're turning our backs on a challenge or that we're flunking a test, we might be struggling with the flip side of the fear of success: the fear of failing.

Imagine you're a little kid just learning to walk. You take a wobbly step out on the middle of the lawn. Your family is watching you. You fall down hard. What happens next? Do your parents scoop you up and put you back on track? Do they yell at you? Point and laugh?

Or imagine you're in first grade, learning how to read. It's your turn to read aloud from *Dick and Jane*. You're having a tough time. Then you come across a word that might as well be in hieroglyphics. What do you imagine happens next? Does the teacher help you sound it out? Does she make you feel stupid? Does she send a nasty note home to your parents?

How we were helped—or not helped—when we were young has much to do with how free we feel to take on challenges throughout life. Dreams in which we fail to make the grade in some way often express some age-old notion of ourselves as not being good enough. We're afraid we'll be judged and found wanting. So ask yourself: Am I afraid of failing? And whom would I be failing, exactly? My wife? My mother? The community?

From the Shadows into the Light

Many of our fears and uncertainties stem from early to current negative life experiences. Hurtful words from others, especially people who are in positions of authority such as parents and teachers, can have lasting effects. Although you might think you've put earlier messages behind you now that you're an adult, fragments of them tend to show up in dreams—often in oblique or cryptic ways. Dream interpretation can borrow from an art therapy technique called an *experiential* to bring these messages from the shadows of your dreams into the light of tangibility so you can explore, understand, and resolve them.

Dream Dictionary

An **experiential** is a type of exercise art therapists use to help people connect to their emotions and feelings, past and present.

For this exercise, you need three or four sticks or blocks of modeling clay and a flat surface in a comfortable, quiet place where you can work without interruptions or distractions. Play-Doh works fine, too! Have your dream journal and a pen handy, too, so you can write down any revelations or ideas that come to you.

1. Close your eyes and think about the family you grew up with. Include your best friend and your pets. Spend a few minutes thinking about each person. Picture your house, your clothes, your school.

2. Open your eyes and take a piece of clay in your hands. Begin to work it, soften it, let it take shape. Let your mind go. Don't think about what your hands are doing; just let the clay take shape. Maybe listen to music while you are working with the clay.

3. Take more clay as you need it, and work until you feel your sculpture is complete. You can sculpt a single item or multiple pieces, whatever comes to you.

4. When you feel that you're finished, explore your sculpture. Look at it, hold it in your hands. What images, feelings, or senses does your sculpture evoke? How does your sculpture resemble the images you pictured before you started working with the clay?

5. Are any of these images or the feelings they evoke showing up in your dreams? Take a few minutes to write some thoughts in your dream journal.

Sometimes surprising and revealing ideas and feelings come to the surface when we are engaged in physical activity. Experientials such as this can be a useful way to bring out, front and center, those parts of ourselves that are so much "us" that we can no longer easily identify where they came from or how we feel about them. Experientials aim to get at the same psychic truths that our dreams attempt to show us.

Gimme That Gold Star

We all like a pat on the back for work well done, or a Grammy Award for that nice rendition of "Come Away with Me" you performed in the shower this morning. It's natural to want validation for our efforts.

Are you having dreams in which you're hoping for—or getting—a prize, an "A" on a term paper, recognition at work? Do you receive the honor in front of your peers? Your family? The community? Or is it just between you and that person you've been trying to please? Is the reward something big (like a 1967 Cadillac, a ranch in Texas, or an elephant) or something small (a nod or a smile from someone who represents your boss, or your father)?

These sorts of dreams might be subconscious messages that we're feeling a bit unappreciated, neglected, or unsure of how our efforts are being received. And it might have more to do with relationships as opposed to work performance. Sometimes this sort of dream is a gentle way to alert us to the disturbing fact that our partner or spouse has lost that lovin' feeling. Once we realize this, we can address the problem directly. What happens when you get that reward? Do you accept it graciously, slip it to the family dog, run the other way? Maybe you create a scene in your dream in which it is stolen from you? How we give ourselves prizes and gifts in our dreams can express how ready we are to accept positive aspects of ourselves.

Crime and Punishment

Are you cheating in order to pass that exam? Do you take a peek at the answer key in your dream test? What happens—are you caught, or do you get the gold star? And how do you feel?

Often, dreams in which we take a shortcut in the marathon or otherwise win by cheating aren't so different from real life's gray areas. They are actions that express a basic lack of self-confidence. Why do we think we can't earn the prize or the recognition on our own? Where did we get the idea that we're inadequate? What are we afraid will happen if we come home without the blue ribbon?

In our dreams, obtaining a reward by cheating can leave us with a hollow feeling, both in the dream and when we wake. It can also make us so anxious that we create *another* dream scene in which we get caught! Perhaps we're punished in front of friends and neighbors. This may be our psyche's way of letting us know that we don't feel worthy of the prize—and we're letting everyone know it.

Sometimes, however, dreams in which we cheat to get a reward can be a more positive sign indicating that we are beginning to see ourselves as "winners," but we're not yet ready to acknowledge that those positive qualities reside deep inside of us. So we have to swipe them from someone or something else.

The best way to decipher what this sort of dream is trying to tell you is to pay close attention to how it makes you feel and what current situation in your waking life it might refer to.

Try, Try Again

How persistent are you? When your dream hands you a test that is indecipherable, do you work at it for hours or do you curse and stalk out of the room? The number of attempts you give to a certain test or task can indicate the importance of the underlying struggle it represents.

If a dream in which you're dodging flying golf balls on a game show is a metaphor for your readiness to get out of your own way and quit your dead-end job, then you may very well be dodging those flying golf balls for a very long time. That is, until you gain the confidence to pursue your waking dreams.

Dreamy

MIT physicist Alan Lightman wrote a best-selling novel called *Einstein's Dreams*. In it, the author imagines a series of dreams the young Einstein, then a patent clerk in 1905, might have had about the nature of time as he worked on his theory of relativity. In Einstein's dreams time is circular, flows backward, freezes, slows down at higher altitudes, and exhibits no relationship between cause and effect. This is a great example of a dreaming mind solving a puzzle or exploring a task.

Lead or Follow

Why are we rarely the ones administering the exams? Wouldn't that be a welcome change of pace? Why are we almost always the frustrated, uncomfortable test-takers? Who's in charge of these dreams, anyway?

How Do You Deal with Authority?

When we take those dream exams, we're often anticipating that we'll be judged poorly. Maybe even punished. The folks we've chosen as judges are those authority figures who exist both in our waking life and in our memories.

We all try to obtain our parents' approval, live up to our community's expectations, realize our biggest hopes and dreams. We keep tabs on how well or poorly we've done those things by consulting with our internal and external judges.

Who's on your judging panel? Think about a recent test dream. Perhaps it was a downhill ski event and you kept wiping out because you had no ski poles. Why did you want to complete the course? Who—in the past and present—would be there to see you either fail or succeed?

All in the Family

Are your parents in the audience when you give that saxophone recital (only you've never played that instrument in your life)? Maybe your kid sister is there, the one who you believe is prettier than you? Maybe it's your stern grandfather who thought that if you weren't in church you were frittering your time away. Are any of these folks sitting in the front row? Or are they backstage, waiting in the wings, ready to show you how the sax was meant to be played? And how does their presence make you feel? Struck dumb with stage fright? Distracted? Supported?

Generally, our family members (especially our parents, or the people who reared us) are the most persistent authority figures in our lives and dreams. It's up to you to figure out to what extent their values and hopes guide and nourish you and to what extent they keep you jumping through hoops.

Dreamwork _____

Ask yourself what people would think of you if you had more or less success. Write down the answers in your dream journal. You may discover some clues about how you respond when you're on the line. Do you sink, or do you swim?

There are many theories regarding birth order and personality. Like all theories, they fit some of us some of the time but not all of us all the time. Whether you're male or female, your inherent personality traits and the natural personalities of your parents, as well as your life experiences, are all factors that influence how your developed personality evolves. Research suggests that your position in the family is among them.

Are you the eldest? Eldest children are often self-confident, ambitious, and competitive—qualities that have probably served you well throughout your life. But these qualities might leave you feeling that no matter what you do, it's not quite enough. You, as the firstborn, bear the brunt of parental hopes and expectations. Parents can find it difficult to separate the real you from the ideal that started taking shape from the moment of your birth. It can be even more challenging for you to break free from definitions that don't fit. And you might find your dreams become the stage upon which these struggles play out as tests and challenges. You might feel overly responsible to succeed, sometimes anxious, and even inappropriately protective of younger siblings.

Are you in the middle? Middle children don't usually have to bear the burden of a parent's hopes and dreams in the same way older siblings do, so they often are less competitive and ambitious. Parents tend to be more relaxed with middle children, so middle children tend to feel freer to explore the world around them with curiosity and leisure. However, if you're a middle child, you might feel like you have the "nots"—not special, not having a specific role in the family, not getting the attention you feel you deserve. Your dreams might put you center stage in dramas worthy of five-star reviews. The more daunting the role, the more impressive the performance. You might awaken from your "test" dreams wishing you could stay asleep!

The youngest child, the "baby" of the family, often enjoys both adoration and leniency. The youngest gets away with everything (no matter how old). By the time this child enters the world, his or her parents have fewer stresses and are more relaxed in their lifestyles and their rules. Youngest children can use this freedom to explore and enjoy their worlds and themselves in ways not available to older siblings. Yet youngest children might feel other family members don't recognize or respect them as adults. If you're a youngest child, you might have difficulty competing because you've never had to "prove" yourself. Or you might be the most competitive of all; you know how to scramble at the dinner table, beating out your older, faster siblings for precious edible resources!

On the Job

I am at work, but it's not my office; it's a swimming pool. My boss dives into the deep end and swims underwater for so long that I get scared he'll drown. But he surfaces and he's not even out of breath. He instructs me to do the same. I know I'll drown.

How often does your boss show up in your dreams? Or maybe the person who has the job you'd like to have? We'd bet that the themes have to do with proving yourself. And failing. Often, the judgment we fear is passed on to us by the higher-ups at work.

This dreamer worked in a bookstore. So why did her dream take place at the pool at the local YWCA? Her father installed pools for a living. He always wanted her to go to medical school or get an MBA, not manage a neighborhood bookstore! So she was left feeling that she was expected to do more, more than she felt capable of.

It's very common for the authority figures from work or school to refer back to our parental authority figures, as in this dream.

Equal Opportunity Friendships

Are you taking the final foul shot against the Chicago Bulls? If you sink it, your team will tie the score and force an overtime. Who's on your team? Who's in the stands? Who is it that you want to witness your moment of glory? Is your high school nemesis watching you? You know, the girl who graduated first (and you came in second … or fifty-second)? If you make the shot, what will you be proving to her? To yourself? What will you finally be triumphing over? In short, she's been out of your life for 30 years, so why is she still in your dreams; what does she stand for?

Feeling the Power

We all have authority figures in our minds and in our lives. They are necessary. They often guide us, teach us the ropes, and give us the feeling that there's always someone to rely upon.

Problems crop up when we listen to these authority figures at the expense of listening to ourselves. Or when those authority figures have been more concerned with making us feel bad than helping us mature and feel proud of our accomplishments and abilities.

What if, in your dream, you showed up for a test, took one look at it, handed it back to the instructor, and said, "Sorry, professor, this exam is wrong. It's supposed to be on astronomy, not astrology." And then you walked out of the room; or better yet, the teacher realized her mistake? What if then you answered most questions correctly? Talk about a hidden reservoir of knowledge! What if you felt that the authority figures in your dreams and waking life *were* there to aid you, not punish you?

Storyboard Your Success Script

Many "test" dreams have endings that if you could, you'd change. Dreams like the associate attorney's: He found himself retaking the law school entrance exam. You can keep the elements of your "test" dreams that you like and change the ones you don't. This feels like going back to class ... but this time no one is going to grade you. This time you're the scriptwriter, the director, and the producer. You even get to pick the cast.

Choose a dream from your dream journal that you'd like to play out in a different way. View it like a script. Use 3×5 cards or cut pieces of paper into 3×5 sections for each step of deconstructing and reconstructing your dream into the story you want to tell.

1. On a 3×5 card, list the characters who appear in your dream who you want to keep. If they are composites, as dream characters often are, write each one separately.

2. If you'd like to add characters, go ahead. You can use real people who you'd like to have in your dream, or you can make up characters.

3. Look at the story of your dream as scenes; divide them however it makes sense to you. On a card, write each scene that you want to keep—one scene to a card.

4. Where you've deleted scenes, what would you script instead? Write new scenes, one to a card. As you create your new scenes, add more new characters if you like (or scratch others that you decide no longer fit with your dream story).

5. Now rearrange the cards into the order you want your dream to follow. You can number the cards and tape them into your dream journal, or glue them onto a large piece of poster board.

6. Read your new dream out loud. Do the words generate clear and vivid images in your mind? Allow your mind to absorb this new story. Read it again before you go to sleep.

7. Record your first impressions when you wake up in the morning, even if they don't seem related at first to the dream you rescripted. Do you see any elements from your new script? You might not dream the whole dream, but you might be surprised to find pieces of your storyboard—characters or elements of plot— emerging in the dreams you do have.

Dreams can be powerful tools for reshaping your attitudes and impressions about yourself. They already reflect the inner you … when you work with dreams, you can make the route two-way.

The Least You Need to Know

- In "test" dreams, we're usually in some way unprepared for the test. This sort of dream leaves us feeling that we're simply not "making the grade."

- The fear of failing and/or succeeding in waking life often plays a major role in our examination dreams.

- We can use "test" dreams to practice and to rescript our fears and worries about meeting the expectations of others and ourselves.

- We can rescript our dreams to prompt unconscious practice at "getting it right."

Head to Toe: Dreams About the Body

In This Chapter

◆ Our bodies, our food

◆ How are we feeling today?

◆ Excuse me, where's the restroom?

◆ Nudity: The ultimate fashion statement

Your body is your calling card to the world and, if you're like many people, you obsess over every detail, over the brightness of your smile, the shape of your calf, the twinkle (or lack of twinkle) in your eye. Your calling card isn't perfect—no one's is. When bodies, body parts, and bodily functions show up in your dreams, you may be sending many different kinds of messages to yourself, depending on the images in the dream, your associations to those images, and your personal history.

Are you physically present in your dreams? Or do you watch the dream unfold from above or from the sidelines? Do you look like someone else in your dreams? Julia Roberts, Uncle Fester, Derek Jeter? Are aspects of your body exaggerated? Are you suddenly three years old again or do you have a really big head? Do you take on an animal form, your brother Bob's form, are your clothes form-fitting, or do you have no clothes at all? And how does it make you feel?

The Nourishing Paradox

Food has the amazing ability to keep us alive and functioning at our best. Too much food makes us fat; too little starves us. It tastes good or terrible. It's sanitized, pasteurized, and prepackaged, or it's fresh from the garden. Maybe as a child you couldn't leave the table until your plate was empty, or had to leave the table before your belly was full. As an adult, you confront even more complex issues and concerns when it comes to food.

Once you heed dream therapist Ann Faraday's commonsense advice and make sure that your dreams about food, hunger, and satiation aren't literal (for example, you dream that all the soda fountain spigots at the drugstore lunch counter will only produce orange juice, not soda—you might need that vitamin C!), and you are current on check-ups with your health-care provider, then you can turn your attention to the personal metaphors of the food-body connection.

Eating in Your Dreams

> *I was so full, but I couldn't stop eating. A third plate of spaghetti appeared in front of me. It tasted so good, but didn't satisfy. I noticed that I was getting thinner, except for my belly. So I just kept on eating ….*

Often dreams in which we feel hunger are about feeling unfulfilled. The "spaghetti dreamer" seems to be trying to fill up a bottomless pit. Perhaps she's been dieting for years and years, trying to attain that impossible female form (which currently, curiously enough, is the form of an adolescent boy) that she sees in the media. Perhaps she's frustrated that all her self-denial has brought her to the point of semistarvation—perhaps she even has an eating disorder, such as *anorexia nervosa*, *bulimia*, or *compulsive eating*—and so, to comfort herself, she dreams of food (for many of us, the ultimate comfort symbol!).

Dream Dictionary

Anorexia nervosa is a disorder characterized by refusal to eat that results in physical emaciation, emotional disturbance concerning body image, and abnormal fear of becoming obese. **Bulimia** is an insatiable craving for food that often results in binge eating followed by purging, depression, and self-deprivation. **Compulsive eating** is continuous eating despite feelings of satiation, often in order to satisfy an emotional need.

Researchers are studying the effects that eating disorders, eating habits, and food allergies have on sleep patterns. Clearly, if what and when we eat affects the quality of our sleep, it will also affect our dreaming:

◆ Anorexics are known to have more Stage 1 NREM sleep, with more sleep disturbances throughout the night and early morning awakenings. Remember, dreams occur primarily during REM sleep, with the longest REM period usually just before waking up.

◆ People who wake up frequently at night and engage in binge eating often suffer from sleep fragmentation, making it harder to reach and sustain dreaming REM sleep.

◆ Infants suffering from an allergic reaction to cow's milk often wake up as many as five times a night (disruptive to parent and child) and get only about four and a half hours of sleep per night, on average. Changing formula often solves the problem.

Okay, perhaps our "spaghetti dreamer" has a healthy attitude toward her body and to food. So what might she be trying to fill if it's not her stomach? Food may be a stand-in for our hunger to gratify our deepest desires regarding love, creativity, spirituality, and meaningful work. That in her dream she seems to be getting thinner despite her overindulgence might indicate that instead of achieving her heart's desire, she's constantly pursuing dead ends.

Is the food in your dream delicious? Is there enough of it? Or does it taste just awful? If it makes you sick or if there is very little of it, who might be the chef offering you this meager or unsavory repast? Your dreams might be letting you know that someone or something in your life is making you feel bad or (heart)sick. Who might be leaving you feeling "starved" for attention? Is it a person, a situation, or a spiritual feeling? Or perhaps you are "starving" yourself by not allowing yourself to make positive decisions in your life.

Life Is But a Dream

Dreams of food and eating are common during pregnancy, and women often find themselves waking from such dreams feeling famished. Doctors believe fluctuating metabolism accounts for these nocturnal hunger attacks, and suggest a light, nutritious snack a half-hour or so before bed to help accommodate the fluctuations. Pregnant women should of course make sure they are getting enough of the right foods to eat, and consult their health-care practitioners if there are any doubts.

If there is not enough food in your dreams, try to think about what might be missing or scarce in your life: love, friendship, joy, ambition. Indeed, sometimes when we feed ourselves in our dreams, it's because we are afraid to eat enough—or enjoy anything enough—in our waking lives.

Wake Up!

If you think you might have a problem with eating in your waking life—eating too much or too little, or a persistent inability to moderate how much you eat—consult your physician or a mental health professional.

In some cases, though, eating in your dreams doesn't reflect a deficit in your life, but rather illustrates your ability to nourish yourself—even as your parents once nourished you. Dream food can be as healthy and comforting as Mom's chicken soup. Because the first people who nourished you were your parents, having a dream in which you are now feeding yourself (and feeling satisfied) can indicate an increasing ability to treat yourself in a protective and loving way.

Have It Your Way

Have you ever tried to feed a one-year-old? Chances are she'll grab the spoon out of your hand and try to feed herself. She'll refuse to open up for the whipped prunes. She wants to put it in her hair instead of her mouth. Perhaps take a few more bites in a little while, or maybe not. Feeding time may represent a battle for control. Is she going to be forced to eat the food you give her in the order given and in the amount you decide? Or will she be allowed to mix the applesauce with the cheese? Will she be allowed to try seven times to get the avocado slice in her mouth?

Often, when we dream of eating, we are revisiting issues of power and control. Are you freely eating in your dream? Are you refusing to open up? What in your current life do you feel you are powerless to change? Who or what is "force-feeding" you?

The Thigh Bone's Connected to the Hip Bone ...

There are about 206 bones in the average adult human skeleton, which support and carry the body's organ systems that keep us alive and moving. In waking life, we might not think very much about what's happening inside our bodies; nevertheless, our body/mind connection is always at work as our nervous systems convey messages to and from our brains. Our subconscious may just "know" our bodies better than we do! And that knowledge often comes through in our dreams. Remember the ancient Greeks who used dreams to reveal illnesses and illuminate cures (see Chapter 2)?

Dreamwork _____

On a page in your dream journal, make a list of your most favorite and least favorite foods. Also write down your eating idiosyncrasies: slow eater, snacker, night binger, big bites, and so on. When you have a dream about eating or food, compare the dream details to the list in your journal. The similarities or differences between your waking and dreaming preferences and habits may surprise you!

The Invisible Body

Our Western approach to the body's function focuses on its physical, tangible aspects. The Eastern view incorporates an invisible "energy" structure as well. In this view, seven energy centers, called chakras, correspond to specific parts and functions of the body and the mind. The chakras are aligned along the spinal column, with the first chakra at the tailbone and the seventh chakra at the top, or crown, of the head.

In the Eastern view, invisible energy centers called chakras influence the body's health.

The chakras release energy to body parts, supporting them in their functions. According to Eastern beliefs, blocked chakras prevent organs and body systems from functioning properly. This can result in unwellness and disease. Releasing blocked chakras restores the free flow of energy. The following table describes the chakras, where they are located, and what body functions they're associated with.

The Chakras

Chakra	Site	Organ/System/Body Function
First or root	Base of spine	Sex organs; survival and basic needs (hunger, sex)
Second or spleen	Low lumbar	Lower digestive organs, spine, pancreas; elimination
Third or solar	Solar plexus	Upper digestive organs, adrenal glands; "taking in"
Fourth or heart		Thymus and immune system; chest emotions
Fifth or throat	Throat	Thyroid gland; speech and communication
Sixth or "third eye"	Forehead	Imagination, intuition, "inner vision"
Seventh or crown	Top of head	Pineal gland (circadian rhythms)

In the Eastern view, there is no division between body and mind. Dreams might be messages related to the health of organs or body systems or energy healing. You can attempt to enhance this link of body and mind in healthful harmony by working with the chakras in waking life using yoga, and before sleep by meditating on the chakras and reminding yourself to record your dreams. For example, if you are experiencing an overwhelming emotional situation in your life, you might try yoga poses that release the heart chakra, such as the prana arch. As you relax into sleep at night, meditate upon the heart chakra, breathing into and out of that space as you invite your dreams to illuminate and heal the conditions surrounding your situation.

Dreamwork

Yoga, from the Sanskrit word for "yoked," is a traditional Eastern practice that represents the union of body and mind through an integration of posture and meditation. Practitioners believe that certain yoga poses aid health by unblocking and releasing the flow of energy from the chakras. Poses such as the corpse pose can aid in reducing stress and inducing relaxation at the end of the day, preparing the body and the mind for a restful night's sleep. Yoga's breathing exercises also enhance calm and promote peaceful sleep.

From Head to Toe

We pay tribute to Freud and his technique of free association in this exercise to help put you in touch with your body. Write down the first thing that comes to mind after you read each of the following words:

	Association	
Feet	_____	_____
Neck	_____	_____
Breasts	_____	_____
Hair	_____	_____
Hands	_____	_____
Legs	_____	_____
Heart	_____	_____
Eyes	_____	_____
Mouth	_____	_____
Abdomen	_____	_____

Read what you wrote. Do your associations refer directly to your body parts and how they look? Did you write "Fred Flintstone" next to "Feet" because yours are wide and square? Do your associations refer to someone else's body parts (Grandpa's hands, your boyfriend's hair)? Or do they refer to the "ideal," or a popular view of what is beautiful or appropriate (such as Paul Newman's bright blue eyes)? How do you feel about your associations? Explore your feelings and their associations in greater detail by writing about them in your dream notebook.

Here's more food for thought: Do these body parts show up in your dreams? If your dream focuses on legs, are the legs crossed (as in "ladylike"), running (as in "like the wind"), or feeling heavy (as in "dead weight")? So why legs? Well, perhaps you broke your leg when you were 12. But that was ages ago, right? Why are you dreaming about legs now? Maybe you're concerned that you're about to be hurt again, as you were when you were 12. But this time it might be an emotional hurt, one that leaves you feeling immobilized.

Did the word "abdomen" spark an image of being punched in the gut? Abdomens are vulnerable and soft, and are home to many of the body's vital organs. The abdomen can represent our physical and spiritual center. At our healthiest, we breathe from our abdominal area and use the great strength of the abdominal muscles to power our bodies. Emphasis on the torso and abdomen in your dreams might suggest a fear of being hurt down to the core of your being.

Jolly Green Giant or Little Green Sprout

Are you bigger than life in your dreams? Dreams in which we make ourselves bigger than we actually are can let us know we're feeling defenseless; we need to "puff ourselves up." How does it feel to tower over the other characters in your dreams? Powerful? Lonely? Could it be that you are, in some way, having difficulty asserting yourself in your waking life, and your dreams are trying to help you "think big" about your current position or your plans for the future?

Dreams in which we are smaller than usual can suggest a desire to hide or to avoid a person, situation, or feeling. Is there some responsibility you're shirking? Or is there someone or some situation in your life that feels threatening to you, causing you to hide? Being small in dreams can also refer to a reduction in self-esteem or a comment about our ideals that we don't uphold. (You know, that difference between what we say and what we do ....) When this happens, we can feel "small." In times of great upheaval, we may dream we're smaller than others as a way to recapture a feeling of safety usually associated with childhood.

Losing Teeth and Other Body Parts

> *I've had this repetitive dream for 30 years since high school, that I keep losing my teeth. I smile and everyone points and laughs because I have no teeth! I am horrified and there's nothing I can do. I see some of my teeth on the ground, and I try to shove them back into my mouth, but they only fall out again.*

This woman recently realized the meaning of her dream. As a high school senior she became pregnant, left school, got married, and gave up her plans to go to college. To her, the losing of her teeth represented a loss of power over her choices. That she loses them in front of others and feels humiliated refers to the stigma that existed 30 years ago when a young woman left school because she was pregnant. The repetition of the dream probably occurs when she is experiencing feelings of powerlessness in her waking life that are as intense as her feelings in high school. In humankind's earliest days, teeth were tools used to bite, tear, and kill. Losing these potent tools of aggression in our dreams generally lets us know we're feeling powerless against current circumstances. What might be going on in your life that would leave you feeling this way? Are you feeling forced into an untenable decision by a domineering parent or partner? And sometimes when we dream of losing our teeth, we are expressing our fears about growing older and growing more dependent on others for our care.

Dreams in which our teeth fall out are very common. These dreams leave us feeling stunned, humiliated, and horrified. How do your teeth fall out? One at a time? Do you spit them out? Swallow them? Are you alone or in a crowd? Do you ask for help or try to hide what is happening to you?

Teeth, in more modern times, are associated with our appearance. If we lose our Pepsodent smile, we are generally expressing a feeling of insecurity about how other people perceive us. We're afraid we'll expose to the world our raw gums (or messy emotions, or stupid ideas) and we'll feel humiliated as a result. We can have this kind of dream when we are undergoing great changes (remember the high school student who suddenly found herself pregnant?) at various points in our lives. We will take a close look at these types of dreams, *signal dreams*, in Chapter 13.

Perhaps you've got all your teeth, but it's your hair that's falling out. In our culture, as well as some ancient ones (the Bible's long-haired strong man, Samson, for instance), having a full head of hair represents strength. So the loss of your hair may indicate that you are weaker than someone else, or are zapped of energy.

Dreams of lost or missing body parts may be frightening. While they can tell us we are not whole on one hand, they can also be a Humpty Dumpty attempt to take all our pieces and make us whole. If you are losing or missing something, what is it keeping you from doing? Are you in some way "cutting off your nose to spite your face?" Often the lost or missing body part represents someone or some type of relationship we want or need. Are you dreaming that your right arm is missing? What does that mean to you? Are you suffering the departure of a dear friend, your "right-hand man?"

> **Life Is But a Dream**
>
> Being unable to hear can be a frightening dream experience. But to millions of deaf Americans, deafness is not a disability. In fact, American Sign Language (ASL) is the third-most-used language in this country. Researchers are studying the hand movements of deaf dreamers during REM sleep to discover whether their finger movements are actually fragmentary ASL signs.

In Sickness and in Health

How do you feel in your dreams? Fit and healthy, deathly ill, or somewhere in between? Do other people who show up in your dreams feel the same, or are they healthier or more ill than you are? Do you or your dream characters get stronger or weaker in dreams that center on health? Do they take place in a hospital where you're apt to get appropriate medical care, or are you felled by the tsetse fly in the jungles of equatorial Africa?

Getting Weaker and Getting Stronger

Are you so weak in your dreams that you can't run from the bogeyman? Or is your energy level so impaired that you can't make a fist, grab the cat, or climb a tree?

When interpreting such dreams, you should first pay attention to your overall health. How are you feeling in waking life? Perhaps a medical checkup is in order. A metaphorical message of such a dream might be that you are feeling "less than," either in terms of what you used to be able to accomplish or what others can accomplish. Often these dreams are experienced more frequently as we age and may well be our psyche's way of processing the natural cycle of life.

The good news: Psychoanalyst Dr. Charles Rycroft points out that if you find you're having dreams where it feels enjoyable to watch someone climb a tree rather than climb it yourself, this might indicate that you are able to accept the passage of time and the different capabilities you now have. On the other hand, if this dream is accompanied by vague feelings of discomfort, it could be a signal to you that you are acquiescing; you're watching from the sidelines rather than doing.

If your dreams are chock-full of images of illness, then you may be feeling some guilt about not meeting some internal or external demands. In your dreams, your unmet goals and high standards are making you ill. But dreams in which you tap into hidden reservoirs of energy, talent, or strength seem to be giving you a nudge, to be telling you you're capable of more than you realize. Ever had a dream similar to the following?

> *I am on display at the grocery store. Patrons line up to have me open jars. They start bringing canned goods, then sides of beef to raise above my head. It feels like there's no end to what I can do!*

Dream Dictionary

Compensatory dreams are ones that are expressions of what the dreamer wishes for but actually lacks in his or her waking life.

In some cases, as with people who are terminally ill, dreams of hidden or unknown abilities may be *compensatory dreams.*

Generally, if there are other people in the dream, witnessing either your feats of strength or growing weakness, there is a theme of competition present in the dream. Who or what are you trying to surpass, beat out, or vanquish?

Caregivers

Do you dream of caregivers, or of being a caregiver yourself? In your dreams are you in need of aid, but no one answers your call? Or conversely, are there too many nurses surrounding your bed? Does the caregiver give the right kind of medicine or TLC? And, indeed, who is that caregiver—a stranger, or someone near and dear?

It's a fact of modern life that most of us have too much to do in too little time, so it's not surprising that caregivers might show up in our dreams and become our own personal angels of mercy.

Are you a caregiver in your waking life? A mother to triplets? An adult now caring for an aging parent? Often we have dreams that express what we can't possibly tell those who depend upon us: that we're tired and cranky and would dearly love a vacation from the ceaseless responsibilities. These are normal feelings, but we generally feel too guilty expressing them in our waking life. So we might have dreams in which we are terrible caregivers, dreams in which we leave our charges unattended, or worse. Clearly, your dreams are letting you know how the repressed part of you feels. Maybe it's a good idea to find some outlet in your waking hours to let off steam.

> **Life Is But a Dream**
>
> Researchers predict that within 50 years, more than one million people will live to be 100 years old. Indeed in the past century alone, the human life span increased from 45 to about 75 years. As we live longer, it's only natural that issues of aging and caregiving will show up more frequently in our dreams.

> **Dreamy**
>
> In her book *Visits* (Three Rivers Press, 1998), Lee Ann Chearney, caregiver to her mother, Gloria, who has Parkinson's disease, recalls a dream where she's accompanied everywhere around New York city by a 30-something brunette woman who likes to have everything her way. In the dream, Lee Ann finally refuses to get on a bus at Rockefeller Center with the woman—who then turns around with the face of her 62-year-old mother. "Don't make me go alone," her mother says. This dream captures the dilemma an adult child faces when taking care of a parent.

Dream Healing

The ancient Greek god Aesculapius was believed to come to people in their sleep, to heal them through their dreams. The sick and the wounded traveled from distant lands to sleep in the temple of Aesculapius at Argos, to let the great healer enter their dreams and cure their ailments. Contemporary spiritual healers, such as *The Hidden Power of Dreams* (Ballantine 1988) author Denise Linn, believe that the power to heal through dreams comes from the dreamer. "Dream healing is a very powerful way to heal yourself and those you love," Linn says. There are a number of methods for dream healing if this is something you'd like to explore; we talk more about them in the chapters in Part 5.

Purging the Urge

Isaac Newton said, "Every action has an equal but opposite reaction." Many years later a pop music group sang, "What goes up, must come down." We highly doubt either was referring to the end result of digestion, but it's rather apt anyway! We eat, then we eliminate. Going to the bathroom is surely as true a law of the physical world as Sir Isaac's law.

Toilet Training

The terrible twos. The era of "No." Luckily, once we pass through them we forget them, our parents forgive us, and we go on with life. But wait … maybe there are some vestiges of this time that we don't exactly leave behind (pun intended!).

Psychologists have spent entire careers studying the period in life during which we graduate from diapers to the potty. No, it's not a weird field of study; in fact, this stage of development encapsulates some of the basic issues we'll face all our lives. They are the issues of power and control and pride and shame. (And you thought it was just about poop!)

Although you might not remember it yourself, it's a real high for a child when she (or he) first learns to control her bladder and bowels, when the child first realizes she—and not her parents or her body—has total say over when she urinates or defecates. This new understanding is accompanied by great pride. If that feeling is mirrored by the parents (how many times have you clapped over little Sophie's "gift" in the potty?), then the child continues to feel like she controls her body and not the other way around. But if the toddler is made to feel that her waste products are dirty and bad, then she will feel ashamed of her creations and of herself.

The power struggle between little Sophie and her parents begins soon after she's successfully toilet trained, ushering in the era of "No." Sophie's discovered this neat ability to assert her independence. She doesn't want her parents horning in on it! They should just be happy to admire her "creations." If her parents displease her, she can forget to use the potty and really make them pay!

As you might imagine, this stage of development remains rich fodder for symbolic—and not-so-symbolic—dreaming throughout the life cycle.

Dreams About Going to the Bathroom

So how does all this relate to dreams in which you're urinating or defecating? Often in this sort of dream, the dreamer is exercising a basic control—or failing to—in his life. He might consider who or what is trying to hijack his basic sense of control. As with the toddler who is made to feel ashamed because the message she's given is that her urine and feces are dirty, these later dreams can often belie a feeling of shame about what we have inside of us.

When you have this sort of dream, you might want to think about what unwanted, "nasty" feelings you are trying to eliminate.

Another common type of bathroom dream is one in which the dreamer relieves himself in public. How do the other dream characters react? Often they simply don't notice. As Dr. Gayle Delaney notes in *In Your Dreams*, this may mean that the dreamer need not fear ridicule for the more private physical and emotional parts of himself.

> **Wake Up!**
>
> Dreams of having to go to the bathroom can also be literal messages. Maybe you're trying to tell yourself to wake up and use the bathroom. To avoid unwanted awakenings, don't drink excessive liquids two hours before bedtime. Remember, fragmented sleep can reduce the length and quantity of dreaming REM sleep.

Nothing but Your Birthday Suit

Have you ever shown up for work naked? Taken all your clothes off in Burger King? Gone to get your hair trimmed when wearing nothing but a pair of shoes? While we would never dream of doing this in our waking lives, we sure do dream of it at night. And we do it often.

Naked as a Jaybird

> *I was on a picnic with different sorts of people, co-workers, friends, and my sisters. I suddenly realized that I was naked. I tried to cover myself up with a napkin, but the wind kept blowing it off. No one seemed to notice.*

In conventional dream analysis, this sort of dream, especially if recurring, is considered an exhibition dream and expresses an ongoing issue with wanting—and failing—to be noticed.

But there are many other ways to look at this dream. Certainly this dreamer must feel vulnerable and exposed, in every sense of the word. Why might feelings of vulnerability and exposure be cropping up now? Perhaps this dreamer is achieving much success and recognition in many spheres: professional, community, and familial. But because her self-esteem is shaky, she's afraid that she'll be exposed as a fraud; underneath it all she feels she's not that good at her job, not that valuable a member of her community, not a particularly interesting friend.

This sort of dream, where we let it all hang out, might also indicate that we're concerned with how our imperfections will be tolerated. Another way to look at it is that we're afraid of how our true self will be seen and what the reaction to this will be.

Dreamy
Writer Elmore Leonard, known for his thrillers, talks of a recurring dream of being naked in public. In his dream there is always bright sunlight and lots of people around him. At some point he would realize that he could simply walk to a nearby doorway or escape in some other way. He understood the message as a desire to ignore other people who were watching him—and get on with his work!

In your dreams of nudity are you afraid that you will be exposed for a fraud, concerned that the honest self you show to the world will be criticized? Does it make you feel defenseless? What are your nudity dreams like? Are you the only one naked? Are you totally or partially clothed? What's the setting? What's the attitude toward you? Do you try to cover up? Are you happily nude in your dreams and suddenly someone shows up uninvited? Does this feel as though your privacy is being invaded, or do you welcome your guest and pour her a drink?

Dreams about nudity can also be wonderful. They can speak to our feelings of being free and unfettered. They can indicate we've "shed" some armor, attitude, negative situation, or behavior. Just remember, it's possible that there might be various elements (fear of exposure, judgment, desire to be noticed) present in the same dream!

Our Animal Nature

If, in dreams, we change into an animal or have animal anatomy and traits, we should look at psychological parts of us that may be clamoring for integration into our personality. We may be expressing primitive desires and needs in a nonverbal way. (Animals don't talk, they just act!) These "primitive" parts are those that we hide from society. Perhaps they are about sex and aggression or a need for nurturance. They are the parts of us that want what we want when we want it, reason be damned!

Native American dancers may honor certain animals in ceremonies designed to symbolize human connection with the spiritual and natural world. Because of the historical centrality of the natural world in these cultures, it stands to reason that animals—as well as sun, moon, stars, wind, rain, water, and other elements—are represented in dreams. What these animals might symbolize depends on the tribes' teachings and the individual dreamer's associations. Obviously, not all tribes view each animal in the same light; for example, Dr. James Lewis points out that some tribes regard the wolf in dreams as the supreme teacher or guide. Other tribes think of the wolf as the male warrior, while still others will interpret it as a feminine symbol tied to the moon's cycle.

Morphing

What does it feel like to be dreaming of your wife and suddenly she turns, or morphs (remember Morpheus, the Greek god of dreams?), into your brother? Shocking? Scary? Delightful? When this happens, it generally indicates that an issue you have with your brother is now cropping up with your wife. It's our creative visual way of saying "Hey— my wife and my brother have something in common for me." Okay, but what? Chances are there is a common emotional button they push in you, even though they are obviously different people.

Dream Body Scan

Before going to sleep, perform a meditative body scan: breathing deeply into each body part as your mind focuses upon it and releasing the breath as you move continuously through your body's organs and appendages, relaxing from head to toe. As you complete the scan and drift off to sleep, reflect on the thought: "Reveal my true self." Upon waking, record your dreams and associations to them in your dream journal

The Least You Need to Know

- ◆ Food and eating in dreams can be metaphors for emotional or physical things we crave.

- ◆ Dreams of sickness or loss of a body part or function might indicate an actual illness or a feeling of being powerless.

- ◆ Dreams about going to the bathroom tend to revisit issues about shame, pride, and self-control.

- ◆ Nudity in dreams generally reveals our feelings of vulnerability and exposure.

Chapter 10

Dream Lovers: Dreams About Sex

In This Chapter

◆ Your steamy dream dates

◆ Friends and strangers ... hidden desire or symbolism?

◆ Sharing your dreams

◆ When famous people visit your dreams

It's as natural to dream about sex as it is to have it. There are many different kinds of sex dreams ranging from the explicit to the obtuse. These dreams can feel sweet, hot, scary, funny, or just plain bizarre. Some sex dreams have little "action" in them but are infused with a strong erotic feel, nonetheless.

What's Love Got to Do with It?

Dreaming about romantic interludes with Mel Gibson, Mel Brooks, or Uncle Mel—or Julia Roberts, Julia Child, or Aunt Julia—probably isn't about sex, per se; it's about what sex represents.

Still, we tend to take sex dreams at face value. Who can blame us? We might resist delving deeper into what it means that we had a romantic tryst with a favorite rock star; we're content to relish the memory intact, thank you very much!

Another reason sex dreams are often viewed as really, truly, and only about sex has to do with our culture's, our family's, and our own personal views about sex. Unlike our views about cardboard, for example, sex has always carried a lot of moral, political, spiritual, and economic weight. Sometimes it feels like a particularly loaded issue to explore. Here are just a few of the powerful issues sex calls to mind:

- Conception, pregnancy, and birth
- Religion, morality, and values
- Homosexuality, heterosexuality, and anything in between
- Infertility
- Self-love or self-loathing
- Adultery
- Freedom
- Control or submission
- Love
- A sharing of souls
- Acceptance
- Rejection

Dreams are elegant expressions of our fundamental needs, desires, and fears. So is sexuality. Let's look at what our dreams about sex might be telling us.

Dreamwork

Jot down some of your free associations, both thought and feeling, about sex in your dream journal. Think about how sex was viewed in your family and among your peers. Were you branded a "good girl" or a "stud"? What were/are your sex dreams like? Do you consider yourself sexy? Why? What qualities in others turn you on? Can you see how your dreams support or refute these waking beliefs?

Dreaming Pleasure, Waking Guilt

I am standing in front of a broken window in my neighbor's kitchen. In waking life I don't find this man particularly attractive, but in my dream I am very drawn to him. I begin to kiss him and suddenly we're making love.

Have you ever had a sexual dream involving a co-worker, your dry cleaner, a neighbor—someone you don't think about too often and certainly not in a romantic way? Why on earth should you be kissing your daughter's soccer coach? Does it mean you secretly want to run off with him?

Maybe yes, but probably no. In *The Dream Game*, Ann Faraday suggests the first thing you might ask yourself is whether you do, indeed, feel an attraction for the lover in your dream. Is it possible that you haven't realized the bank teller is sexy? Is that why you've been showing up at her window every day with checks made out to cash in the most romantic penmanship?

Maybe you're working 300 hours a week, rearing triplets, running the household, and trying to be a good spouse. You and your partner haven't had a romantic rendezvous in memorable history. In other words, are you simply too busy to pay waking attention to your libido? Sometimes a dream about sex is our body's way of letting us know it's been too long.

Or maybe you're just not comfortable feeling turned on by anyone other than your spouse or partner. We're taught that fidelity includes our actions—and our thoughts. (Former U.S. president Jimmy Carter roused national interest when he acknowledged "lusting in his mind" in the 1970s.) We lose sight of the fact that it's natural to have all sorts of feelings—including sexual—for all sorts of people, places, and things! It doesn't make you a *nymphomaniac* or a *Don Juan*. Our biological yearnings don't go away just because we are in a permanent relationship.

In fact, some dream theorists note that we can feel erotic toward a project, a sunset, a piece of music—anything that moves us. Still, we judge certain feelings as unseemly; we block them out. So we shouldn't be too surprised when they pop up in the less-guarded dream state.

Dream Dictionary

Nymphomania, defined as "excessive sexual desire by a female" (**Don Juanism** is the term used for men), originally referred to nubile, unmarried, young women. During the Middle Ages, these women became represented in art and literature as fairies or sprites. The nymphs' reputed orgies during seasons of the moon contributed the sexual connotations we attach to the word today.

While excessive day and night dreaming about sex with partners other than your spouse might indicate that you should explore what bearing this has on your current relationship, more often than not, sex dreams involving surprising lovers may be enjoyed guilt free. Some people have even found that in such dreams they're less inhibited sexually and then can bring that sense of adventure to their waking relationship.

But what if, after a few soul-searching moments, you come to the conclusion that in reality you do not harbor sexual feelings for your neighbor? Well, then, we've just crossed over into the land of metaphor.

Perhaps our dreamer found herself having sex with the neighbor because to her, sex can be a metaphor for reconciliation. It's a "coming together." As it turns out, this dreamer had a minor argument with her neighbor a few days prior to the dream, and this was symbolized by the broken window. If the argument had been with the neighbor's wife, then the dream may have been a metaphorical revenge, a "taking" of something that doesn't belong to her.

A Symbolic Union

Suppose you dream you're having sex with your partner, and he or she turns into a tiger or a piece of furniture or a beautiful rose. What does it mean when you're coupling with your own personal *satyr?* You'll need to consider what the morphing symbol means to you, as well as how the experience feels—in both dreaming and waking states.

You may be delighted in your dream to be making love to your partner-turned-tiger. But upon waking, perhaps the dream seems more unsettling and frightening. Dream symbols are specific to the dreamer (you); always evaluate them in terms of their personal meaning, not what you might read in someone else's dream dictionary.

Dream Dictionary

In Greek mythology, a **satyr** is usually half-horse, half-man (or half-goat, half-man). Like nymphs, satyrs are spirits of the woods, and they're lascivious, riotous creatures.

Here's another powerful symbol to think about in sexual dreams. Where is the union taking place? From the top of the Eiffel Tower to your bathroom floor, *any* setting is possible in dreams. Do your sexual dreams usually take place in the same place, or all over the place? Are you comfortable, uncomfortable, perhaps thrilled? Your setting may figure dramatically into the total dream experience, or it may be a nondescript or nonexistent feature of the dream with the emphasis instead on what you're doing and whoever you're with.

A Blast from the Past

It's very common for dreams about sex to involve an old love. But this probably doesn't mean you wish to rekindle a long-ago romance. In some dreams, an old love might emerge only to vanish in a puff of smoke. Maybe as things really heat up, this old love tells you it's all over and waves good-bye. Does this mirror what happened when you broke up way back when? Or maybe you weren't as, well, mature then and you threw her over the day before the senior prom. And so dreaming that she disappears on you this time is your way of lessening your guilt!

It's common for aspects of old relationships to pop up as we embark on new ones. This makes sense; we're nervous about once again revealing so much of our selves both emotionally and physically. Or perhaps we feel the resurgence of old, familiar dynamics in the relationship. And it seems the more serious the new relationship is, the more serious the sex dreams involving old loves can be. Dreaming of a long-lost lover might hearken back to earlier romantic rejections. The dreamer (who feels confident and full of enthusiasm in waking life) is having the dream now, just as he or she embarks on a new relationship. This may highlight hidden insecurity. Getting dumped again may be real fear … and perhaps a deep-down expectation.

There are a few things to note about such dreams. What did you feel and think in waking life while you were in this relationship??

- Ignored
- Intimidated
- Aloof
- Cherished

How did you feel and think in the dream? Upon waking?

- Controlled
- Shut down
- Adored

Next, try to associate these feelings and ideas with someone or something in your current life. Who in your life intimidates you, leaves you feeling controlled or shut down? You might be surprised to find that your dream describes not a current sexual relationship, but perhaps a business or platonic personal relationship.

Finally, ask yourself, "When was the first time I felt this way?" Chances are the feeling goes way, way back to Mom or Dad. Or even someone in the family or neighborhood who didn't observe good sexual boundaries. Armed with this knowledge, you can clearly see this pattern and begin to do what's necessary to choose other, more successful ways of relating to the problem person or situation.

> *I dreamed about my best friend in elementary school, a boy named Bobby. In real life, I'd loved him since second grade, but he always chose girls who were thinner and prettier than me. So I settled for being his sidekick. In the dream we were young, still, but high school age. I was so happy to see him, thrilled really. He told me he'd come back for me. We kissed and it was so pleasurable.*

This dreamer has found a nifty way to rewrite history! Here, as in earlier examples, the blast from the past (Bobby) is a metaphor. It's as if the dreamer's unconscious is telling her that the attributes she felt she *didn't* have when she was around Bobby—being pretty, desirable, and sexual—were now hers. The dream shows the dreamer that finally she's found a way to feel confident regarding her sexuality. This dream is not only a reunion with a lost love, but also a reunion with parts of herself that she had difficulty believing were hers.

Will You Be Rejected or Embraced?

When we present ourselves sexually, we're usually in a pretty vulnerable state, naked in most senses of the word. We might wonder if we'll be good enough or do it right or start laughing or any number of things, all of which can result in either a humiliating rejection or a sweet embrace. Which kind of dreams do you have and when? What's going on in your life that would give you such a dream? Some possibilities include:

- You got into the law school of your choice.

- Your book is rejected for the 6,747th time.

- You just heard that your brother's getting divorced.

- You're getting divorced.

- The folks in the Sales Division did/didn't invite you to the annual Karaoke Festival.

- The grocery store clerk remembered your name.

- You just happened to hear through the grapevine that Brad Pitt, George Clooney, and Michelangelo's *David* are fighting over you.

Now it's your turn. In your dream journal, make a list of a few things that have happened to you in the last week or so that felt like rejection or acceptance. It can be something large or something small—and it certainly doesn't have to be about sex.

Did any of these things trigger a sex dream? (Now that you've been through the exercise and have started thinking along these lines, we wouldn't be surprised if you had a dream about sex related to something on this list!) If so, explore it in your dream journal. Consider the people, places, and plot of the dream. Can you identify other symbolism?

Life Is But a Dream

Freud postulated that dream images often represent the male and female genitalia. For example, swords, tree trunks, and umbrellas are penises, while doorways and rooms could symbolize vaginas. Exciting dream activities could even be metaphors for sexual intercourse. This kind of symbolism might be more prominent in cultures and times in which sexual subjects can't be discussed in society, as was the case in the Victorian England of Freud's lifetime. Even Freud, later in his career, moved away from strict interpretation of such symbols as sexual. Contemporary dream analysis puts less emphasis on the items themselves and more on how they appear in the context of the dream and what they mean to the dreamer.

Feeling embraced by your dreamy date can indicate that there are parts of him or her that you're able to acknowledge as your own. One dreamer, a rather high-powered, almost ruthless commodities trader, told us that she had the most tender sexual dream about a friend of hers whom she describes as "sensitive, honest, almost ridiculously spiritual." That she was able to "embrace" these qualities was a clue to her that she was ready to pay more attention to nurturing those qualities within herself.

Dream Lover, Come to Me

How often are your dreams the setting for intimate trysts with your waking-life lover? People in close relationships often find that their partners appear in their dreams. The dream might be a replay of a sexual encounter that actually happened, a fantasy filled with metaphor, or anything in between. You might find that you dream about your lover when you are separated, such as when one partner is away on business. How do such dreams stack up against your waking sex life? Do they highlight the aspects of your relationship that satisfy you or that you enjoy, or draw attention to challenges or perhaps changes you might like to see in your relationship?

Sharing your dreams with your partner is a way to open dialogue between the two of you. You might find sharing your fantasies (sexual or otherwise) adds intimacy and even excitement to your relationship. Because dreams reflect the inner, uncensored, and sometimes unknown you, it's important to have some ground rules in place for the respect with which you treat each other's dreams. You don't want to worry about your partner laughing at your REM adventures, for example, or telling them to dinner guests.

Two as One: Shared Energy

Some Eastern views, such as Tao and Tantra, perceive sexual union as the blending of life energy (called *prana*) as well as body and mind. When bodies join, according to these traditions, so does energy. We talked about chakras in Chapter 9; the first or root chakra, located at the base of the spine, is the body's channel for sexual energy.

During lovemaking, in Eastern traditions, the union of bodies activates the first chakra. Energy flows freely between the lovers, strengthening and intensifying the connection between them. This connection extends beyond the physical joining of sex to a melding of minds as well. The couple's thoughts and dreams mingle, too, a state that envelops them even after their bodies separate and they drift off to sleep.

Intimate Communication: Shared Dreams

The Tantric tradition often uses shared meditation to encourage and open the flow of energy between lovers. But you don't have to subscribe to Tantric or Eastern views to try variations of this method yourself. Whether you accept the philosophy of energy exchange or simply enjoy feeling close to each other, this exercise can help you set the tone for sharing each other's dreams. Do this right before going to bed.

1. Sit cross-legged (in yoga's lotus position), facing each other.

2. Look into each other's eyes. Take three slow, deep breaths in unison—breathe in over a count of five, hold the breath for a count of five, and breathe out over a count of five.

3. Still looking into each other's eyes, each of you place one hand over the other person's heart. (In the Eastern tradition, this opens your heart chakras.) Join your other hands together, fingers intertwined.

4. Invite each other, through your thoughts, to appear in each other's dreams. Visualize the dream you want to have with your partner, if you like. (It doesn't have to be sexual.)

5. When you feel ready to disengage, take three slow, deep breaths in unison. Release your joined hands, and then remove your hand from the other's heart.

6. Go to sleep.

When you awaken in the morning, each of you write down what dreams you remember. Then compare notes. Do you see any similarities? Did your dreams have common themes, even if you didn't appear in them?

Like a Virgin, and Beyond ...

Remember Freud's breakthrough remark, the one that sent polite Victorian society into an uproar, that even kids are sexual? The truth of this can be seen in our sexual dreams which span a lifetime.

The First Time

Can you recall the first dream about sex that you ever had? How old were you? Do you, in fact, have sex dreams? How often? Some of our earlier dreams about sex may have been triggered by the physiological changes taking place in our bodies. Still other dreams may have pointed toward a developmental change. For instance, a pre-teen's dream might focus on dating rather than on long, involved sexual trysts. Read more about this in Part 4.

For adults, sexual dreams that feel like "the first time," either with a particular person or in terms of a new setting or feeling, can be messages that there are important beginnings ahead.

> *Lately I've begun to dream that I am the one initiating a sexual encounter. At the age of 41, it strikes me as odd that until now, my dreams about sex have always been ones in which I was passive; you know, where sex just sort of "happened."*

This dreamer thought the change from passive to active participant referred to new, positive feelings he'd been having about his self-esteem in waking life. So a "first" dream can really be about fresh beginnings, no matter how old we are or how many lovers we've had.

The "firsts" you have in your life are many and ongoing: the first day of school, your first sexual encounter, your first marriage, the first day of a new job, the first experience of parenting, and the day you retire are just a few. We're apt to remember all our important firsts. The excitement, anxiety, and joy you feel can be reflected in all your dreams, including your sexual ones.

Consummation: Satisfaction Guaranteed

Does your dream partner run off just as things are getting really heated up or does he or she stick around? Are the two of you interrupted by a marching band? A sexual dream that leaves you feeling frustrated might be a metaphor for some relationship or situation in your life that has left you feeling abandoned or out of control.

Dreams that are sexually satisfying could be a sure indication that you're getting what you want even in your dreams—or it could highlight the fact that it's only in your dreams that your sex life is pleasurable.

On a more pedestrian note, having a successful sexual union with your grocer (in your dream, of course!) might refer to your positive feelings about your recent promotion and raise; now that you've got more money, you can stop buying only generic brands!

Are your sex dreams wildly fulfilling and exciting? Sometimes we're uncomfortable with the nature of, or the passion in, our sex dreams. You might want to ask yourself why. Is it because such passionate dreams don't fit in with the serious, buttoned-down image you have of yourself (and the serious, buttoned-down sex you're having in waking life)?

Physiologically speaking, researchers have discovered that during dreaming REM sleep, males experience erections and females experience increased blood flow to the vaginal tissues—no matter what the content of the dream. In fact, "wet dreams" may be more a function of sleeping than dreaming—most nocturnal emissions do not coincide with overtly sexual dream recall. But some dream research shows that if someone is awakened while sexually aroused, he or she will likely recount a sexual dream story.

There's a lot of research going on regarding physiology and REM sleep, and it's clear that both men and women can often achieve orgasm while dreaming. However, it's too early for researchers to say with certainty that this physiological behavior during REM sleep has the same sexual connotations that waking arousal has. Whatever it means, know that it's perfectly natural.

> **CAUTION** **Wake Up!**
>
> Repetitive, disturbing sexual dreams in which we feel forced and/or violated may be our dreaming mind's way of letting us know there has been some sort of sexual abuse in our past. We urge you to discuss this with a mental health professional.

Some sex dreams aren't satisfying because of the setting of the dream. Perhaps you're about to make love in your dream only to discover that you're in a public place or the entire Senate just walked into your hotel room. Maybe you're trying to make love in the bleachers at game seven of the World Series. This might reflect a feeling of frustration in your waking life with a partner or with a totally unrelated, nonsexual situation.

Was your sexual union interrupted by a roving pack of puppies or by a three-alarm fire? Why do you suppose you're creating a dream in which you stop the action? Are you scared of the intimate moments in your dream (and how does that apply to your waking life)? Do you feel on some level that you don't deserve pleasure? Or are you sending yourself a wise message that there's some situation or relationship you need to curb?

The "I" Word (Impotence)

Viagra aside, both women and men have impotence dreams. The first order of business in deciphering such a dream is to consider the obvious: Are you having a problem with sex in your waking life? Could this signal a difficulty with your sexual or reproductive capacity that you're not quite conscious of?

Once you and your health-care professional rule out the physiological, you might discover that dreams about impotence signal a fear of losing power. Maybe you're afraid you won't measure up to a particular person or task in your life. Often, dreams of impotence occur as you launch yourself into uncharted territory—and you're not particularly confident about your navigational skills. Are you having this sort of dream as you re-enter the dating game after a divorce or breakup?

Impotence dreams leave us with a feeling of having been thwarted, even cheated. We simply cannot perform the way we wish to. Perhaps your closest friend just snagged the lead role out from under your nose in the community theater's presentation of *The Sound of Music*. Hell, you'd been lip-syncing the album for years; Maria was yours; you were born to play that part! But instead, you've been asked to move scenery.

Impotence dreams can also be dreams in which you can't quite get your clothes off or you can't turn your dream date on. Maybe she turns into a statue just as you whisper sweet nothings in her ear.

Being Pregnant: The Moment of Conception

Both men and women can have pregnancy dreams. We've found that often, dreams of conceiving or pregnancy refer to some aspect of the dreamer, or some aspect of the dreamer's work or personal life, that is growing and developing but might not be ready to be talked about or acted upon. In fact, the dreamer might not even be able to put into words what this new life growing inside him or her might be. Just like living creatures, ideas and feelings have their own gestation period.

The most important thing to consider is how the dreamer feels upon discovering that he or she is pregnant. That's right, even men can dream of being pregnant. Sometimes the dreamer feels unsure of how he or she became pregnant. This surprise can be a welcome one or one curiously devoid of feeling. The dreamer can feel a sense of excitement or bliss, or the dream realization that one is pregnant can be frightening ("How will I care for this baby?"), or repulsive ("What on earth is growing inside me and taking me over?"), or exhausting ("How will I carry all this extra weight around?").

> **Life Is But a Dream**
>
> Women in their third trimester of pregnancy often don't sleep as well and report more strange and evocative dreams. At this stage in pregnancy, many women take longer to fall asleep and have more trouble getting back to sleep if awakened during the night.

Another metaphorical aspect to dreams of pregnancy has been noted, but only recently. With the advances in reproductive science that make it possible for peri- and postmenopausal women to have babies, dreaming of being pregnant can also herald a feeling that anything is possible, that there are no impediments to your heart's desire.

Oh, and let's not forget the obvious: There's the possibility that women of childbearing age are letting themselves know through their dreams that they *are* pregnant! And sometimes it's the partner whose concerns emerge under cover of metaphor, as was the case with this dreamer:

> *I—not my wife—am pregnant. I can see through my own skin that I am carrying rotting vegetables. I know that if I don't go into labor immediately, the vegetables (babies) will die. But I don't know how to do this.*

Pretty disturbing, right? But very normal. When women or men are awaiting the birth of a child, it's common that they'll have bizarre dreams in which anxieties about pregnancy, birth, and becoming parents are expressed. This dreamer feels quite out of control with regard to the changes going on in his life, and he can't seem to figure out what to do to help with the birth process.

You're Having a Baby?!

So you're giving birth! Never mind that in your waking life you are 64, male, and celibate. While pregnant women often dream about giving birth in anticipation of the upcoming event, dreams of giving birth may have more to do with a sense of being reborn, of fresh beginnings, of ideas coming to fruition.

Sex with Someone Who Isn't Your Spouse or Partner

Okay, so you've been in a happily committed relationship for 10 years. We still want to know: Who else are you doing it with at night?

Sex with Famous People

We tend to think that sex dreams about famous people can be a simple wish fulfillment and/or a way of emulating or incorporating aspects of the star's particular talent. For instance, an aspiring vocalist may dream of having sex with Barbra Streisand. But another man or woman who can't hold a tune in a bucket might also dream of a romantic tryst with Barbra. The sought-after quality here might be her passion for political causes.

In a recent, highly unscientific poll of American adults between the ages of 30 and 45, we've compiled the following list of famous people—in no particular order—who are most frequently dreamed about in a sexual context. See how many have popped up in your dreams:

Bill Clinton	Bill Gates
Mel Gibson	Boyz II Men
Sharon Stone	Luther Vandross
Denzel Washington	Michael Jordan
Robert Redford	Alex Rodriguez
Madonna	Candace Bergen
Gwyneth Paltrow	Grace Kelly
Whitney Houston	Cary Grant
Toni Braxton	All supermodels
Brad Pitt	Jesse Helms
Matt Damon	Alan Greenspan
Tiger Woods	George Steinbrenner
Bruce Springsteen	

Sometimes the famous people we dream about are really stand-ins for the people who aren't so famous, the people in our day-to-day lives.

Oedipus, Schmedipus ...

In addition to death and taxes, we'd bet that one other thing we can count on in life is that folks just don't like to dream about sexual encounters with parents, siblings, children, or any sort of first-degree relation. Such dreams can leave us feeling shocked or ashamed.

Perhaps you're dreaming of having sex with your wife and suddenly she turns into your mother! Such dreams are common and not necessarily a cause for alarm. They can suggest a wish or a desire to return to maternal comfort and warmth. Jung has also suggested that dreaming of sex with the father is a way of getting in touch with our masculine side. These dreams can also serve as a signal that dynamics in the sex dream are being re-created in current relationships. Didn't your father make you feel like you couldn't do anything right ... and voilà! Dad shows up in your sex dream. Once you get over your shock, you realize that your current lover makes you feel the same way!

If your dreams about sex with older or more powerful family members are violent, coercive, and frightening, it's possible that these dreams are memories. And they may not be memories of sexual abuse, but of emotional abuse that, in your dream, expresses itself in sexual imagery. Pay close attention to how the sexual situation unfolds and, most important, how it makes you feel. Again, *please* see a therapist if you have recurrent dreams with disturbing sexual content.

One last word about Oedipus and Electra: It's most often quite normal to have a dream in which you're having sex with one or the other parent. As she grows up, for instance, a young woman may begin to see her parents as real, separate sexual beings, and dreaming of one or the other in a sexual way might have everything to do with her growing understanding of herself as a maturing person.

Dreamy

Freud once wrote that all neurotics are either Oedipus or Hamlet. Oedipus was a legendary king of Thebes who fulfilled a prophecy made at his birth to unwittingly murder his father and marry his mother. The hero of Shakespeare's famous tragedy, Hamlet seeks to avenge the murder of his father. "O God, I could be bounded in a nutshell and count myself a king of infinite space, were it not that I have bad dreams." (*Hamlet*, II, ii)

What's Your Orientation?

Dreaming about a homosexual encounter if you're straight or a heterosexual encounter if you're gay or lesbian does not mean that you've been mistaken all this time about who turns you on.

Certainly, recurrent dreams about sexual orientation might indicate a discomfort about lifestyle choices. Unfortunately, gay and lesbian people have much homophobia to contend with and these attitudes can be internalized, resulting in dreams where they choose a partner that Mom, Dad, and the rest of the world would seemingly approve of.

But remember, most sex dreams aren't about sex at all. So it's more important to consider the content of the dream. What could the steamy dream date be a stand-in for? Are aspects of the dream date's personality really unrecognized aspects of yourself? Dreams with themes of sexual orientation can also point out to us that even though by young adulthood most of us clearly understand our sexual identity and what gender we wish our sexual partners to be, we can be sexually attracted to all sorts of people of both genders. As long as we feel we're being true to ourselves in our waking life choices, perhaps we should just enjoy our same- or opposite-sex dreams and regard them as forays into either end of our *sexual continuum*.

> **Dream Dictionary**
>
> Alfred Charles Kinsey (1894–1956), American biologist and author, studied human sexual behavior. He coined the term **sexual continuum,** which refers to our propensity to be sexually attracted, in varying degrees, to members of either sex; our sexual response is not rigidly fixed on one sex or the other.

Who Was That Masked Stranger?

Do you dream of sex with a stranger, someone you've never met? What is this person like? How does the event unfold? Sometimes it can feel safer to risk being rejected or accepted by a stranger rather than someone for whom we have deep feelings. Or perhaps dreaming of sex with a stranger is a message you're sending to yourself that you long to get to know hidden parts of yourself.

> **Life Is But a Dream**
>
> Some people believe the same-sex sexual dreams (if you're straight) or opposite-sex dreams (if you're gay or lesbian) are presentations of prior life experiences. After all, it stands to reason that you haven't been the same sex (or sexual orientation) in all of your lifetimes, right?

Sex with Someone You Love the Best, Yourself!

We're very quiet about some aspects of sexuality and very noisy about others. Sex to sell anything from detergent to socks is the norm. Heterosexual sex, that is. Probably not gay or lesbian sex and certainly not … masturbation! So what if the latter surfaces in your dreams?

First of all, such dreams are about you pleasing you. Even if your religion, family, or culture has taught you that masturbation is wrong, your dream might be telling you otherwise. Ask yourself what you'd like to happen in your waking life that would give you that much pleasure. It might be some form of sexual encounter or something totally nonsexual. What is the emotional feeling that your dreams of masturbation leave you with? Do you think you're simply discharging sexual energy or is it more related to a need to "peak" in some area of your life?

Your Famous (or Not-So-Famous) Dream Lovers

Take another look at the list of famous people most often dreamed about. Who's been showing up in your dreams? Make a list of your personal dream lovers in your dream journal, and jot a few words that come to mind when you think about them. Is there anyone in your life who has the traits you associate with the dream lover? Or does your list suggest a person you'd like to be?

Imagine yourself in a sexual encounter with one of the people you've listed as a dream lover, or with someone else who is not normally a part of your life. Close your eyes, daydream, and watch yourself with your dream date for a minute. Then write in your dream journal a paragraph about what you thought, felt, and experienced—and what you're thinking, feeling, and experiencing right now.

The Least You Need to Know

- Because we're all sexual beings, it's natural for us to dream about sex.

- Often our sex dreams are metaphorical expressions of all we desire to develop in ourselves and/or in our varied relationships; they're often not about sex at all!

- Sharing your dreams with your partner, either through talking about your respective dreams or inviting each other into your dreams, can enhance the intimacy of your relationship.

- What sexual dreams say about our desires, hopes, and fears depends on how we feel about ourselves, our dream partners, and dream stories.

- Repeated, disturbing dreams of sexual abuse indicate a need to consult with a mental health professional.

The Art of Losing: What Was Lost Is Found

In This Chapter

- ◆ Losses big and small
- ◆ Hiding, disguising, and hoarding
- ◆ A matter of trust
- ◆ Draw your own dream mandala

What we lose in the span of a lifetime, muses American poet Elizabeth Bishop's poem, "One Art," runs the gamut from the mundane—letters and keys—to the irreplaceable—places, friends, and time. It seems the natural course of existence. Losses start so small we barely notice. Not consciously, anyway. But the stresses of the ongoing changes that define our waking lives often play out unconsciously in our dream lives. Can your dreams help you find what you've lost?

The Shell Game

I can't find my house keys. It's dark and rainy. I could have sworn I'd put them in my purse. I can hear my son yelling for me inside of the house. I'm becoming frantic to get to him. Then I hear what he's saying: that his father took my keys and locked me out.

In this sort of dream, we often feel frustrated, anxious, frightened, or sad. That makes sense: We've lost something that's of meaning to us, either in and of itself, or as a stand-in for something more important and perhaps less tangible.

When You Just Can't Find It

The dreamer who lost her house keys might be expressing her feeling that she can't protect her son, or that her son and husband seem to be leaving her out (literally!). And because our dream messages can run counter to what we feel in waking life, we might have no conscious awareness of our strong and undeniable underlying feelings in the same way that this dreamer does not.

In our dreams nothing's sacred; we can lose anything:

- Limbs, or other parts of our bodies
- Keys, or other items that give us access to things
- Houses, cars, clothing, or other personal items
- Communities, jobs, organizations, or other places or things we "belong" to
- Money, jewelry, or other valuables
- Letters, messages, or other communications
- Other people or pets

What we lose or misplace in our dreams can, on a basic level, alert us to something we may be in danger of losing or something we have recently lost but don't yet realize. In an earlier chapter, we mentioned dreaming of losing a wallet or purse as a way of sharing that unconscious knowledge with the conscious mind. Or maybe this sort of dream is a more general reflection that we're feeling overwhelmed or distracted in our day-to-day lives. It could be time to clean the house or buy that organizer!

If our dreamer considered her dream again, she might find she views the dream story in a different light. Remember, she's locked out of her house (either purposefully or inadvertently by her husband) and can't reach her son. This time what becomes clear to her is that there's a part of her that wishes her husband would take more responsibility in their home life, freeing her to pursue her career. Or considering the same dream yet again, the meaning it holds for her may have more to do with the part of herself that feels she should lock herself out of her house (and her husband's urging her along!) and get back to her career. In this last reading, she's feeling guilty about not measuring up to her own concept of Super-Mom.

We all feel, at times, pushed and pulled by various impulses. It's in our dreams that all these impulses can be depicted at once in a single multilayered image!

Dreamwork

Dreams are a little like onions. They have many layers. Looked at from varying perspectives, at different times, they reveal different aspects of our personalities and struggles. Reconsider one of the early dreams in your dream journal. Do you understand it any differently now? It can be rewarding to return to the same dream repeatedly.

Playing for High Stakes: Losing Big

Let's say you dream of losing something insignificant, such as a newspaper or a tennis shoe. Yet in your dream you feel the most profound grief. What's going on?

Dreams of losing items are often metaphors for losing opportunities, relationships, or parts of ourselves. It's only in our associations to what we've lost that we can unmask the emotional meaning of the dream. For example, a tennis shoe might represent youth to an elderly person concerned with aging. Or a newspaper might represent a person's deepest desire to become a journalist. Giving up that dream, that part of yourself, is surely a cause for sadness and regret.

The best way to ascertain what you're really losing or fear losing is to pay attention to how you feel in the dream:

- ◆ If you're relieved, you might be telling yourself you're not ready for a certain challenge or that the place or situation is not right for you.

- ◆ If you're afraid, it could be that you don't feel confident or worthy enough to meet a challenge in your waking life.

- ◆ If you're angry or frustrated, it's possible you are conflicted about the opportunities before you.

What about when you can't find an address, when all the street numbers are a jumbled mess? Or when the writing on highway signs is just gibberish, or you're not where you're supposed to be? These might be metaphors for feeling you've "lost your way" in the grand scheme of life. Is there anything going on in your waking life that would trigger such a dream?

Your dream story may, on the surface, seem totally unrelated to whatever issue is bothering you. But once you begin to examine your dream more closely, you may find "clues" that reveal interesting and, perhaps, unexpected insights into your deeper feelings and concerns.

It's Too Late, Baby

The bell has rung. The gate has closed. The train has left the station. Every taxi is off duty, all flights are booked, and the boat has set sail without you. Your friends gave up on you hours ago. In other words: You're late.

Often, dreams of being late highlight our ambivalence about seizing an opportunity. Not getting to the subway on time reflects the part of us that's afraid to change; that part of us that feels unready, unworthy, or unsupported. We may also be feeling forced in our waking life to metaphorically get on the subway that takes us to that new job, and it's only in our dreams that we can rebel against the pressure. Yet feelings of sadness, frustration, and regret when the subway departs give voice to the part of us that wanted to hop onboard.

Who Can You Trust?

Gaining or losing trust is a deeply intimate matter. When you're having trouble in relationships, trust issues may surface in many ways in your dreams.

In your dreams, are you surprised to find that you're telling your best friend that no, you haven't seen the bouquet of flowers (and all the while you're holding it behind your back)? Or do you share the bouquet with her, knowing she won't run off with it and leave you flowerless? In your waking life, are you secretly afraid your friend's got an eye on your significant other?

Hiding and Hoarding

Sometimes we play a frustrating game of hide-and-go-seek with objects or people in our dreams. We create situations in which we hide things, then set off in search of them. Why do we do that to ourselves?

Sometimes we may be afraid of losing something important to us so we hide it to keep it safe. Remember when you were a kid and hid your "treasures" so that your younger siblings never got their hands on them?

So what are you afraid of losing? Perhaps you're getting to know someone in a deeper way. Or approaching intimacy in a new way. Maybe you have been close to someone before, but it was a hurtful experience.

We all have vulnerabilities, parts of ourselves that we protect. Often we learn as kids that we need to keep parts of ourselves secret, nonvisible. We take sensitive issues "underground," to *avoid* being teased or worse.

Our dreams can reflect this. We may lose something and know that it's missing and not really be sure that we want to find it. We may hide something because it's dangerous to have it. Secretly, though, we may covet our private treasure.

Dream Dictionary

When we exhibit **avoidant** behaviors, internally or externally, we are psychically (or even physically!) running away from a fearful, anxiety-provoking, or shaming set of circumstances or feelings.

> *I am aware that there's a bright gold key hidden behind the painting on the wall. I can see its glow through the canvas. I have put the key there. I feel drawn to it, but I have no intention of going near it. It excites me to know it's there, but if I got any closer to it, I'd feel endangered.*

What in this dreamer's life feels beautiful and exciting and is a little too dangerous to face? Perhaps this dreamer secrets away the gold key because he doesn't want to share with anyone else what it unlocks.

If you're falling in love for the tenth time and you reach a point where you begin to sabotage the relationship just like you did all the others (with anger, or distance, or refusal of appropriate closeness), ask yourself why you equate growing close with pain or confusion. There may have been a good reason in your past for you to protect yourself by hiding and hoarding, and your mind and body do not yet recognize that such behavior is not needed anymore.

But dreams of hoarding and hiding can also signal that you feel guilty about some personal attribute or stroke of luck. This makes sense. It doesn't always feel good to let our friends and family know how happy we are when they're having hard times.

The nature of hoarding or hiding in dreams varies generationally. Most of the adults of the generation that fought in World War II also have terrible memories of an economic depression and an earlier war. People born just after World War II grew up hearing stories about poverty and hunger. People in these generations often talk about hiding or hoarding things in their dreams. They never quite count on there being enough to go around, and this is reflected in their dream life. So feelings of needing to hoard and hide can come from cultural situations as well as familial ones.

A wealthy Texan who had made a bundle in the oil industry had a dream in the early 1980s as the rumblings of the oil crash were beginning:

I was frantically trying to hide valuables only to turn around and have them popping out of their hiding places again.

The dream haunted him, and it seemed to him to be a predictor of the oil crash that later came to be. Paradoxically, the people who are often the most concerned about monetary wealth are those who have it. They have to protect it.

We may feel that we have been given or even earned something that we don't deserve. We may feel guilty or that we're impostors with our newfound status or possessions. In our dreams, we may try to hide something that represents the thing(s) that make us feel awkward.

Hiding or hoarding in dreams is a very natural response to threats in everyday life. And it may also be a response to underground feelings in our psyche that are reaching for daylight.

Revealing and Giving

If hiding is a response to a threat or to stress, then what is giving? Oddly enough, it also can be a response to stress. Or it can celebrate a new freedom from stress and self-imposed limitations!

Maybe you're in a relationship and you're growing closer and closer to someone. Your psyche says okay, here's something to celebrate. You have a dream of giving away bags full of gold, rainbows, French roast coffee beans, or seashells. Who cares! The point is there's a celebration of trust, and you're suddenly free to give in a new and exciting way.

Or maybe we want to be recognized for a new talent or skill achievement. So we dream of standing on the street corner and giving away our underwear. See what we have gone to the very essence of our soul and earned? See how hard we worked and what it meant to us? In our dreams, we show it all!

Maybe we're giving ourselves a midnight pep talk about a new endeavor. Or about trusting in someone we've not trusted before. Or learning about the humanness of our parents and choosing to love them in a more adult or mature way. Or launching that new designer line of cell phones and hoping that they'll be a big hit.

Again, these situations may spark dreams of bringing something out of ourselves and giving or displaying it. We're taking a risk and we want to be noticed and reassured. Even if it's only in our dreams!

But the giving or revealing dream also comes into play when we're a little nervous or tenuous. We may be saying, "Look, I'll show you mine, if you'll show me yours." Risk for risk. "But," you tell yourself, "I'll do it in my dream first to see how it feels."

Dreamy

John Nichols, the author of *The Milagro Beanfield War,* tells of a dream in which he wandered around a field full of damaged bodies trying to get them restored. He never really understood the message of the dream, but remembers it as profoundly disturbing. The theme of lost, missing, deformed body parts recurs in Nichols's writing, and he often finds ways to make people whole.

From a different angle, we may be getting ready to "give away" a bad relationship, a confining job, a child ready to move out on her or his own. There's some reluctance to our giving, but we do it nonetheless. We don't want to give away our crayons in the dream, but we walk around the classroom and solemnly give a red one to this person and a blue one to that. Slowly, we allow ourselves to let go.

"You Jump, I Jump"

In the movie *Titanic,* Kate Winslet's and Leonardo DiCaprio's characters find in each other true and everlasting love. That they never get to argue over who left the cap off the toothpaste or whose turn it is to take out the trash only helps crystallize the notion of finding a perfect love. Who said, "It's better to have loved and lost than never to have loved at all"? Hey, it's that trust thing again.

Finding True Love

So how do you know when the right one comes along? And do you have to "go down with the ship" in order to recognize true love? We often have a feeling of being in deep, foreign, and exciting waters when we think that we've found our potential life partner. But if your dream takes you out onto a lifeboat and you sit and shiver and watch the cruise ship go down, then maybe you're sensing something about this relationship that's not quite right. Are you "in over your head"? Treading dangerous, shark-infested waters? This might not mean you've chosen unwisely. You just might be proceeding too fast; you're swimming in the deep end when you should spend a bit more time in the kiddie pool.

Separation and Divorce

If you're seeing a parting of the seas in your dreams, does it mean that your marriage is headed for disaster? Not necessarily. But there may be some serious trouble that you're not quite willing to face. There are all kinds of "parting" dreams, such as traveling fast in a vehicle, away from the familiar; running or walking through a dark house or park; or that old standby, coming to a fork in the road and being forced to choose one path or another.

In any event, your dreaming mind is letting you know that something needs to be done. In the case of losing a relationship, such a dream might signal that something is not quite right and you need to pay attention in your waking life. Perhaps you have smelled an unfamiliar perfume on your sweetie's sweater and dismissed it as meaningless. That night you dream of being ambushed by the Chanel ad in *Cosmopolitan* and dying a cruel death. Better rethink the perfume signal. Your *inner self* is not so ready to let the perfume smell go.

It's possible that on some level you recognize an impending separation or bad news before your conscious mind comes to terms with it. After all, your dreams are your creations! The signals come to you from the outside, and you make sense of those signals as best you can in your dreams. Dreams form an important part of your intuitive awareness. Trusting your own intuition—and that means trusting the messages of your dreams—can help you gain confidence in accepting life's wonderful finds and its heartbreaking losses.

Who's Telling the Truth?

Have you ever had a variation of the old standard dream of being before a large audience and trying to give your speech or presentation or speak your part or sing your song and nothing, we mean nothing, comes out of your mouth? This dream may be an indication that you're not "telling the truth" about something either to yourself or to someone else. Or perhaps someone else is not telling the truth to you and you're hesitant to recognize it.

Staying Honest

Maybe you're standing on a corner in your dream and selling newspapers and your name and picture are on the front page; you're the lead story. And you want everyone to pay attention. So in your waking life are you finally being honest about something? Are you standing up for something you believe in, perhaps a new product for your company, or that your daughter would make a better tree than tomato in the spring school play? You want others to pay attention to what you believe is the truth!

Maybe you've caught the boss in a compromising position with a co-worker, and that co-worker is fudging statistics on the annual statement. So, in your dream, you sell your newspapers from under a barrel. You want to be honest, but you don't necessarily want people to know that you're the whistle-blower. After all, we're conditioned that being a tattletale is very uncool.

Being honest can feel good and have positive results or it can cause real problems (or seem to!). Suppose you have a dream about rescuing the wonderful, handsome, charming man who's tied to the railroad tracks, and then he introduces you to his wife and five kids. Unfortunately, virtue sometimes has its price.

What a Tangled Web We Weave

Are you dreaming that you're a little person with a spider body and a human head caught sitting in the spider's web while someone sneaks up on you with a fly swatter? We may lie out of convenience or laziness, or for an opportunity, and we may try to mitigate the consequences in our conscious mind. But the dream that comes that night tells us that the deception is not as innocuous as we thought it to be … or wanted to think it was. Maybe that "little white lie" you told wasn't so little or so innocent. The spider dream might tell us we're afraid that our waking dishonesty bothers us more than we anticipated.

Or maybe we have a dream of snorkeling or scuba diving to commune with the dancing dolphins, and all of a sudden a shark takes off our arm! We'd best think of who we might be innocently trusting or believing that we shouldn't. Or pay closer attention to the job that seems to be going smoothly, but we don't understand why our co-worker seems to be looking at us funny and spending a lot of time with the quality-control officer. In short, are we trusting or believing folks that our dreaming mind insists we shouldn't?

Who's Overwhelmed?

Who isn't? We all go through phases of feeling like a gerbil on an exercise wheel—running, running, running, and getting nothing back for it but elevated blood pressure. We probably don't need to tell you that these feelings show up in our dreams. When we're overwhelmed, we can struggle with the burden of having it all—and holding on to it!

Losing Direction or Being Swallowed Up

We all have scary dreams in which we're drowning or falling out of a boat into a lake or a pool. Perhaps the water's clear and we can see the bottom but not tell how deep it is. Maybe the water's ominously murky and dark. Or maybe there's no water at all, but instead the lake or pool is filled with chocolate pudding and is teeming with alligators or every boss we ever had, each holding a knife and fork and looking awfully hungry. Such dreams tell us that we need to look for the areas of our lives in which we feel overwhelmed. And we probably don't need to look very far.

Water is often a symbol for our emotional life or for life itself. (After all, biologists say that the human body is 98 percent water!) So if in your dream you're about to be hit by a tidal wave just when you've settled down to read a good book, are being given the Chinese water torture, or are having a lethal squirt-gun fight with Godzilla, you might want to take a moment and a deep breath. What's happening in your waking life that feels out of control? Ask yourself what you can do to feel less overwhelmed.

Then, if your dreams show you giving Godzilla the lethal squirt, you just might be telling yourself you're triumphing over the stresses in your life.

> **Wake Up!**
>
> Excessive stress isn't healthy emotionally or physically. Try something simple like deep-breathing exercises, or better yet, if you have time, try yoga or moderate exercise—after you get the okay from your medical doctor.

Additionally, clues to how we want to resolve the stress in our lives can show up in our dreams. Perhaps there's a giant open book and you're standing in the middle of it and it begins to close. You scream in terror and run like hell. Maybe you don't really want to get that second graduate degree or marry again or adopt a child or buy a new house, or ....

Turning Water Into Peaceful Dreams

Do you find that stressful life events are keeping you awake at night and fragmenting your sleep with troubling stress-filled dreams? Consider a warm bath or an aromatherapy bath right before bed to help you relax and prepare for restful sleep. Aromatherapy uses fragrances to soothe your body and calm your mind. It can take the form of scented candles that you burn during your bath, or essential oils that you add to the bath water. Fragrances that encourage relaxation and peaceful sleep include lavender, rose, jasmine, chamomile, marjoram, and sandalwood.

During your bath, imagine that the concerns and tensions of the day are coming to the surface of your skin, where the water gently lifts them from your body and carries them away. And if you're not the bath type, try a warm shower. As the water flows over your body, envision it washing away your worries and stresses.

Getting Back on Track

Certainly dreams about standing on the side of a train track and then jumping in a railroad car that takes you to Vegas where you become rich and dethrone Wayne

Newton tell you that something good is happening to you … well, depending on how you feel about Wayne Newton. And Vegas. But generally a train to somewhere delicious is a pretty good sign.

What if the train (or the car or boat) is running backward? It's possible you're getting back into a familiar mess that you aren't quite through with yet. How many times have you noticed that you've been romantically involved with the same sort of selfish, domineering woman? Repeating bad experiences is what Freud called a *repetition compulsion*.

Or maybe you have come to a phase in your life where you are repeating a good experience, like having little children in your life again, only this time it's your grandchildren.

Does it feel like you're facing Dante's seventh circle of hell? Are you feeling like you're on the fast track to nowhere—again? Is there any way you can slow the train down and get it going in the right direction?

Dream Dictionary

The act of repeating past behaviors, in particular ones that aren't fun or healthy, is called **repetition compulsion**. It's our minds' flawed but best-guess way of trying to go back and replay events, hoping for a better outcome.

On a more positive note, just as fast-moving transportation can tell us that we're going a little too fast and in the wrong direction, it can also tell us that we're finally going in the right direction.

Perhaps you have a dream of driving in a red convertible or riding an exquisite bay horse next to a serene ocean. Maybe that proposal that you did last week really is *good!* Or maybe the career change that you're contemplating will work out quite well. As always, our dreams can affirm our aspirations and inner changes well before we have full confidence in them. One of the reasons that we can weather the stress of putting ourselves "out there" is that we can stand on our dreams. They're our personal proof that we're on the right track.

Dream Mandalas: Visualizing Patterns

Archetypes were an important aspect of dreams to psychologist Carl Jung, and later in his career he became intrigued with the *mandala* as a representation of archetypes and began having his patients craft mandalas to help interpret and understand their dreams. The mandala, Jung believed, presented a dream in its purest form and free from conscious encumbrances. The images the dreamer draws reflect the quest for wholeness (symbolized by the circle) and the elements of challenge or conflict standing as barriers to such wholeness that are currently confronting the dreamer.

Create your own dream mandala. Mandalas have many designs but share common characteristics of a circle containing symmetrical patterns, usually balanced quadrants.

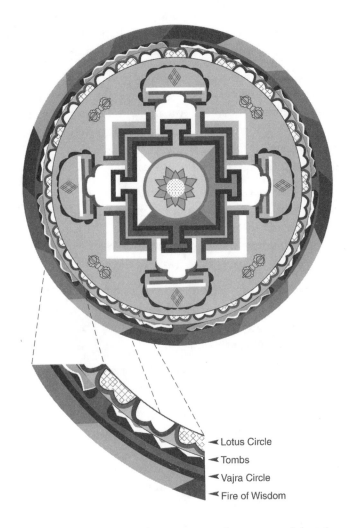

◄ Lotus Circle
◄ Tombs
◄ Vajra Circle
◄ Fire of Wisdom

Dream Dictionary

Originating from Hindu and Buddhist culture, a **mandala** is a circular configuration that represents the cosmos. Jung interpreted the mandala as a symbol of the effort to reunify the self.

You can make your own dream mandalas. A mandala is most effective for gaining insight into the messages of dreams that seem significant to you, such as dreams of loss (particularly ones that repeat with the same general imagery or even as the same dream). Here's how to make and use a dream mandala:

1. You need paper and colored pencils, markers, crayons, or paint. Draw a circle on the paper. (You can trace around a bowl or a plate to make it precise, if you like.)

2. Sit in a quiet place where you can be comfortable and work without interruptions or distractions.

3. Think about your dream. Try not to censor, revise, or restructure the dream's imagery. Let your dream fill your mind, pushing aside all other thoughts.

4. Begin to draw geometric patterns within the circle that represent your dream's images and what or how those images cause you to feel. Draw as though there is a direct connection between your hand and your dream. You can be as simple or intricate as you like. Try to maintain symmetrical balance. Use whatever colors appeal to you.

5. Keep drawing until you feel your dream mandala is complete.

When your dream mandala is finished, hold it in your hands. What is the first thing you notice? Write down your answer in your journal. Follow these guidelines:

♦ What is the first thing you notice about your dream mandala?

♦ What strikes you about the patterns and colors of your dream mandala? Write some observations in your dream journal.

♦ What feelings, sensations, or thoughts does your dream mandala evoke? Write them down.

♦ Do you get any "aha!" reactions as you explore your mandala? Note them in your journal.

Making and using a dream mandala for the first time can be an intense experience. You might want to come back to your dream mandala later, and use it as a guide for meditation. Whatever the twists and turns, discoveries or losses, celebrate your dream journey!

The Least You Need to Know

♦ Dreams in which we lose things let us know we're concerned about letting go, losing parts of ourselves, our fantasies, or the people in our lives.

♦ Dreams in which we're too late tell us that we're either overwhelmed or conflicted about an opportunity before us.

♦ When we feel scared or unsure of ourselves, we might have dreams in which we hide or hoard objects.

♦ When we feel excited or expansive, we might have dreams of sharing our abundance.

♦ A dream mandala represents your dream in primordial symbols. The process of drawing a dream mandala can be as provocative as the completed result.

Part 3

Decoding Your Dreams

Who *was* that masked man? Sometimes we can't figure out what the strange images in our dreams mean or we can't shake the spooky feelings that linger even after we wake up to realize, with great relief, "It was only a nightmare …." In yet other dreams we just can't believe the boss said *that!*

The language of dreams often is mysteriously—and sometimes frustratingly—metaphorical. What appears real … isn't. And what seems implausible … happens.

The most important thing to remember: *All* your dreams are about your personal growth and enrichment. Viewed through that lens, your dream experiences—painful, puzzling, or pleasurable—can only help you on the path to greater self-knowing.

Chapter 12

What a Nightmare!

In This Chapter

- The physiology of nightmares and sleep terrors
- Recurring nightmares
- Returning to sleep after a nightmare
- Confronting your night demons

Just *mentioning* the word *nightmare* conjures images of monsters, criminals, ex-lovers who chase us, the tornadoes, the rivers, the quicksand that swallows us, the deep and dark passageways that beckon us. Do we *really* need to be afraid of these dreams? Let's take a look at what nightmares really are and how we can use them to our waking advantage.

It Seemed So Real!

Nightmares generally describe our scary, painful, and unpleasant dreams. But for dream and sleep researchers, this definition is too broad. Researchers have discovered that most people report two kinds of "nightmare" dream experiences. Either they wake up with a general sense of fear or distress but can't remember what it was that scared them (perhaps recalling just a "crushing feeling" or "a menacing shadow"), or they wake up from a vivid dream story, usually at the most frightening or threatening part of the dream. The first isn't technically a nightmare; the second one is.

Wake Up Screaming

Sometimes what you think of as a nightmare really isn't, even though it's just as scary. Do you know which of these scenarios is *not* a nightmare?

1. When you know you're dreaming.

2. When you begin to turn the tables on the villain and it looks like maybe you'll scare *him*.

3. When it's a night terror.

If you answered number 3, go claim your prize; you're right. *Night terrors* are not *nightmares*. They're not even dreams. Also called sleep terrors, night terrors happen during non-REM sleep, not during dreaming REM sleep. They usually occur within the first two hours of going to sleep, in Stage 3 or 4 NREM sleep. A person experiencing a night terror will wake up for about 20 seconds and most times, just settle back to sleep. Night terrors are considered to be "disorders of arousal." Dr. Sonia Ancoli-Israel, Professor of Psychiatry at UCLA-San Diego Medical School, Director of the San Diego VA Sleep Disorders Clinic, and author of *All I Want Is a Good Night's Sleep* (Mosby-Year Book, 1996), tells us they're characterized by:

Dream Dictionary

Night terrors are sleep disturbances during non-REM sleep that produce physical feelings of fear and anxiety; they're not dreams. **Nightmares** occur during dreaming REM sleep and are characterized by frightening dream content, but dreamers do not exhibit the physiological arousal common during night terrors.

Wake Up!

In adults, alcohol and drug use, stress, fever, or lack of sleep may trigger night terrors. Some experts say that more than four episodes of night terrors in a month might indicate that the adult dreamer is suffering from an anxiety disorder. Your doctor or mental health provider can help you evaluate this.

- Abrupt, but partial, awakenings

- Increase in heart rate, blood pressure, and respiration

- A classic physiological response to fear, with dilated pupils, confusion or panic, and sweating

- Screaming or yelling, flailing arms and legs, or sitting up straight in bed

- The recall of a single image or feeling ("I was suffocating"), if the night terror wakes the sleeper up

- No recall of the night terror if the sleeper returns to a sleep state without fully awakening

The cause of night terrors is not known, but it's generally accepted that they're not a metaphorical depiction of a psychological issue (the way dreams are). Rather, they probably have their basis in purely biological functions. Indeed, during night terrors, subjects studied in sleep laboratories show elements of both wakefulness and sleep.

Night terrors are most common in children between the ages of three and eight. Dr. Sonia Ancoli-Israel suggests that parents curb their instincts to rush to their child to awaken and/ or comfort him or her. This effort tends to fail or to aggravate the intensity or duration of the night terror.

Let the night terror run its course, and the child rarely will recall the event. Occasional night terrors are considered normal in children at this age, and there's not much evidence that these episodes reflect deeper psychological problems. Still, this can be quite an upsetting event for the parents.

> **Life Is But a Dream**
>
> In a 1972 study, researchers found that when 23 children suffering from night terrors had their adenoids removed, 22 of them immediately ceased having night terrors! (Adenoids are masses of lymphoid tissue at the back of the pharynx; when they become enlarged, they can obstruct breathing.)

The Science of Nightmares

Nightmares, like other dreams, most often occur during the REM stages of sleep. Nightmares generally cause dreamers to wake up from a long episode of REM sleep that's lasted about 15 minutes or so. If you don't wake up, is it still a nightmare? Well, not technically. You might just want to call it a bad dream.

Nightmare dreams are most often characterized by the following symptoms:

◆ A sense of dream dread or fear that may stay with the dreamer for hours or days upon awakening.

◆ The physical paralysis, called *atonia*, which signifies dreaming REM sleep (as opposed to the physical arousal common in night terrors), but perhaps with more eye movements than usual and slightly elevated pulse and respiration rates.

◆ The ability to recall all or part of a frightening dream story. Commonly, the dreamer is threatened or actually harmed in some way.

◆ A recognition of powerful, personal dream themes, or a repetition of the dream itself for months, years, or even decades.

Dream Dictionary

Atonia is the lack of muscle tone during sleep, particularly during dreaming REM sleep.

Dreamwork

Rate your "bad" dreams on a scale of 1 to 10, with 10 being the most frightening. Can you see a progression of anxiety that prods your dreams toward nightmares? Is there a problem you're avoiding in waking life? Or that seems to be going out of control? Your dreams may be an effort to alert you to pay closer attention to the issue at hand.

The hallmark of a nightmare is that it's scary. It's often long, intricately detailed, and among the easiest of our dreams to remember. Nightmares aren't considered sleep disorders, as are night terrors. It's interesting to note that while people with night terrors exhibit frightening physical symptoms such as screaming or kicking, and are inconsolable during an episode, they don't remember anything later if they're allowed to settle back into a sleep state.

Nightmares, however, are a different story. The dream content of nightmares has much to reveal to us, if we're courageous enough to take a closer look at what's scaring us. As novelist Gail Godwin writes in *Dream Children*, "I believe that our dreams transport us through the underside of our days, and that if we wish to become acquainted with the dark side of what we are, the signposts are there, waiting for us to translate them."

Life Is But a Dream

Nightmares are most frequent in children from ages three to six, and become less frequent with age. Yet 30 to 50 percent of adults report having occasional nightmares; those age 25 or older report having 1 or 2 nightmares per year. Only 5 percent of the adult American population is bothered by nightmares at any given time.

Many factors—including drugs, alcohol, excessive stress, and lack of sleep—can alter the quality and quantity of REM sleep. It should come as no surprise that one possible outcome of this is to give rise to fewer dreams, unusual dreams, or nightmares. While these things can raise our incidence of nightmares, it's often a struggle in our daily lives that bring on scary dreams. Many people swear that eating pizza or too much spicy food before bedtime causes nightmares, but we're not aware of any hard scientific evidence supporting that hypothesis.

The Dreaming Mind Requests the Honor of Your Attention ...

We've differentiated nightmares from night terrors. But experts also tell us there are two different kinds of nightmares:

♦ REM anxiety dreams

♦ Post-traumatic stress nightmares

Post-traumatic stress nightmares (PSNs) are different from your average REM anxiety dream or run-of-the mill nightmare. They're usually experienced by people who've lived through a traumatic event, and the dream content and story will closely resemble that event. So there's very little disguised imagery. Robert Van de Castle points out that the dream is recurrent with little alteration from time to time, except that elements from the dreamer's current environment may gradually be incorporated into the prescribed dream plot.

POWs from World War II and concentration camp survivors have been known to suffer from post-traumatic stress nightmares up to 50 years after the traumatic event. PSNs usually occur during REM sleep, but can also occur during Stage 2 non-REM sleep. Unlike during "normal" nightmares, these dreamers can experience significant physical symptoms, such as an increase in respiration and heart rate, and muscle twitches with more than one arousal, or interruption, during REM sleep.

One psychological theory holds that post-traumatic dreams are the body and the mind's joint way of replaying the event in the attempt to master it within the "safe" context of the sleeping body and dreaming mind, where the event can be re-experienced without harm. Eventually the anxiety and stress associated with the traumatic event diminish as the dreamer regains control and confidence in waking life. Adults might experience other traumatic events in their lives, too, that continue to play out, sometimes over years, in the form of nightmares.

The more standard REM anxiety dreamer, however, has frightening dreams about stress relating to work, school, or relationships. The threat here isn't to one's life (although we sure can feel powerless against dreams of imminent danger), but to one's sense of self and self-confidence. These kinds of nightmares tend to be the ones that you're relieved to realize "It was only a dream!"

> **Dream Dictionary**
>
> **Post-traumatic stress nightmares** are caused by traumatic events considered out of the range of common human experience, such as war atrocities, natural disasters, kidnapping, or extremely violent acts either witnessed, experienced, or even perpetrated, which overwhelm the dreamer's defensive mechanisms.

Dreamy

The Spanish painter Francisco de Goya (1746–1828), the painter to the Bonaparte court during the French occupation of Spain from 1808 through 1813, experienced extreme nightmares, which he painted on the walls of his house in the early 1820s. Goya's scathingly satirical political etchings and paintings reveal his sensitivity to human suffering. Contemporary art enthusiast Sister Wendy Beckett expresses the hope that in painting his nightmares, Goya was somehow released from the burden of their pain.

Dr. Ernest Hartmann, director of a sleep laboratory in Boston, has found that many long-standing nightmare sufferers have "thin boundaries." That is, they are emotional, creative, sensitive, and often prone to depression. These people have difficulty insulating themselves from internal and external stresses. People who report frequent nightmares often see more indistinct, diffuse, or torn images on Rorschach ink-blot tests.

A sensitive but somewhat moody artist who gets much inspiration for his or her work from dreams—including nightmares—might be just the sort of person researchers describe. And such a person might use the nightmares to fuel his or her creative spark.

Nothing in Nightmares Can Hurt You

The thug pointing the gun at your head; the man at the top of the volcano laughing maniacally as he lets go of your hand, dropping you into the magma; the inability to run, to move, or to shout as the truck bears down on you—none of these or any other nightmare images can kill you, injure you, or leave tire tracks on your back. Nightmares are not external events. They're internal ones. The stage of your subconscious mind offers a safe place to work through challenging or scary ideas or situations.

Remember, *You* Create Your Dreams

You're the producer, director, and cast of the nightly movies you attend. Even the thrillers. As with all the other kinds of dreams we've mentioned, nightmares are messages from one part of the self to another. Their meaning is disguised. Often, the level of fear or anger in our dreams and nightmares mirror equally strong feelings in our day-to-day lives. Sometimes the issue at hand is particularly volatile, and so we have dreams that include a lot of negative emotion.

Many of us are taught that our aggressive tendencies are bad. When we were children we were told to "be nice." We were punished for our tantrums and rewarded for our smiles. So it shouldn't come as a huge shock that we're not too terribly comfortable with anger or aggression in ourselves or in others. We push it away. When it shows up in our dreams, it can get distorted, and what we end up with is a nightmare.

Perhaps you're furious with your boss for not giving you a promotion. You may have a nightmare in which you're pursued by strange henchmen who plan to immolate you. Is that your dreaming mind's self-punishment for having waking thoughts of wanting to wring your boss's neck? Or is it that you bowed and scraped to the old fart who cheated you out of your promotion, and it's only in your dreams that you dare to vent your rage? And what a scary, threatening, red-hot thing it seems to you!

What Scares You Most About Your Bad Dreams?

In our experience, the most common types of nightmares are ones of being chased or ones of being hunted down. One explanation: Being chased or stalked as prey are primal memories from our human collective unconscious, and they refer to primitive times when our ancestors were chased by wild animals. Back then, being caught meant certain death.

What things, people, characters, and events scare you most about your bad dreams? Some common responses are:

- Menacing, intrusive strangers
- Careening over a cliff
- Dark rooms, woods, alleys
- Heights and depths
- Land or sea storms, tidal waves, earthquakes
- Friends or family who are suddenly old or disfigured
- Friends or family who suddenly become cruel and dangerous
- Guns, knives, and other weapons
- Car or plane crashes
- Being lost

These examples might leave a dreamer with the overriding sense that his or her place in the world (or the actual terra firma!) is violently shifting. The dreamer's totally out of control in a big, big way. Could it be that this is a metaphor for feeling on "shaky ground" in how we define ourselves at work or at home? Our self-confidence or self-concept is being put through the meat grinder (now *that's* scary ...).

What else do we have in life, if not our own view of the world and our self-conception? When considered from that angle, it makes a lot of sense that dreams in which our world—meaning our confidence—is rocked signal nightmares of the highest magnitude! What images or scenes show up in your nightmares?

> **Dreamy**
>
> Sue Grafton, creator of the *Kinsey Millhone* mystery series, says that becoming successful creates its own problems. She worries constantly that her current writing project won't be up to the standards that people have come to expect from her. This fear and anxiety shows up in vivid REM anxiety nightmares.

Using Nightmares for Creative Problem Solving

When we wake up from a nightmare, our hearts pounding and minds racing, it's sometimes hard to believe that what we were dreaming about wasn't really happening. It's also hard to remember that *we* are the authors of our nightmares—they don't just happen to us. We create them. What could this possibly mean, and how can we use this knowledge to make nightmares less scary and more helpful to us in our waking lives?

When we have nightmares, our unconscious could be sending us such a loud message that we have no choice but to "wake up" to it. Examining the dream content of our nightmares usually provides clues to troubling events or issues we're not ready to face consciously, or that we're struggling with on a daily basis. Nightmares may even hold solutions or new ways of thinking about difficult situations.

For example, you dream night after night about ironing a perfect white blouse. You think you've done a good job, but when you go to put on the blouse, it's all wrinkled, wet, and scorched. You turn to see the iron blow up to a giant size and spray harsh steam at you, hissing and sputtering as you bolt awake, afraid you'll be burned.

> **Dreamwork**
>
> Remember what Jung called our "shadow side?" Choose a bad dream or nightmare recorded in your dream journal and look at it from a Jungian shadow perspective. Could the dream's elements represent parts of yourself you'd rather keep hidden? Are you recognizing this side of yourself for the first time?

What could it mean? You hate to iron; you're a career woman who buys "dry clean only." Perhaps the iron is your internalized voice of perfection, hounding you as you put in 12-hour days to get that report exactly right. Or perhaps, just perhaps, you really *do* want to make sure that blouse gets ruined despite the perfect iron! Meanwhile, your parents are asking you when you and your partner are going to settle down and start a family ....

When the Nightmare Recurs

Because our nightmares tend to depict issues that threaten our sense of emotional safety and well-being, we often dream of the same event, person, or setting over and over again.

Bad Dreams from Childhood

Can you remember a nightmare from childhood? In our experience, most people can. These dreams stick with us. Some researchers say that children can begin to have nightmares at age one; others say age five. We tend to think children begin to have nightmares as they start to experience anxiety and fear and have the cognitive capacity to make mental pictures.

There are lots of things for children to be anxious about once the lights go out. Dr. Charles Rycroft points out that to a small child, the utterly new daytime world can be a strange and scary place. There can be huge dogs that bark, loud thunderstorms, strange faces that loom over them, loud noises that startle, parents who argue. And because a child's ability to differentiate reality from fantasy isn't well developed, the "monsters" that attack might feel completely real. Also, because they have a hard time putting their fear into words, it's more difficult for us to convey to a child that the scary dreams aren't real.

> **Life Is But a Dream**
>
> One theory holds that dreams with recurring subjects or themes may coincide with life's developmental passages, or are responses to an underlying psychological stress such as divorce or changing jobs. Women are more likely to report recurring dreams than men.

What's Going On in Your Waking Life?

The bedrock of our fears is laid down during early childhood (except for later, unexpected catastrophic events). Basically, a very small child fears abandonment (without the parents' nurturing the child would literally die), and later, as a child beginning a tenuous path toward crawling and then walking, the child fears bodily harm. These two issues recur again and again throughout the life span. A 40-year-old man in the midst of a divorce might dream of the sky crashing in on him as he frantically searches for shelter. This hearkens back to abandonment fears.

If you're being chased in your nightmare, it's important to think about the attributes of the frightening pursuer and then ask yourself if there's anyone currently in your life or any aspect of your personality that reminds you of the pursuer. Are you wrestling with a masked stranger whom you would describe as "overpowering, insistent, part human, part animal, and somewhat sexual"? Perhaps that's a disowned aspect of your personality, and you need to pay more attention to your animalistic, untamed sexual desires.

Of course, nightmares that present you with undisguised imagery—the roof falling in on you, your car stalling on the highway—may be warning signals that you need to pay attention to the care and maintenance of the things around you.

Getting Back to Sleep

Waking from a nightmare can be quite disturbing. You might find it difficult to go back to sleep, or you might not want to go back to sleep for fear you'll return to the nightmare. Although returning to a bad dream is one method for understanding what it means, sometimes you just want or need to go back to sleep. You can analyze the dream in the morning.

Because scary dreams offer windows into the worries and fears that are on your mind, you don't want to simply dismiss them. When you awaken from a nightmare, take a few moments to orient yourself to the reality that, no matter how frightening the events of the dream, they are not real and cannot hurt you. But before you let the nightmare images slip into oblivion, write down the dream. Capture as many details as you can. When you've written all you can remember, set your dream journal aside. You can come back to it in the morning; for now, you need to go back to sleep.

There are two ways you can return to slumberland: with or without your nightmare. Do you want to further explore the nightmare, confront its demons (as we discuss in the next section)? As you are lying there in bed, preparing to go back to sleep, hold a particular image from the nightmare in your thoughts. What about this image intrigues you, or scares you? Form the questions you have about the nightmare, and let them "wrap around" your thoughts about the dream. As you drift back to sleep, keep your questions about the nightmare foremost in your thoughts for as long as you can. This exercise increases the chance that you'll return to the dreamscape of your nightmare with a fresh perspective.

Do you want to try to forget the nightmare and move on to more pleasant dreams? As you're lying in bed, focus your thoughts on something that makes you feel safe and content. Try to push all other thoughts away, and let this "happy" thought completely fill your mind as you return to sleep.

There's no guarantee either way, of course. But holding in your consciousness what direction you want your dream to take is sometimes a powerful way to manifest what you desire. When you wake up in the morning, write about the experience in your dream journal.

Confronting Your Demons

What if you didn't shake yourself awake or realize *in* the dream that it was only a dream? What if you stopped running from the monsters and turned to face them instead?

In *Living Your Dreams* (HarperCollins, 1996), author Gayle Delaney, Ph.D., states that by getting to know these nasty nightmare people, places, or things, we can harness their energy and take back into ourselves those aspects of our personality we disown. She believes that it's not a good idea to run after the monster, attack him, and beat him to a bloody pulp: While we might awaken feeling victorious, we'll never know what the monster wanted from us or what his message was! Instead, we learn so much more from our frightening dreams if we train ourselves to bravely inquire …

- What do you want?

- Why are you in my dream?

- Why are you chasing me?

This is the central dilemma in the *Nightmare on Elm Street* movies: how best to understand why the monster is on a rampage, but not get killed in the process!

Dreams of Violence and Anger

Are you the perpetrator of violence or the victim? Are you screaming bloody murder, or are you being screamed at?

Dreams in which we really tell someone off or slap someone across the face can let us know that we're holding on to our anger and not finding a healthy way to express and resolve it. Sometimes it's easier to tell off our spouse, boss, child, or neighbors in our dreams, but when we're face to face … we cave in—big time.

So you've had a dream in which you've told your friend's husband to drop dead? But in waking life you aren't particularly upset with him? Well, what is he like? Passive, shut down, meek? Does that describe anyone else in your life, or does it describe how you've been acting in relation to your job? Maybe you're angry with yourself for not "looking alive" at work.

If you're the victim of others' tirades or even violence in your dream, this could suggest that you feel guilty about some achievement in waking life. Maybe you're finding some way to beat yourself down so that you don't surpass the image you have of your older, more successful sibling. Then again, recurring dreams in which you're physically hurt might indicate some sort of past abuse. You might choose to talk to a therapist about this.

CAUTION

Wake Up!

If your dreams are consistently frightening, disturbing, or violent—to the degree that they seem to "haunt" your waking life and affect your daily routine— consider talking them over with a therapist.

Dreams of Drowning

Are you sinking slowly but inevitably into a pit of quicksand, or are you swallowed by an angry sea? Do you actually go under for the third and final time or are you treading water? Are you alone or are you with others? Anyone you know?

This kind of dream usually represents a not-so-subtle signal that you're feeling overwhelmed in waking life. You can be "flooded" by your emotions or flooded by real-life tasks.

Dreams in which you're caught in a tidal wave might indicate the strength of the emotion, perhaps accompanied by tears that you're holding back in your waking life.

We know a writer who juggles hectic manuscript delivery schedules, unpredictable cash flows, and the stress of life in a big northeastern city. In her quiet moments (and there aren't many), she daydreams of a peaceful beach house and a good book (one she hasn't written herself!). Okay, here's her nightmare. The minute she's curled up on the front porch swing reading a wonderful novel, she notices a huge tidal wave approaching the house, ready to engulf everything. The hectic pace of her waking life is really a hedge against the disastrous tidal wave that she fears would surely arrive to sweep her away should she ever dare to slow down!

A Failure to Communicate or Take Action

Almost everyone has had a dream of being paralyzed in some sense. While researchers suggest that this is a reflection of the fact that during REM sleep we *are* paralyzed, it doesn't really explain why we don't *feel* paralyzed in other sorts of dreams in which we fly, run, dance, skip, or jump. So what's the missing element that can help us understand dreams of paralysis?

Usually, such dreams are expressions of feeling pinned down or paralyzed in some aspect of our lives. We may feel torn about which path to pursue, or how to resolve the part of us that wants to settle down and have children with the part of us that wants to play the field. A paralysis dream can be an expression of this conflict.

Animals, Monsters, and Shadows

Which kinds of animals torment you in your dreams? What do they look like? Who do you suppose is behind those creepy shadows?

By and large, animals are thought to represent the untamed, uncivilized aspects of ourselves. If they appear in your nightmares, baring their teeth, ask yourself what it is in you that you've been ignoring for the sake of propriety. Of course, your personal associations to animals are of primary importance. Did you grow up next to a zoo and did you make friends with the lion? Or was your father a big-game hunter who was mauled by a lion?

The shadow is often that part of ourselves we keep hidden. Perhaps we're afraid to bring vulnerable parts of ourselves into the light of day; perhaps our parents taught us that there were certain behaviors that were unacceptable, and we relegated those to the shadows. It's possible that the appearance of the scary shadow in our dreams is even a positive thing; it's our dreaming mind's way of reintroducing the cast-off parts of the self in an effort to make us whole!

Nightmares of Death and Destruction

Does a corpse pop up in your dream? Are you being killed or are you killing someone else in your nightmare? Is it a slow death or a quick one?

What Happens If You Die in a Nightmare?

Well, nothing. Dreams of one's own death don't mean that you actually die during the dream, or that you'll keel over the next day. However, you may wish to take stock of your physical health and act accordingly.

Many dream experts believe that dying in a dream, especially if you're not upset about it, can signify a rebirth, a shedding of the old and a heralding of a new begin-

ning. In our experience, however, this has not been the case. Usually these dreams represent involvement in deeply painful relationships or unhealthy behaviors. There's a feeling of being strangled by a situation or a person.

It may be that taking a hard look at what is unhealthy in your life and taking the brave measures to correct it can lead to a fresh, new beginning, but the presentation of the nightmare usually indicates a self-destructive situation.

Wake Up!

Dreams of actually killing others or of getting killed are not terribly common. If this sort of dream persists, you may wish to talk it over with a mental health professional as it might indicate deeply unresolved issues that are plaguing your dreams—and your waking life, too.

What Happens If You Kill Someone Else in a Nightmare?

Again, nothing. In our experience, that person you killed last night doesn't die, or if the person does die, it has nothing to do with your dream. This kind of dream can indicate that there's a part of you or your life that feels dead or out of control, or that there's a part of you or your life that you wish would leave you alone—for good.

This sort of dream can express rage in the most powerful way. Is there some situation or person or aspect in your life that needs to be snuffed out? Can you describe the person you've killed and how you feel about it? Are you in mourning? Afraid of being caught? Remorseful?

The Story Behind the Dream

One way to figure out what your nightmare means is to continue the story line while you're awake. A good way to do this is to write it out in script form. So, for example, if you're dreaming of a helicopter that keeps swooping down on your head, write out the dream plot as it occurred. You can do this in your dream journal.

Then keep going. What happens next? If you hold your ground, do the helicopter blades turn into feathers and tickle your face? Have you been continuously running away from positive things to the degree that they have to literally get up in your face for you to pay attention? If the ending of the nightmare as you dreamt it isn't satisfying, write a new ending. Is this new ending *really* a more satisfactory resolution to the dream?

Now, à la Gestalt, put yourself in the place of the most threatening person, place, or thing in your nightmare. Rewrite the dream plot from that point of view. What is it that the menacing character wants? Why is the menacing character in your dream? This is kind of like asking Herman Melville to rewrite *Moby Dick* from the point of view of the white whale!

Imagine that you can have a conversation with the helicopter, masked stranger, tiger, or white whale that's chasing you. Write it down. You may be surprised by what you read.

Try to associate the patterns and urges you've uncovered in your nightmare to conscious, waking issues and events.

As we have mentioned in previous chapters, this kind of dreamwork may bring up deeply disturbing issues that are best not handled alone. If you feel quite upset or don't see any kind of meaning or possible resolution to your nightmare, please see a therapist.

The Least You Need to Know

◆ Night terrors are not nightmares, but are sleep disturbances that occur during non-REM sleep.

◆ Nightmares occur during REM sleep and can either be products of anxiety or, more seriously, of traumatic life events.

◆ Our nightmares, just like other kinds of dreams, send us messages about ourselves. Usually nightmares have a lot to do with "negative" or cast-off emotions.

◆ You can *try* to shape your return-to-sleep experience to go back to the nightmare so that you better understand what it means, or to dream another dream and return to your nightmare analysis when you wake up in the morning.

◆ Once we face and understand our scary dream images, we may be able to diffuse or even use nightmares to make beneficial changes in our lives.

13

Learning from Signal Dreams

In This Chapter

♦ Important events, important dreams

♦ Getting to know your signals

♦ Exploring your signal dream through a three-dimensional dream mandala

♦ Red Light, Yellow Light, Green Light: dream signals for life situations

We may rejoice in the idea that at some point we're through "growing up." Maybe when we turn 18, get married, have our first child, finish graduate school, or … you fill in the blank. But it doesn't take long to realize that life is all about transition. Change never ends. We constantly change direction— sometimes subtly, like grains of sand in the wind, and sometimes with the force of a landslide. We might expect to miss the signs of subtle change in our waking lives, busy as we are, but not be surprised in the least to find them surfacing in our dreams. However, even those landslides sometimes escape our conscious detection.

Transitions

Our physical, emotional, intellectual, and social selves change all of our lives. All that we can count on *is* change. Sometimes these changes go unnoticed.

A little slowing down in our 30s from what we could do in our 20s. An attraction to a different type of person than we were drawn to in the past.

But some changes are rapid, or startling, or confusing. Changes like this can be disconcerting. They're so common in our culture that we have nicknames for many of them. Here are just a few:

- **The terrible twos,** to explain the rapid change in our 18-month-old from cute, gurgling baby to insistent, stubborn little person who's exercising his or her will

- **Sweet sixteen,** to describe a young girl's blossoming transformation into a young woman

- **Honeymooners,** to celebrate the passage of newlyweds into marriage

- **Midlife crisis,** to note a time of reconsideration and re-evaluation as life approaches its midpoint

- **The seven-year itch,** to describe one partner's sudden disinterest in a long-term marriage or relationship and possible infidelity

- **Empty nest,** to signify the transition from parenting to retirement, as children leave the home and set out on their own

The big changes may not all have names, but are nonetheless recognized as something new and different while we're going through them. They may be lightning fast—we may wake up one day and simply say, "I think I'll go and get that second degree after all." Or, they may brew over time so that the decision to have children or move to a retirement community is front and center of our waking and dreaming life for months or even years.

Even though you may not have paid much attention, your dreams will help you prepare for and acknowledge all sorts of changes. After all, you create your dreams, and they give you information that your psyche keeps hidden during waking hours. Because dreams are formed from the events of your current waking life, your conscious and unconscious thoughts and feelings about those current events, and your great storehouse of memories culled from similar past experiences, feelings, and events, what better place to look for guidance in times of transition and decision making? Dreams can synthesize your past, present, and future in one dense, rich burst of highly personal intuition.

Navigating Life's Passages

Dreams are a wonderful way to explore new options and to examine how you're responding to the changes and challenges of the life cycle. We call dream images, content, or themes that occur repeatedly *signal dreams*. They tell us that a change is coming or taking place. Since we go through changes constantly, these repetitive symbols often alert us to the fact that we're going through a certain phase or coming up against a specific dilemma again.

Our own, personal, individualized, signal dreams are important to recognize and appreciate.

Dream Dictionary

Signal dreams tell you something important is happening within yourself or within your life. They often occur when you need validation of a new direction. And they may be repetitive.

"Every Time Something Important Happens, I Dream About ..."

Make a short list of recent events that have been new, different, exciting, scary, or potentially difficult. For example:

 ◆ You got a new job.

 ◆ You totaled the car.

 ◆ You purchased your first two shares in a mutual fund.

 ◆ You brought home a puppy.

 ◆ You agreed to chair the local fundraiser.

Have you noticed that each time you take steps along the path of life—either giant steps or smaller ones—you dream a dream from which you awaken with the feeling that you've just been visited by an *old* dream friend (or enemy)? We've said that dreams can often be traced back to the previous day's events. So when you have that same dream over and over, what sort of issue is repeating itself?

Maybe each time you ponder the idea of getting serious in a relationship, you dream that you buy an engagement ring but then lose it. That you manage to lose it in a different way with each replay of the dream doesn't mean this isn't a signal dream; the theme of ambivalence about intimacy and commitment comes across loud and clear!

What sorts of life events trigger signal dreams for you? Here are some big-change events that can trigger signal dreams:

 ◆ Birth

 ◆ Death

 ◆ Moving

 ◆ Entering into a committed relationship

- Divorce

- A new job

- Buying a home

- Applying for a grant, new job, scholarship, prize

Of course, your signal dreams are highly personal and specific. The appearance of a brown dog may have powerful meaning for you, and he might trot through your dreams the night before you leave on business trips. Perhaps he signals to you that you need to watch out not to lose sight of him—of yourself, really—and lose your way on the trip.

We know someone who grew up in a white room with white furniture, white walls, white curtains, white everything! As an adult, white freaks her out. She's noticed that whenever she's going through a stressful life event, she'll dream of a beautiful Jamaican woman who wears brightly colored clothes and jewelry—truly a woman of color! This woman of color always shows up to urge the dreamer to relax and have a good time. "Come out dancing," she'll say. It took our friend three years of keeping a dream journal to recognize the meaning of this signal dream symbol and connect it to the room in which she grew up!

Learning to Recognize the Dream Symbols in Your Signal Dreams

Take a few minutes to list in your dream journal the dreams that have recurred for you over your lifetime. They may not always come in exactly the same form, but there will be familiar elements in each. As you're compiling this dream list, don't be surprised if some of the signal dreams are unsettling or disconcerting. Those nightmares do command your attention, don't they?!

Now look at the dreams you jotted down and see if they fall into broad categories. Are there lots of dreams in which you attempt to fly? Dreams of moving fast? How do these dreams relate to the big life events we discussed earlier in this chapter? Begin to look for the clues of cause and effect between your life events and your signal dream stories.

CAUTION Wake Up! _____

If your signal dreams are horrifying or contain elements of being hurt or in pain and feeling helpless, they may be real signals of mistreatment by others—either in the past or in the present. These dreams may be telling you that you need to deal with this abuse before you can go on with your life. Please consult a mental health professional about troubling recurrent dreams.

What common symbols or themes pop out? People, places, or things? Do you dream of animals or red apples on a tree when certain types of change are in the air? The variety is endless; after all, it's your dream creation. But somewhere along the line, your mind learns to give you your own encrypted messages. The symbols and themes you discover are the hallmarks of your signal dreams.

As you look for your signal dream symbols, it's important to notice what emotion you feel in your dreams or when you remember them afterward. Are you elated, cautious, afraid, peaceful, calm, happy, or do you feel no emotion at all?

Another important clue about our signal dream symbols is how we feel physically when we're having the dream and when we wake up: tense, sore, heart beating too fast, sluggish, like you haven't slept at all and are exhausted, or haven't slept at all and are elated?

Also, how do you feel about your signal dream symbols themselves? Perhaps you dream of a beautiful rose, but in your signal dreams the rose scares you. Why would something beautiful seem threatening? In dreams, emotional responses and reactions may not be so clear-cut. Examining those uncomfortable gray areas of feeling reveals surprising information about yourself—things you may not have realized before!

Expanding the Picture

The images that appear in signal dreams sometimes seem obscure and even trite— pieces of things like walls and doors, items of clothing, colors, objects such as trees or flowers. We know these images are important because they continue showing up in our dreams, yet we struggle to make much sense of them. We can return to a method we introduced to you in Chapter 11, the dream mandala, as a way to draw out (literally!) these symbolic representations to help give them context.

Because signal dreams often dive deep into your subconscious and represent matters that remain unresolved in some way, we're going to make a three-dimensional dream mandala. To get started, first gather these materials:

- Two pieces of heavy paper or lightweight poster board in whatever colors appeal to you
- A ruler or straightedge
- A pencil
- Optional: markers, crayons, paint, or colored pencils
- Scissors
- Glue or tape

◆ Magazines with photos and pictures that you can cut up

◆ Notepaper to write on

Next, find a quiet place where you can work without interruptions or distractions, and where you can make a bit of a mess. You might want a flat surface such as a desk or counter, or be content to work on the floor. Think about your signal dream. If you want, jot yourself some notes or thoughts about the dream to help remind you of the dream's key images. Keep these notes brief; you want them to jog your memory, not explore the dream.

Let your signal dream float around in your thoughts while you prepare your dream mandala. Follow these steps:

1. Draw two identical circles on the heavy paper or poster board and cut them out.

2. Using the ruler or straightedge, draw a line across the center of each circle. Next, draw a line perpendicular to this line so the two lines intersect at the circle's center and divide the circle into four equal parts.

3. With the scissors, cut one leg of a line to the center of the circle. Do this for each circle.

4. Slide one circle into the other at the slots you just cut, so you end up with an eight-sided "globe." You can use tape to hold the sides in place if necessary.

5. Go through the magazines. Cut out whatever images seem to connect when you think about your signal dream. They can be fragments, colors, whatever. Let your subconscious mind direct the process—don't think about your choices, just follow your intuition.

6. Tape or glue the images you cut out onto the segments of your dream mandala. Consider the balance of your dream mandala in its three-dimensional form as you do this. Let the story of your signal dream unfold without censorship or structuring from your conscious mind.

7. Do you feel that you want to add color? Go ahead—use paints, markers, crayons, or splotches of color that you've cut out of the magazines.

8. Keep working until you feel your dream mandala is finished.

When you're done, sit back and relax for a few minutes. Take several deep, cleansing breaths. Don't be surprised if you feel exhausted. You've been doing some intense dreamwork, even if it just feels like arts and crafts!

When you're ready (and it is okay to save this part for another time), begin to explore your dimensional dream mandala. Have your dream journal or notepad handy so you can write down your thoughts and reactions. You are likely to find that your dream mandala evokes long-forgotten memories and images, and that your responses are deeply emotional. This is both okay and normal. Signal dreams have special prominence for good reason. Therapist Jeremy Taylor, author of *Where People Fly and Water Runs Uphill: Using Dreams to Tap the Wisdom of the Unconscious* (Warner Books, 1993), holds that those "aha!" responses tell you that you're on the right track and you've tapped into your subconscious (buried) memory. And remember Taylor's guiding philosophy that "all dreams come in the service of health and wholeness" however difficult it is to receive the dream's message. If you struggle with any of the issues brought up by this exercise, talk to someone you trust about it.

Red Light, Green Light

The "traffic light" system for sorting through signal dreams is a good way to further understand how you're coping with the tumult around you. Consider your list of signal dreams and assign one of the following:

- ◆ **Green Light.** This dream affirms you as you grow and change, and you welcome having it. It tells you your gut feeling is right and that you are progressing nicely.

- ◆ **Yellow Light.** This dream feels pretty good every time you have it, but you have some questions about certain elements in the dream, or how you feel when you wake up. You need to take a closer look.

- ◆ **Red Light.** This dream scares the hell out of you and you keep having it, or one like it.

Are you beginning to recognize a certain class of dreams that comes to you when you're undergoing change that might leave you feeling unsure of what to do? Look again at your dimensional dream mandala. Do you see more elements of a Red Light, Yellow Light, or Green Light signal dream?

> **CAUTION** **Wake Up!**
>
> A Red Light dream lets you know that it's time to either figure out what's triggering the dream or talk to a mental health professional who can help you do that. This kind of dream is not one you want to replay over the course of your whole life!

Survival of the Fittest

Your unconscious self often knows more about trouble than your waking mind. Perhaps a work situation is like a long-ago bad school situation. A bully runs the yard/office. The similarity may not seem apparent to your waking self, but the dreaming self says "Whoa there, I've been here before and it's not fun."

Easing Through the Tough Times

So are your dreams giving you signals such as a blue car going over Niagara Falls? Or is William Tell trying to shoot an apple off your head with a bow and arrow and his hand keeps shaking? Or is your beloved grandmother burying you up to your neck in sand and you see the bucket of ants next to her? These dreams can warn us about dangerous situations.

The first time we touch a hot stove burner, we learn not to touch it again. The first time we're in an embarrassing social situation that does us harm, part of us learns not to place ourselves in such a position again. And that part of us manifests in dreams as hesitations that we don't understand or perhaps in what we experience as intuition.

Sometimes it's hard to decode the meaning of these "mixed-signal" or Yellow Light dreams because they may have pleasant as well as unpleasant components. You love your grandmother, right? So why is she going to torture you? Could it be that even though you feel loved and accepted—the way Grandma made you feel—by your boss, there's part of you that knows his caring is keeping you prisoner in an otherwise stifling situation? It's much easier to learn not to touch a hot stove than to learn how to negotiate complex interpersonal situations that, in the long run, may be bad for us.

The good news is that as you learn to recognize your Yellow Light warning dreams, you learn to trust knowledge that you have picked up on but not consciously recognized. So if you dream time after time that the ant bucket is coming or your car is really going over the falls, you will learn to get out of a bad situation more quickly.

Celebrating the Good Times

As we have discussed, our dreams can tell us that we have grown and changed in a positive way before we recognize it consciously. Dreams can also tell us that we have resolved a difficult situation or made a good decision before we recognize the truth of it. As we become more familiar with our signal dreams, we can take a shortcut to acting on them. Let the good times roll, right?

So suppose you've struggled with the choice of starting a new job right away or taking a year off and seeing the world. You've looked at the positives and the negatives every way that a sane person could. You've even tried to look at what's happening in the world weather patterns or in the stock market. After driving yourself crazy, you finally decided to take the year and travel.

> **Dreamy**
>
> According to Veronica Tonay in her book *The Creative Dreamer* (Celestial Arts, 1995), the writer Isabel Allende dreams of her protective, soothing grandmother when her writing is going well.

But there are some nagging doubts. Driven to your wit's end, you think about consulting a Magic 8 Ball. But then you have a dream that night that's similar to other dreams you've had.

In this repetitive signal dream, you're in an airplane and you're flying through a violet-colored sky, happily navigating without having to think about what you are doing. When you wake up, feelings of peace, joy, and excitement fill you. Congratulations! You have just had your Green Light dream. You may have it, or a close variant, several times before your waking self connects this to the difficult decision you are trying to make. And you may even forget the dream, but eventually, you will learn to recognize the affirmation that this dream represents.

Does that mean that life after making a difficult decision will be trouble free just because you dreamed your Green Light dream? Of course not, but all things considered, you've probably made a good choice.

In our experience, Green Light dreams come because a person has struggled to grow and change. You might not be quite sure that you've achieved this growth, but you're ready to step on the gas.

Evolving with Your Signal Dreams

Your signal dreams may evolve over time. As you reach new ways of understanding and dealing with your environment and your relationships, the images in your recurring signal dreams may change. Although most of the themes will stay the same—flying, soaring, moving fast, beauty, peace—the symbols may reflect a new "altitude." You may have a larger plane, or a sturdier car, or move faster, or start from a different place. Or some of the people and places may be different and the settings will remain the same. As you work with the variants of your signal dreams, you'll learn to recognize the symbolic forms that they take. And remember, these are very special, very potent dreams that may occur infrequently over the course of your lifetime.

An Opportunity for Self-Healing

If your Green Light dreams are opportunities to celebrate, your Yellow and Red Light signal dreams are your invitation to focus on problem solving and healing. Thankfully, for most of us, most of the time, our dreams that tell us of the need for growth and change are of the Yellow, proceed-with-caution variety.

Perhaps you divorced a few years ago and now feel that you are ready to marry again. You've found the perfect person, but something is holding you back. You know that you sometimes have a dream about being in a stalled car when you need to attend to your inner feelings. And whattya know, you have your stalled car dream two days before marriage number two! But instead of a minivan, your stalled car is a Mercedes S-class sedan. Because you love Mercedes, that tells you that, yes, this is a good relationship; it's special and precious. But you had your Yellow Light signal dream, so that means you need to see what leftover material from the last marriage might get in the way of this one.

With some thought, or a list on paper about attributes of both partners, you discover that there's something about the new partner that overlaps with the old partner. Maybe they both sleep on the right side of the bed, which is your side. Maybe it's something more important to you; maybe they want demonstrated physical affection when you would rather be left alone. The point is that your dream is telling you that something from the last relationship, which ended somewhat painfully, factors into this one, too.

Opportunities for growth appear in our signal dreams in relation to all parts of our lives. Perhaps you have been considering a return to school. The only problem is that you have a learning disability that dictates working with your professors more closely in order to achieve your goals. Perhaps you have one of the signal dreams that signifies caution for you.

Keeping your signal dream in mind, you go to the university and talk with the learning center folks and realize that the archaic attitudes and methods of 20 years ago are long gone, and you will have more help this time. You have paid attention to your dream and acted on the message to investigate before you leapt. Maybe a Green Light celebratory signal dream will be your reward, to accompany the waking pride and excitement you feel. You've opened up new possibilities partly as a result of paying attention to your Yellow Light signal dream. So Yellow Light signal dreams can mean be careful, be mindful of what you're doing, but please do proceed!

Amazing Grace

Sometimes we go through times in our lives that are difficult and demanding, and that don't always bring out the best in us. Perhaps we've had an adulterous affair, cheated on a major exam and cost someone else a scholarship, or told a lie about someone else that caused that person to lose his or her job. It all seemed logical at the time, perhaps just a response to overwhelming stress, but it brings feelings of shame and guilt now.

Feelings of shame and guilt are useful only for the amount of time that it takes to recognize the source and begin to make amends. Either feeling can come from within, or by the words or actions of others.

Because no one lives a perfect life, grows up in a perfect home, or works in a perfect job, there are times when *guilt* and *shame* are appropriate emotions. These feelings alert us to something that requires action. If we have wronged or shamed someone else, we can apologize and ask for forgiveness. If someone has wronged or shamed us, we can consider going to that person and working toward conciliation by discussion and agreement. Sometimes we are not aware that we have hurt someone else or that we have been shamed.

Dream Dictionary

Guilt is remorseful awareness of having done something wrong or having failed to do something required or expected. **Shame** is a painful feeling brought about by a strong sense of guilt, embarrassment, unworthiness, or disgrace.

We may have signal dreams that tell us when these feelings are cropping up. Perhaps we dream of eating an ice-cream cone that is vanilla on the outside but is filled with worms. Or we appear nude in front of everyone and watch ourselves turn beet red as we discover our birthday suit condition. Whatever the cause of our guilt or shame, our signal dream can tell us that we need to deal with it in order to go on with our lives.

Claiming the Treasure

The good news is that once we have discovered these problems, we can do something about them. So if we apologize, take responsibility, ask for the respect due us, then the wormy ice-cream cone we dream about might turn into the most delicious ice-cream sundae in the world.

By paying attention to your signal dream images, symbols, and situations, you can gain a deeper understanding of how and why you react to waking events the way you do. You'll grow more confident about trusting your intuition and, hopefully, life's changes won't seem so daunting anymore. Rather, you'll see them as new opportunities for change, growth, and self-awareness.

Give the "Go!" to Your Green Light Dreams

In your dream journal, make a list of all the Green Light signals that recur in your dreams. Examine your list and identify how many of these items, people, events, and other elements are derived from your waking experience and how many are fanciful or wishful images.

Would you like to incorporate your Green Light signals into your waking life? Is this possible? Try not to think too literally. If your most wonderful dream is of flying over a meadow, perhaps in waking life you want to move out of that cramped studio apartment and buy that country house! The pleasure of your dream flying (which you can't do during the day!) becomes the pleasure of an evening walk through the wildflower patch. So make a list of what your Green Light dream might be giving you permission to do!

As you work with your signal dreams (and with dreams in general), you may gain the confidence and insight to heed internal messages and feelings and make new decisions about your life. This, in turn, can make you more satisfied with your life and can filter down into your dream life. The result of this may be fewer Red and Yellow Light dreams and more Green Light dreams. If you need help and support to do this, think about working with a mental health professional.

The Least You Need to Know

- ◆ Recurrent dreams or dream themes sometimes visit us when we're going through a time of great change.

- ◆ Learning to recognize signal dreams and understanding their messages can help us decide how to handle new and changing situations.

- ◆ Red Light signal dreams alert us to potential or current troubles, and prod us to pay attention to resolving something that's bothering us.

- ◆ Yellow Light signal dreams tell us that some ambiguity or confusion exists, or that we need to make an important decision.

- ◆ Green Light signal dreams bring positive, life-affirming messages. A green light means "Go!" and that's often what Green Light signal dreams are telling you it's okay to do.

The Language of Dreams: Wordplay and Numbers

In This Chapter

- ◆ Look who's talking
- ◆ The laugh's on you!
- ◆ The story behind the numbers
- ◆ He/She/It said *what?!*

Our dreams express our emotions in pictures. We might dream of a lamb at a disco dance. Why *that* image? Could it be that the dreamer, a divorcee re-entering the social world, is frightened of feeling like a lost lamb as she begins dating once again? Maybe, maybe not. The point is, can you see how that one image conveyed what it took many more words to do? Sometimes, a picture really is worth a thousand words. But what about the words behind the pictures?

Who's the Narrator?

Do your dreams have a narrator? Is there someone else describing the action or guiding the characters? Or is that your job? Perhaps you're taking direction from the narrator. If you are the narrator but not one of the actors, it could indicate that you need to maintain a certain distance from the action. Maybe you're dreaming of a bunch of kids playing in mud. Maybe you're the narrator because you don't want to get your hands dirty. This is an example of a visual pun, which we'll get to in a moment.

If you are not the narrator but a major player in the dream, that might suggest you feel more comfortable under someone else's direction. Perhaps you wish to be in the middle of things at all times. As with anything regarding dreams, it is impossible to uncover specific meaning without understanding the feelings associated with the dream. If you were the narrator, did you feel distant? Safe? Aloof? If you weren't, did you feel controlled or warmly guided?

> **Life Is But a Dream**
>
> In his book *Seeing Voices* (University of California Press, 1989), Dr. Oliver Sacks writes that a daughter observed her elderly deaf mother making fragments of signs with her fingers after nodding off for an afternoon nap. For the profoundly deaf, who have never heard spoken language, the visual image *becomes* the linguistic building block of language itself. Images *are* words and concepts.

Silence Is Golden—Or Is It?

The amount of music, dialogue, monologue, or plain old noise varies from dreamer to dreamer and from dream to dream.

> **Dreamy**
>
> At 19 months old, Helen Keller had an illness that left her deaf and blind. Later in her life, she said that in her dreams she visited foreign lands she had never been to and conversed with people in languages she had never heard.

Do you think that a person who grew up in the isolation of the Arctic would have less noise in his dreams than a person who grew up smack dab in the middle of Rome? Would you imagine that a native Italian, known for physical and verbal expressiveness, might have more dialogue in his dreams than a strong, silent Swede? Does music fill a musician's dreams?

We can't say for sure, but it makes sense that your dreams reflect your environment. It could also be, however, that your dreams express a strong wish for quiet or noise.

Word Games

It's time to play ball, step up to bat, sign on the dotted line, put all your ducks in a row, tee off, and pass Go. It's time to check out the word games we play in our dreams.

Very Punny!

Have you heard the one about the dreamer who woke up laughing because she was singing an aria in a battered tent in the middle of the forest—in her dream, of course? Upon awakening, this woman realized that she was "intent" on giving the annual report at the investor's meeting, a task that she felt exposed her as much as someone on stage is exposed.

Or how about the dreamer who knows that each time "suede" appears in his dreams he's being "persuaded" against his better judgment?

Finally there's the dreamer who woke up with rigid arms because he'd just spent an entire dream trying to fit a huge boulder under a child-sized chair. It turns out this expressed his fear about how "unfit" he felt about becoming a father!

Dream Dictionary

Puns are the humorous usage of words to suggest associated meanings or applications of words having similar sounds but different definitions.

We are able to joke and *pun* because we are able to use abstract thought—we're able to create symbols that serve as stand-ins for the original object or idea. Once we are able to state, for example, "In that dress she looks like a pink flamingo," or "He walks as if he's on roller skates," and know that we are not saying that she *is* a pink flamingo or he *is* on roller skates, we are cognitively ready to roll up our sleeves and pun till the cows come home—figuratively speaking, of course.

According to Ann Faraday, author of *The Dream Game*, our dreams can treat us to different kinds of puns:

- Pictorial puns

- Verbal puns

- Colloquial puns

Pictorial puns, or visual puns, use dream images whose meaning corresponds to a certain word and association, but in an unexpected way.

For example, consider the following dream:

> *I am at a weekend retreat. I check into a bed-and-breakfast. The building is rickety and falling down. The bedroom has tattered sheets. I am aghast that this is a place of business and know I have to get out.*

It is only several hours after awakening that the dreamer uncovers the meaning of the run-down bed-and-breakfast; it refers to her ex-lover whose initials are B. B., his nickname. This dream lets her know that the "B&B" is ruined and uninhabitable.

> **Dreamwork** _____
>
> What are your dream puns? Look through your dream journal, noticing unusual or perplexing images. Is the icebox a stand-in for an icy feeling toward someone? A teddy bear a possible reflection that you feel bare or vulnerable? Try to keep a list of your puns. We bet it'll soon be a long one!

Other dreamers might find that when their dreams contain hands—hands clapping, reaching, grasping, holding—that indicates they are in need of a helping hand, or feeling handled" (manipulated). Another person might report a dream in which he was dating himself; maybe he met himself at his own front door and took himself out to dinner! This dreamer could be letting himself know he's feeling old. When he's around his more youthful co-workers, he's often saying things to "date himself."

Here is a short list of other possible puns. This list is just to get your own creative punning juices flowing:

- **An airplane.** Are you feeling rather plain?

- **First in line.** Are you being "up front?"

- **A buoy** _bobbing_ **in the ocean.** Are you thinking about your old boy (buoy)-friend Bob?

- **A whale.** Are you wanting to wail on someone?

- **Making dinner reservations.** Is there something you're hesitant or reserved about?

- **Putting many ribbons on a package.** Are you concerned with putting too much meat on your ribs?

- **Dreaming of urns.** Are you worried about how much you earn?

- **Dreaming of a highway's bypass.** Are you concerned about being passed by in life?

The list, as they say, is endless. The goal is to get you to start looking for the puns—puns based on visual images (the whale), words (the dinner reservations), friends' names (Bob), syllable reversals (the bypass), and common sayings (up front)—in your dreams.

Freudian Slips

Way back in Chapter 4 we said that Freudian slips are everyday occurrences in which we express strange or unacceptable thoughts or urges. For a split second the censoring aspect of the self goes on the fritz, and what is really on your mind pops out in a seemingly bizarre and unexpected way. These slips happen in everyday speech as well as in our dreams. These verbal mistakes tell us something about our unconscious wishes.

We said that in waking life you might run across your elementary school teacher from 1970 and say, "Why Mrs. Pernokas, I thought you were *dead!*" What you mean to say was *retired*. But you always hated her, ever since she made you sit in the corner and miss the Friday afternoon science movie on mollusks.

It is likely that in your dream, however, you'd dream of Mrs. Pernokas laid out in the funeral parlor. Since our dreams come to us in images, the image revealed in our dream would be the uncensored one. But it is quite possible to have a dream in which you say the most unexpected, embarrassing, but secretly true thing to a dream character.

You're Joking!

We believe our sense of humor is one of our greatest gifts. It gives us pleasure—who hasn't watched an *I Love Lucy* episode and laughed?—and it helps us ride out the rough times in our lives. A friend of ours read the entire Sue Grafton humorous mystery series as a antidote to the sadness she felt after a bad breakup.

Jokes pop up in our dreams, too. One dreamer walked down the aisle only to find Tom Cruise, the actor, waiting to marry her. She laughed out loud, even in her dream. Now, her fiancé is a good-looking man, but, well, Tom Cruise is Tom Cruise. "I'm not supposed to marry you!" our friend exclaimed in her dream. "Have a little faith, why don't you," Tom assured her in the dream.

It took our friend about a week to realize that she'd been worried about her fiancé's feelings for an old girlfriend. She was afraid her guy would keep on "cruising." Happily married five years now, she still jokingly calls her husband "cruise."

Spelling It Out

Have you ever been on the highway and looked at other cars' license plates? Did your eye ever get caught on a vanity plate that seemed like a random bunch of numbers and letters, but when you spelled it out, there was a whole new sentence? You know, like RU40?

Our dreams can give us letters and numbers to decipher. Road signs, store signs— signs and slogans of all kinds can suddenly appear in our dreams telling us we're going the wrong way or that we're on the right track. They can be straightforward, like an arrow, or be more like those automobile vanity plates that say BM9 or 4U. The important thing is to take the time to puzzle out the meaning of the sign you are giving to yourself in your dreams.

Sounds Like Greek to Me

Are the words in your dreams unintelligible? Are they a throwback to the high school Latin you thought you'd forgotten? Or is someone speaking in Greek? You? Another character? What does it mean to you that you can't understand the dialogue in your own dream?

While some people might say that this is evidence of our past lives emerging into our dream life (a past life in which you were a Greek sailor or a Turkish seamstress or a Hindu merchant), we tend to think that it is either a replaying of a bit of foreign conversation you might have heard but not have been aware that you were picking up, a memory of your own foreign language experience, or a metaphorical message that there are parts of yourself that you cannot understand, that you can't talk to.

Wake Up!

If your dreams are filled with words you cannot understand and you also find that in your daily life you have difficulty deciphering others' speech, see your doctor to rule out a physical problem!

As always, it is important to try to decipher the confusing aspects of your dreams. You might find that speaking the phrase aloud after you wake up jogs some unexpected realization. Just like those car vanity plates, some confusing phrases, when spoken aloud, suddenly make sense.

Secret Messages

When you were a kid, did you and your friends have a secret language that you used when passing notes back and forth in class, so if the teacher intercepted any of them they'd just appear gibberish? Yet you all knew to replace every "y" with an "e" or to cross out every seventh letter to reveal the note's message. Hiding words within words can be as simple as such children's games or as elaborate as *anagrams* in which you rearrange the letters to form entirely different words and a new sentence.

Or your hidden message might appear in the form of a *homonym* (different words that sound alike) or be an example of *polysemy* (a word that has multiple meanings). These are two common "wordplays" that show up in dreams. The words "tale" (a story) and "tail" (an extension from the backside), or "navel" (belly button) and "naval" (pertaining to the navy) are examples of homonyms. The word "suit" is polysemous; it can be something you wear, one fourth of a deck of cards, or acceptable ("suits me fine").

Dream Dictionary

An **anagram** is a word puzzle in which you rearrange the letters of the original word or phrase to create new words or phrases. **Homonyms** are words that sound alike but have different spellings and meanings. **Polysemy** refers to a single word that has multiple meanings.

If your dream's linguistic messages don't make sense at first, look for a hidden code! Write the mysterious word or phrase at the top of a piece of paper. Are there other words that sound the same but mean something different? Are there other meanings for the word? Can you rearrange the letters to form different words or another phrase? Generally, if you play around with the words and phrases from your dreams that confound you, you'll figure out their secret (or not-so-secret) meanings.

Putting Words into Their Mouths

What dialogue do you write each night? Who do you cast in the various roles? Who we choose to deliver our juiciest lines can say a lot about who we'd like to be—and who we'd hate to be.

Whose Dream Is This, Anyway?

No doubt about it, it's your dream. But sometimes it can feel like someone else is running the show. People and animals can appear that we certainly did not invite into our dreams!

Both Carl Jung and Fritz Perls believed that each dream character and object is an aspect of our cast-off selves. They believed our character is multifaceted and strives toward wholeness. The goal is to understand the odd character and reintegrate him or her into our personality. So if your dream has many brutish thugs in it, you might consider that their raunchy vocalizations are trying to get your attention. Maybe you need to listen more closely to the parts of you that are forceful, pushy, and even downright lewd. Maybe your vision of yourself as totally peace loving and polite isn't the whole story!

Or perhaps you dream of a beautiful dolphin jumping through the salt spray. Maybe the dolphin is making unintelligible noises. What's going on, and how did the dolphin get into your dreams?

Animals in general (and we do mean in general) are thought to express the more primitive sides of our nature and the raw urges having to do with sex and aggression—all the things that polite society curbs.

What does a dolphin call to mind? That, of course, depends on whose mind we're asking. But let's say for a specific dreamer the dolphin calls to mind a wise, gentle, playful animal swimming freely and unencumbered.

> **Life Is But a Dream**
>
> As newborns hear different patterns of spoken sounds, different clusters of neurons in the auditory cortex are wired to respond to each phoneme, or smallest unit of sound. By 12 months old, a baby's auditory map is pretty well formed.

Okay, fine. Now, what might this have to do with our dreamer? Well, perhaps she is boxed into a dead-end, 9-to-5 job. Worse, she doesn't think much of herself, and so stands little chance of making a huge and positive change in her life. Maybe her parents drilled it into her head that she was a mousy sort, destined to a drab existence. But her dreams! Her dreams are filled with the other parts of her personality that were not given room to flourish. If only she can learn to pay attention to her dreams and the parts of herself that the dolphin represents.

"Do You Know What You Said in My Dream Last Night?"

How is it that your sweet old granny told you to "Get up off your big butt and wash the damn dishes, for once in your life"? Wasn't it surprising when your least favorite co-worker told you he worshipped the very ground you walked on and in fact was nominating you for sainthood? Or how about when your doctor informed you she was leaving the medical profession to do paint-by-numbers?

Sometimes we should just expect that our dreams will dish up the unexpected. People, animals, and objects can say the most unusual things. As we've said, when we dream our mind is free to use images metaphorically. But here's the new twist: There's no rule that says we can't mix metaphors, even heap them one on top of the next. So we can end up with dreams in which our dear, sweet granny is telling us not to be so lazy (a deep, dark concern of ours) *and* that we need to get off our "big butt." See, we've also been worried about the 10 pounds we've gained that's centering on our, um, backside.

At other times, an unexpected utterance by a dream character may be giving rise to something we aren't ready to say ourselves or to hear. Does your best friend appear in your dream only to tell you that she wants you to fail the CPA exam? Maybe you're not an accountant at all, but a chef. Still, this statement might reflect a buried feeling that your friend isn't so supportive after all.

Or these surprising words might indicate that you yourself have mixed feelings about succeeding at work. Perhaps this dream has come to you just as you're about to ask the boss for a raise. Sometimes we put our own words, or fears, into someone else's mouth.

Lastly, your friend's statement, her wish that you fail, might be an ingrained expectation you have of yourself. Who used to make you feel like a failure? Does your friend resemble that person in any physical, intellectual, or emotional way? It could be that your friend is pulling for you 100 percent, but there are old issues and negative voices you attribute to her in your dreams.

By the Number

Instead of counting sheep to fall asleep, are you counting them *when* you're asleep—in your dreams? Do numbers dance across your dreamscape? Numbers, like words, can be symbols for many unexpected things. Here are a few examples of the different ways numbers may appear in your dreams:

- ◆ Anniversaries or other important dates
- ◆ Math problems
- ◆ Addresses
- ◆ Weights or measures
- ◆ Phone numbers
- ◆ Prices or money

Sometimes dream numbers are metaphors bridging the past and the present to bring insights about both, as was the case for this dreamer:

> *I was at a bar, ordering a martini. The bartender told me it cost $15. I thought that was outrageously expensive and told him so, at which point he became insistent and grabbed the fistful of bills from my hand, pointedly counting out 15 $1 bills. My anger melted and I felt embarrassed and chastised.*

Later, this dreamer realized that at age 15 she had a bad experience with algebra in which her teacher made her feel stupid (and embarrassed and chastised). She was able to relate that old experience to her current life; her boss Martin (represented by the martini!) was asking too much of her at work. He was costing her too much in the way of the quality of her life. She was afraid to confront him for fear she would feel incompetent—as she did when she was 15 years old.

Another dreamer we know recently took a Ph.D. qualifying exam. On one night she dreamed she got a 23 on the exam; on the next night, she dreamed she got a 67. It turns out she got a score of 90—the sum of the two numbers in her dream. Perhaps these dreams expressed her anxiety that she would get a low score while also expressing her gut feeling that she really did very well. Or perhaps this was a precognitive dream, which we discuss in Chapter 19.

Maybe you have a dream in which you are about to buy a beautiful diamond necklace. You feel very anxious that it will cost a fortune. You're about to bolt from the store, but then the bill is handed to you: It only costs $40! And guess what? It's your 40th birthday. This dream might be letting you know that you are now ready to reap the rewards and riches that life has to offer. What a great birthday gift!

Perhaps you see a road sign in your dream with a stream of numbers. In the dream it makes no sense. Upon awakening you realize it is the phone number of a friend you've been neglecting. The dream may have been a sign to the waking mind that it's time to renew old ties.

As with other symbols and dream images, the goal is to determine the personal significance of the numbers that appear in your dreams. While the winning lottery ticket might not be forecast in your dream, you may find that other enriching material can come your way as easily as 1, 2, 3!

Dream Numerology

Numerology is an ancient system of interpreting the relationships between numbers that stems from the work of the sixth century B.C.E. Greek mathematician Pythagoras (yes, of geometry's Pythagorean theorem fame). Pythagoras believed that numbers could define the natural world. From this belief has evolved the modern system of numerology that assigns certain archetypal meanings to numbers. In numerology the number 1, not surprisingly, represents leadership and independence—the start of things. The number 9, coming at the end of the cycle of numbers in numerology, symbolizes completion and conclusion. Double-digit numbers such as 11, 22, 33, and so on are numerology's "master numbers" that symbolize greater potency.

When numbers show up in your dreams, make note of their context and obviousness. It could be that hidden numbers are telling you something you don't want to confront … or that you're missing the obvious.

That's My Lucky Number!

Is there a number that you consider your "lucky" number, that whenever it shows up in your life good things happen? Maybe things are coming up sixes and nines, or the third time's a charm. You might have a number you consider unlucky, too—a lot of people aren't especially fond of the number 13, for example. Or maybe whenever the number 5 appears, things get rocky for you. Numbers show up far more often in dreams than we realize, and sometimes we miss their symbolic significance because we're trying to figure them out at face value.

What Are Your Dream Numbers Telling You?

Consider your dreams from a numeric perspective. Numbers in your dreams may appear simply as numbers—as in addresses, phone numbers, grades or scores, dollar values, roulette winners, and the like. Or they might be more obscure, such as a particular number of items or objects. Do you walk up seven steps, see two cats, run from a pack of five angry dogs? Choose one dream from your dream journal (or from last night) and write down all the elements that are somehow numeric. Does your interpretation of the dream change when you add up the numbers?

What numbers are important to you in your waking life? Anniversaries? Birthdays? Your MCAT, LSAT, or Regence score? The street address from childhood? The date of your high school prom, the first time you made love, the day you bought a condo (or the price of the condo), the date of Grandma's death, the date of Martin Luther King's death, or even the number of S&H Greenstamps you saved to purchase the washer/dryer way back in 1967?

In your dream journal, make a list of *all* important numbers, for whatever reason, and note what they signify. How does each one make you feel? Finally, be on the lookout for them in your dreams.

The Least You Need to Know

- Dreams contain metaphors that are visual and linguistic.

- Puns are common dream symbols in which one word or image is humorously compared to another.

- You have a sense of humor in life. It's only natural that it will show up in your dreams.

- Characters who say strange things in our dreams may represent something we are afraid to say or know directly.

- Numbers may present archetypal symbolism.

Visual Metaphors:
Dream Pictures

In This Chapter

◆ Picture this: Your true expressions

◆ Your primary dream colors

◆ Using all five senses to understand dreams

◆ Your dreamwork canvas

We've explored many ways in which our feelings and wishes are expressed by the images in our dreams. But have you ever wondered, why *images?* Why don't sounds or words serve as the primary mode of communication in our dreams?

Understanding Is Seventy Percent Visual

Chances are, we think in images because we had images before we had words. Think about it. When we were infants, we could see our parents and even anticipate their appearance before we could say "Mama" or "Papa."

The region in our brains most responsible for speech, the frontal lobe, develops gradually in the newborn. Around the end of the first year of life, a baby is able to access higher cognitive abilities such as speech and reasoning. But the parietal lobe, that part of the brain most active in developing our ability to recognize objects, is active much earlier—from the second or third month of life.

Because our visual sense gets up and running so quickly, our preverbal thinking takes the form of images. Certainly the other senses—smell, touch, hearing, and taste—figure prominently into our early development and our dreams, but it seems that biology and society both have attuned us most sensitively to images.

Primary Process

Scientists have shown that this early visual perception (preceding linguistic acquisition) paves the way for our lifelong tendency to take in information visually first, and then verbally later. So right from the start, we are ultra-sensitive to color, shape, and movement.

In Chapter 4 we talked about secondary process. Now let's talk about its predecessor, primary process. This is a Freudian term describing how urges and untamed impulses—our id instincts—are expressed without benefit of logic or repression. The id doesn't know from logic or language or societal rules. It is that part of us that wants what it wants when it wants it. Because we are little bundles of 'id' as babies, when our early expressions and perceptions are imagistic, it stands to reason that images are more closely aligned with primary process functioning than other modes of expression.

This adds extra importance to our task of trying to understand our dreams. The images in our dreams can contain the most significant clues to the very earliest and deepest parts of ourselves.

A New Way to Be Articulate

When artists paint or draw, they are not only using their secondary process mode of thinking (that part of our thinking that follows rules of logic and reason, telling us to paint within the bounds of the canvas), but also their primary process thinking. That is what can be so viscerally moving about a painting and also so hard to articulate in words. Artists have remained in touch with that part of themselves that is unself-conscious and preverbal. Artists are very good at articulating in a way that many of us are out of touch with; they speak with images.

If you could ask Pablo Picasso, Georgia O'Keefe, and Andrew Wyeth to draw a red flower, each would draw something very different. Each work of art would articulate something distinct and precise, something that communicates with us and that we are able to understand on a visceral or gut level. This type of communication activates the vestiges of our communicative, preverbal self. Even if we are out of touch with this ability, even if we stopped taking art classes in junior high, our dreams present us with the opportunity to put on an artist's smock, grab a palette, and return to our creatively visual beginnings!

The pictures in our dreams refer us back to our richest source of meaning. As we look closely at the pictures moving across the nightly dream screen, we become articulate in the same way visual artists are articulate—through image. Our particular dream images are utterly personal and come from the depths of our being.

Dreamy
Surrealist painter Salvador Dali often attempted to paint his dreams by falling asleep in front of the easel with a brush in his hand. Immediately upon waking, he set to work. Dali had a profound interest in the metaphorical power of images in the esoteric arts; he painted his own version of the Tarot, another highly visual tool for self-awareness.

Painting Our Primal Pictures

For most of us, verbal expression becomes our primary mode of communication fairly early in life. As adults, we're fairly adept at emotional editing: conveying what we want and holding on to what we think might not be appreciated or sound appreciative to an audience's ear. We are less masterful at conveying (and not conveying) our feelings in images.

So in our drawings and our dream pictures, the feelings and wishes that emerge can be surprising and "primal." We might readily say that we're a bit annoyed with Mr. X, but our dream image might show Mr. X dangling out of a seventh-story window as we are about to close the window on his fingertips. We're much more than annoyed; we're furious!

According to Harriet Wadeson, art therapist and author of *Art Psychotherapy* (John Wiley and Sons, 1980), another reason that a dream (or waking) picture can be so powerful is because it's not bound by the rules of sequence or space. If we are talking about a scene, we must say something like, "The boy had a fish in his hand. He was running down the street. Mr. Jones emerged from a stairwell and asked the boy what time it was. Then the boy's mother poked her head out of a second-story window and said she was ready to fry the fish." As you can see, this is a linear story; several things happen in close succession, but they happen one at a time, nonetheless. In a picture, all things can happen at once. The canvas, the dream screen, can depict the whole scene simultaneously.

Life Is But a Dream

Hypnagogic and hypnopompic hallucinations, those visual bursts we see before falling asleep and shortly before waking, are characterized by a quick series of snapshotlike images. Unlike dreams, these images are speeded up and don't unfold in the normal sequence of time in which dreams mirror waking life. Zen meditators often move in and out of hypnagogic and hypnopompic states and attach importance to the images they see.

Color Theory 101

What are your dream images? Do you often dream of the countryside in beautiful green tones? Or is the countryside in perpetual autumn, filled with red and gold? Do your dreams take place in the gray alleyways of London? Are your dreams filled with violence and stark colors, or are they soothing and painted in pastels? One thing's for certain: The colors of our dream images can tell us a lot about our emotions.

Can You Feel It?

In sleep-lab experiments, most people report dreaming in color most of the time. This might be because sleep researchers tend to ask about color; otherwise, a person might not recall color or lack of it in his or her dreams.

Wake Up!

Just because you don't recall dreaming in color does not mean that you dream in black and white! As you begin to recall more dreams and in more detail, you should be able to recall more color.

In a study of 3,000 dreams by sleep expert and psychologist Calvin Hall, he found that 24 percent of men and 31 percent of women reported dreaming in color. Scientists can't say for sure why this difference exists, but some people think that the reason men tend to have achromatic (lack of color) dreams more often than women is because men are either acculturated or biologically predisposed to be somewhat less sensitive to all the shades of gray, emotionally speaking.

Dreamwork

How can you try to understand, to *feel* the images in your dreams without attaching words or descriptions to them? In our verbal world, it's not easy! Imagine what it might be like to be deaf from birth and never able to attach spoken words to objects. You understand primarily through image. Language is also a part of the mix, but often it is sign language—and that's visual, too!

Interestingly enough, in a dream study conducted by Robert Van de Castle, children report color more often than adults. This supports the idea that when we are young we're more in touch with that powerful part of ourselves expressed in vivid imagery.

There are times, however, when we might dream in black and white. As we mentioned in Chapter 1, this can happen if we are feeling depressed or if our dreams are trying to let us know we're seeing things in an all-or-nothing, black-and-white kind of way. At these times, our dreams might give us images of penguins, piano keys, or tuxedos. When we are depressed, though, our dreams seem to have muted colors or a lack of color.

The great postimpressionist painter, Henri Matisse, trapped in an unhappy marriage, often painted male figures in black-and-white–striped outfits standing in the midst of the bright colors of a lyrically painted room.

You Are Picasso

Think about a drawing or painting that you like. What message does it convey to you? Wait. Don't say it; *feel* it. Does that sound odd? Probably.

Suppose you are picturing a painting of a field of wheat being brushed by the wind. When you look at it, it will give you a feeling of some sort. Maybe you'll hate it, or maybe it will remind you of your beloved uncle's farm where you spent childhood summers. But once we put words to our feelings, we're doing something other than, or in addition to, feeling. We're organizing, compartmentalizing, defining. All wonderful things, but a frame ahead of our focus.

We need to learn to open our minds to the other ways we can know things—through our sense of smell, taste, touch, and sight. Sometimes in order to do that we need to tune out that ceaseless "radio" of language and feelingly understand the images we see.

Your Common Color Symbols

The *colors* in our dreams can be full of meaning. They can refer to some emotional attitude, to a particular person, or to a body part or object. If your dream is filled with greens, could you be dreaming of someone with the last name Green? Or Brown, White, or Black—all common surnames?

Here are some common color symbols in our culture. This brief list is not meant to define what these colors represent. Only you can decide what, if any, meaning these colors have for you. We offer them in the hopes it might spark your own interest in the colors in your dreams.

Color	Emotions	Objects
Red	Passion, lust, anger, violence	Blood, sports cars
Yellow	Cowardice, distrust, clarity	Flowers, urine, the sun
Green	Envy, abundance	Money, trees, grass, nature
Blue	Sad, calm	Water, sky
Purple	Passion	Royalty, bruises
White	Purity, hope, emptiness	Hospitals, weddings, virgins, snow
Black	Fear, calm, peace, evil	Night, coal, outer space
Gray	Wisdom, ambivalence, gentility, calm, confusion	Clouds, hair (associated with aging)
Orange	Assertive, powerful, lively, conceited	Pumpkins, carrots, autumn leaves, gold
Brown	Shame, languor, comfort, nurturance	Feces, earth

Dream Dictionary

That portion of the electromagnetic spectrum that's visible to the human eye, we call light. Light varies in wavelength and so appears as different **colors** to our eye. From the longest wave to the shortest, these are the colors in the spectrum: red, orange, yellow, green, blue, indigo, violet.

Consider this recurring segment in a 45-year-old woman's dreams:

I noticed that I often dream of a pink basketball floating up into a gray sky. It makes me very sad.

When she began to explore this repetition by writing about it in her dream journal, she was able to associate both with how the color and how the shape of the image made her feel. She discovered that pink— the color of girls, the color of the dresses her mother tried to make her wear when she was a child—gives her the feeling of being constrained. But why a basketball? It is round, earth shaped. This statement led to the realization that she'd felt she'd had to give up her love of playing basketball after college, something that meant the *world* to her, because it wasn't considered feminine enough 20 years ago.

What About the Other Senses?

Can you smell someone's perfume a mile away? Does that soft clicking sound that no one else seems to notice drive you nuts? Does the feel of velvet give you goose bumps? Or are you the only member of your family who can distinctly taste 17 spices in a stew? Remember Proust's Madeleine?

Our sensitivity to our other modes of feeling and processing information varies from individual to individual. Sometimes this is due to cultural norms. (It's not polite to go and sniff the guests.) But since our dreams don't obey the constricting laws of society, it's possible that your senses are very present in your dreams.

How often do you recall tasting, touching, or smelling in your dreams? Remember, just because you don't remember these sensations doesn't necessarily mean you didn't experience them. As you pay closer attention to your dreams you just may find that you taste delicious desserts, touch all sorts of fabrics, and smell delicate flowers in your dreams. When we discuss lucid dreaming in Chapter 21, you'll find the tools you need to "program" yourself to experience sensations in your dreams beyond visual and auditory.

> **Life Is But a Dream**
>
> In the 1890s, Dr. Mary Calkins and her Wesley College students conducted a major study on sensory images in dreams. They found that visual imagery was present in 85 percent of dreams, auditory sense in 68 percent, tactile sense in 11 percent, sense of smell in 7 percent, and taste in 6 percent of dreams studied.

In the 1800s, dream researchers paid a lot of attention to sensory-induced dreams. They made the sleeper's room very warm to see if he or she would dream she was suddenly in the middle of a hot desert. Or they made buzzing sounds to see if that introduced a swarm of bees into the subject's dream.

Perhaps the most famous account of a sensory-induced dream was the one conducted (and experienced) by the famous French dream researcher, the Marquis d'Hervey Saint-Denys. Oddly enough, he spent several weeks of vacation in the countryside of Vivaris smelling a handkerchief sprinkled with a particular cologne. When he returned home, his servant placed drops of this same perfume on his pillow after he fell asleep.

This only happened on certain nights and without his awareness. He reported dreaming of Vivaris each night the servant placed the perfume on his pillow. In this way, he was able to test his belief that our senses—in this case, smell—might induce certain dream events.

Take a moment to conduct your own experiment. In the following list, let the first thought or feeling you have come to mind. Does it spark any memories? What feelings are associated with them?

♦ The smoke from pipe tobacco

♦ The first bite of a tart apple

♦ The sun's rays on your back

♦ The aroma from a barbecue

♦ Squishing sand through your toes

♦ Lemonade with no sugar in it

Scientists are still exploring how external sensations while we sleep can or cannot enter into our dreams. But if Freud is right that one of the goals of dreaming is to protect sleep, then it makes sense that the annoying bark from the neighbor's dog might get incorporated into our dreams as a drumbeat or something else that makes sense in and prolongs the story line of our dream.

The Objects of Our Desire

What objects populate your dreams? Does it seem like there's everything but the kitchen sink in your dreams? Or are your dreams filled with open and airy spaces? And how does that make you feel?

Dreamwork

Try drawing in your dream journal any common dream objects you are aware of, paying close attention to the ones that confuse you because they seem out of place or unrealistic. What, if anything, does the object remind you of? How did you feel when you were drawing it, and after you drew it?

Are there spirals, circles, spheres, arrows, containers, cylinders, triangles, rectangles, or five-pointed stars in your dreams? Try to begin to notice what shapes and specific objects make appearances in your dreams.

You might notice that even though you work as a computer programmer, you never, ever have computers in your dreams. This might be important, depending on how you feel about your career and how you feel in the dream. Perhaps repetitive images of round objects might indicate that a person wishes to be pregnant. Or maybe the appearance of an empty jar suggests that the dreamer feels an emptiness in his or her life.

Are the objects in your dreams fantastical or realistic? Are they out of place, like a car inside the refrigerator? Or does it feel that everything is in its right place: The stove is in the kitchen, the car is in the garage, the chair is by the table? Try to notice if the shape of the object or the object itself attracts, pleases, repulses, or intrigues you.

Touch the Colors of Your Dreams

Do you remember finger painting as a child? Remember the wonderful squishiness of the paint between your fingers, those vivid colors, the delight there was in such messy creativity? You might have been too young to manipulate a paintbrush, but you sure could use your fingers and hands to express your feelings and emotions in primal images and primary colors! You might think finger painting is for preschoolers, but we invite you to reconnect with this tactile, artistic part of yourself with a finger painting exercise to explore a dream that intrigues or puzzles you.

First, of course, you need finger paints and finger paint paper. It's a good idea to actually use finger paints, as they are thick and clean up easily with soap and water, without staining. You can buy them at arts-and-crafts stores, department stores, toy stores, and sometimes even grocery stores—all these many years it's been since you were a child, finger painting remains a favorite activity. Pick up some finger paint (or heavy) paper, too.

Choose a place and time when you can indulge your creative expression without interruptions or time constraints. Finger painting is messy, even when adults do it, so you might want to cover your work surface and wear old clothing. Open the lids of your paint jars or pour the paints into containers you can easily get your hands into (a difficult task once you've started and your hands are covered with paint).

Before you dip your fingers into the paint, focus on the dream you want to express. Take a moment to feel what is going on inside you. Let the dream images wash over you. When the dream is vivid in your mind, let your creativity loose. Dip your fingers into the paint and have at it. Let the colors, and the shapes you form with them, capture the images of your dream. Engage your senses of sight, smell, touch, and hearing as you let your dream express itself. Don't be concerned with painting the story of the dream; simply allow your hands to express what you feel.

If you're not in the habit of expressing yourself in the visual arts, this might be a difficult exercise for you at first. Be patient and persistent. Above all, don't judge or criticize your efforts! When you are finished, give your painting a title.

After you get cleaned up, look at your painting. What was the experience of painting like for you? Did it connect you to your dream in different ways than thinking or writing about the dream? Does the title you gave the painting fit as the dream's title? If not, why? What might you title the dream, if not the same as the painting? What feelings come to you as you look at your painting? Does looking at your painting (or did the process of creating it) bring forth any "aha" reactions? If you'd like to return to words, you can write about your finger painting experience in your dream journal.

The Least You Need to Know

◆ Humans primarily take information in visually.

◆ The images in our dreams are some of the most potent sources—and representations—of our feelings.

◆ The shapes and colors in our dream images can convey many meanings.

◆ Our other senses—smell, taste, touch—as well as sight and sound can figure prominently in our dreams, especially as we pay more attention to them.

Part **4**

Dreaming Through the Life Cycle

"Can babies dream? What on earth about?"

"I can hear the bogeyman breathing under my bed!"

"What do you mean, I'm having pregnancy dreams? It's my *wife* who's expecting!"

"I'm 68 years old and retired. Why am I dreaming about sixth grade English class?"

No matter your age, dreams are an important part of life. As we grow up and grow older, we encounter a host of new issues and signposts for each stage of the life journey that challenge us to the fullest. Joys and sorrows, successes and setbacks, the experiences of living play out on the stage of our dreams, evolving and changing as we do.

Chapter 16

Kids! Dreams of Children and Adolescents

In This Chapter

♦ Birth and before

♦ The first years: Early dreams

♦ Growth of dreams

♦ Teen dreams

"One step at a time," right? "You have to crawl before you can walk," isn't that so? And we'd bet you learned addition before you learned fractions before you learned calculus, didn't you?

These are pretty standard, obvious thoughts and sayings (except the one about crawling first; 20 percent of babies skip that stage altogether). The point is that we learn, mature, develop, and grow in stages. Unlike the Greek goddess Athena, we don't spring forth from Zeus's head fully formed.

During the course of our lives we are faced with many developmental challenges: emotional, intellectual, spiritual, and physical. These challenges, when met successfully, help us mature. They also trigger some pretty interesting and cogent dreams, some of which help us to meet those challenges and pass on to the next stage of development.

Dreams Through a Lifetime

We know that our dreams reflect our deepest concerns and desires. So it makes sense that as we grow and develop, our dreams comment upon our struggles to adapt to the challenges we face. You'd expect the standard concerns of a 3- or 13-year-old to show up in their dreams, but exactly what these concerns are and how they are represented in the dream world depend upon individual differences, sleep patterns, and cognitive ability.

The amount of time a child, young adult, and elderly person spends in REM sleep differs. Newborns spend as much as 50 percent of their sleeping time in REM stage, while toddlers spend about 30 percent in REM sleep. From our 20s through about our 50s, we spend about 25 percent of our sleep in the REM stage. As we continue to age, our circadian rhythms change and we spend even less time in REM sleep. Since REM sleep is the stage of sleep in which we do the bulk of our dreaming, it makes sense that the amount of time we spend dreaming changes as we age.

Life Is But a Dream
REM sleep, as we've said, was first discovered in 1953 by researcher Nathaniel Kleitman. He noticed that the eyes of his sleeping eight-year-old son periodically moved about, back and forth, as if he were watching a silent movie inside his head. Using an EEG (electroencephalograph), Kleitman recorded his son's brain waves. The readings revealed a brain so active that it might as well have been awake.

Lights, Camera, Action!

Have you ever wondered what your one-year-old dreams about? Have you watched him sleep, noticing that he makes sucking motions with his lips and clutches at the air? (Could it be that he's dreaming of his next meal?) Or does it seem like your six-month-old is having a nightmare? (Could she be worried about the flying thing above her bed, which is only a brightly colored mobile?) Could that be the explanation for her sudden, violent awakening, since she's not wet or hungry?

Since your infant can't explain what's going on, you can only wonder about the images and feelings she's exploring in her dreams. Scientists wonder about the same things.

In addition to (probably) having significant emotional and psychological content, we know that dreaming performs an essential biological brain function. So it makes sense that there is dreaming right from the beginning; indeed, even in the womb there is REM sleep, which may mean that even fetuses dream. However, recent research suggests that the role of REM sleep in the womb might have something to do with the development of eye muscle movement. But other scientists challenge this theory by asking why we continue to have REM sleep during the course of our entire lives, even after eye muscles have been completely developed. Still other scientists think that REM sleep is simply the by-product of electrical discharges in the mid-brain, even for the fetus, and *never* means anything more to the human psyche or condition.

Since the brain of a fetus isn't anywhere near fully developed, it seems unlikely that dreaming as we know it is within a fetus's capacity. In fact, the brain of a baby is still forming long after birth. It is not merely growing bigger, but building the neuronal connections needed for thinking, feeling, remembering—and at an extremely rapid rate. At birth, a baby's 100 million or so neurons form more than 50 trillion *synapses*. In the first months of life, the number of synapses will increase to more than 1,000 trillion.

This astounding development takes place with proper feedback (studies show that proper emotional nurturing actually stimulates brain growth!), encouragement, care, and, yes, rest. A newborn usually sleeps at least 16 hours a day, spending approximately 50 percent of that time in REM sleep.

Dream Dictionary

A **synapse** is the gap between the endings of two neurons (nerve cells). For a message to pass across the synapse, it needs help from special body chemicals called neurotransmitters.

Because we don't yet know exactly how dreaming works at any age, we cannot say what sorts of dreams an infant can have. Scientists don't agree on whether an infant can dream at all! Depending on how much of her capacity for memory has developed, she may be replaying remnants from the day during REM sleep. Perhaps this takes the form of mere sensation: the sense memory of being fed, held close, growing cold and being wet, floating in the womb.

From a developmental standpoint, such images and emotions coursing through the brain may strengthen newly acquired brain functioning as well as lay the groundwork for new neuronal pathways. One thing is clear: An infant is busy developing 24 hours a day; up through the first decade of life, an infant's brain uses twice as much energy as an adult brain. So the role of dreaming, however rudimentary, probably has a powerful developmental purpose.

The Growth of Dreams

Have you ever wondered why the game peek-a-boo is such a hit with the two-and-under set? Besides being a simple and fun game, it is an incredibly important learning tool for the growing baby. Each time the adult hides his face and then reveals it, the baby is working to develop her memory. She is learning how to remember, as well as picture in her mind, the face that is suddenly out of sight.

At first, it is both out of sight and out of mind: Once it's gone, she's forgotten it altogether, which may explain her delight at suddenly seeing it again! But soon, the baby can keep the image of the face in her own mind and predict its "return."

What does this have to do with learning how to dream? A lot. Studies reported in the *Encyclopedia of Sleep and Dreaming* (Macmillan, 1995, edited by Dr. Mary A. Carskadon) suggest that before the age of three, dreaming is pretty much nonexistent. One reason for this may be a small child's inability to conjure up a host of objects, thoughts, and memories when the object or situation is not present. For this little child, the peek-a-boo game has not been mastered. And in order to dream, it must be mastered on some level.

These studies also show that between the ages of three and five, dreams usually have no real story line; they are fragmented, without strong emotional accompaniment, and without the child depicted in the dream as the main character. This begins to shift between the ages of five and seven when the child has developed the intellectual ability, directly involving the maturation of the brain, of *representational intelligence*. However, even though most children by the age of nine have the visual and intellectual ability to have adultlike dreams, some of the more sophisticated aspects to dreaming (the self as both the participant and observer) may not appear until adolescence.

> **Dream Dictionary**
>
> **Representational intelligence** refers to the developmental ability to recall conscious events—to symbolize them—when those same events aren't present in the child's environment.

But wait. What about the fact that children between the ages of three and six are most likely, according to Dr. David Foulkes, to report nightmares? And do we really believe that children under the age of three don't have the capacity to hold on to a visual memory? Dr. Richard Ferber, Director of the Center for Pediatric Sleep Disorders, Children's Hospital, Boston, and author of *Solve Your Child's Sleep Problems* (Fireside, 1986), says that children as young as two report dreaming when awakened from REM state! He also says that a child under the age of two doesn't understand the concept of a dream, so we can't ascertain if the child is really dreaming or not. So one thing is certain: The study of dreams, especially as it relates to children, is far from over.

We think that as children begin to experience strong emotions—anxiety, fear, pleasure, joy—and develop the capacity to represent ideas and emotions in their dreams, they begin to become aware of dreams. And generally, the dreams reflect waking life concerns. While dreaming may be something present from the beginning, it will be experienced as something *received* rather than *perceived*. The ability to distinguish between reality and dreaming, between "me" and "not me," are later developmental milestones whose attainment will mark the ability of the child to perceive her dreams as something that goes on in her own sleeping mind.

Dreamwork

Every child's needs are different. Some children need little more sleep than a night's worth and 20 minutes to recharge after lunch. Others require much more sleep and take multiple naps until they are four or five years old, while others may give up napping altogether at age two or three. However, if your child is irritable, inattentive, and impulsive, sleep deprivation may be the reason. Talk to your child's doctor if you need more advice.

But we don't see such an attainment as a single milestone, but rather as a one-step-forward, one-step-backward type of progression. That's why a toddler sometimes will have a hard time believing that the monster in her dream isn't really downstairs one night, while on other nights she will readily accept this. So, in our opinion, dreaming, like learning to walk, takes time and practice.

Early Dream Themes

D. W. Winnicott, a famous British pediatrician and psychoanalyst who practiced in the mid–twentieth century, once said, "There's no such thing as an infant." What he meant was that the infant doesn't exist on his own but instead exists as a team with his mother. Over time, the infant develops into a separate human being with an awareness that he is indeed an individual. This process of developing a sense of self takes time, and when this has happened, the child will be able to perceive rather than receive his dreams. As the baby learns to do things for himself, he is less dependent on a primary caretaker for literal survival.

Erik Erikson, author of *Identity and the Life Cycle* (Norton, 1980) along with other groundbreaking works, conceptualized this growth process in discrete stages. Each stage is mastered, mastered in part, or not at all. Each stage is cumulative; one must come to terms with the psychobiological tasks in a specific order. Erikson calls the first stage "Basic Trust v. Mistrust." In short order, this means a baby's first task is to be able to trust in his world. He needs to be fed, bathed, changed, picked up, and put down for naps in a consistent and predictable manner. If this happens, he will emerge into toddlerhood with a firm sense that the world is a welcoming place that he can participate in.

Life Is But a Dream

An infant's sleep patterns change dramatically during the first year of life. At one month of age, about two thirds of babies wake up more than once per night. By six months of age, most infants sleep through most of the night, and only about 15 percent of infants wake more than once a night.

Dream Dictionary

Cortisol is one of the body's stress hormones that acts to speed up the heart and respiration rates and tense muscles during a physical or emotional challenge.

Dreams, assuming he has rudimentary ones, might center on the sensate memories of being fed, being cradled, or of the anxiety aroused when he is hungry or uncomfortable. Dr. Ferber says that a one-year-old can have nightmares of simple content: a bee sting or a recent blood test. Further, because of an inability to distinguish between dreaming and reality, he might have trouble understanding that the dream is over. Remember, he's still learning to *perceive* rather than *receive*.

In talking about abused children, Dr. Bruce Perry of Baylor College of Medicine said in the spring/summer 1997 issue of *Newsweek* that trauma elevates stress hormones such as *cortisol*. High levels of cortisol during the first three years of life may make the baby's brain acutely sensitive to even the replaying of the trauma in dreams. Normal levels of anxiety in babies may work in much the same way. Perhaps the stress associated with being left with a strange baby-sitter, feeling hungry, cold, wet, or too warm is re-experienced in simple dreams that are the earliest forms of nightmares.

The Age of "No!"

A toddler is master of the universe, or so she would have you believe. She has discovered the magic of "No," and has proceeded to drive her parents crazy with using it. She has discovered that she has control over her body, including her bowels and bladder. She has the power to please her parents by using the potty or not. She explores her surroundings with a confident pioneering spirit. But in a flash, she becomes scared and clingy, no longer a tiny version of Amelia Earhart.

Erikson calls this stage "Autonomy v. Shame and Doubt." During this stage, a toddler must come to feel that she can move about in the world freely, but not so freely that she feels alone. It is her parents' job to admire her abilities but not heap on more demands, which will make her doubt herself. Conversely, the parents must be sure not to ridicule or ignore her accomplishments, or else she might become filled with shame and have little confidence in her abilities and creations.

Dreamwork

Vicky Lansky, in the online newsletter "ParenTalk," suggests creating a dream jar. On slips of paper, write all the good dreams you and your child can think of. Be sure to include good dreams you remember from your own childhood if you can. Place them in a jar and let your child pick out a slip of paper each night. This is a pleasant bedtime ritual as well as an aid to inspiring enjoyable dreams.

Dreams at this stage will reflect this balancing act of feelings: shame, doubt, pride, invincibility, and dependence. Because child development experts believe that one hallmark of this phase is representational thinking, it stands to reason that two-year-olds have the capacity to dream. It is also about this time that children learn to speak, and so, dreams can be described. Dreams will reflect impulses toward independence, but may also contain fears about too much independence.

The Age of Nightmares and Beyond

From the ages of three to about six or seven, nightmares are common. In Chapter 12, we talked about all the things in the world (strangers, loud noises, parents fighting, the evening news …) a young child has to fear. But there are things inside a young child that are scary, too. For instance, his wish that Daddy would disappear so he could have Mom all to himself is quite a frightening feeling. Or perhaps it is a new sibling he'd like to do away with. This strong wish is a scary one because he anticipates being punished for it.

You can help your child with nightmares that awaken her by assuring her that you will protect her and make sure nothing bad happens to her. You may wish to open the closet to demonstrate that there's no monster in there, but as Dr. Ferber points out, this isn't really what matters to her. It is more important that she get the firm sense that you will not let any harm come to her. During the day you might talk to her about the difference between reality and dreaming, but depending on her age, this may be an impossible concept for her to grasp. You can also ask your child to draw the scary dream or creature and then make a second drawing of how she would like the dream to end, allowing her to triumph over or make friends with the monster.

From the ages of three to six, a child has to come to terms with many sexual and aggressive impulses. She may be playing "doctor" with other children, or with herself. Dreams at this *Oedipal* stage are likely to be of monsters, animals, and other primitive beings running amuck. Children are often giants or lions—or are being chased by them. As we've said before, animals in dreams tend to represent our wilder sides, sides that are normally present in everyone, no matter what our age.

Dreamy

Steven Spielberg's sister, Anne, says that Steven used to tell her wonderful stories as a child. In one story, Steven told Anne that the moon was alive and would come down outside her window when it was full to take a look inside. This image was so vivid for Anne that it became the theme of recurring, frightening dreams for her. Steven used this theme in his movie *Close Encounters of the Third Kind*.

It is also from the ages of three to six that children have the deepest nondreaming sleep. In fact, in one experiment, children sleeping with headphones on could not be aroused during deep Stage 4 sleep, despite extremely loud buzzing sounds—123 decibels, a sound level similar to that of a loud motorcycle—in both ears. Most likely, it is this deep Stage 4 sleep that allows for sleepwalking, sleep talking, and night terrors. (Remember them from Chapter 12?)

Dream Dictionary

According to Sigmund Freud, the **Oedipal** stage of development involves a child's hostility toward the parent of the same sex and attraction to the parent of the opposite sex. It usually arises when a child is between the ages of three and five.

Wake Up!

If your child continues to have frequent nightmares after the age of seven or eight, she might still be struggling with earlier conflicts. Talk to your child and find out what's on her mind. Because it's difficult for some children to put feelings into words, you might do this while taking a drive or a walk.

Children tend to outgrow nightmares by age seven or so because many of the issues we've discussed are mastered. Dreams now tend to have more characters in them—including the dreamer and his parents—and depict realistic scenes from school or play. It is during these years that a child, newly freed from the issues we've mentioned earlier, can concentrate on physical, intellectual, social, and creative learning. A child may have many dreams about how he is learning—or not. Perhaps he's nervous about a test or anxious about homework. Perhaps he dreams he's scored 10 goals in 1 soccer game.

One of the Gang

Children develop a strong peer network around age seven. Concerns over popularity may emerge in children's dreams. Friendly interaction is a dominant theme during this time, although a main concern in the dream is with his own physical state; dreams take on themes of hunger, thirst, and sleepiness. This, coupled with the child's focus on social interaction, places him on the developmental cusp of nearly being able to shift his attention away from his immediate needs and wants.

Whether he's picked first or last to play in the soccer game will probably affect him emotionally, as well as influence the content of his dreams. Is there a bully at school who steals his lunch? Is there a teacher who intimidates him? Perhaps he will have trouble letting you know this, but if you create a home environment where dreams are welcome, you will hear about his concerns as they show up in his dreams.

Dreamy

In some native tribes, such as the Cuna Indians and the Senoi, children are expected to report their dreams to their parents at the morning meal where the dreams are discussed, respected, and heeded. James R. Lewis reports in *The Dream Encyclopedia* that in the Zezuru culture in Zimbabwe, children's dreams are considered extremely important; often they are viewed as direct messages from the spirit world.

Gender differences begin to crop up in dreams during this time, although according to Robert Van de Castle, gender differences in dreams are evident much earlier. But by late childhood, characters in the dream tend to be of the dreamer's own sex. Boys' dreams are more likely to contain acts of aggression, while aggressiveness in girls' dreams declines. Girls' dreams also contain more familiar characters—in fact, their dreams contain more characters overall—than boys' dreams, which contain more inanimate objects. Whether this is due to nature, nurture, or some complicated interplay of both remains to be seen.

The Power of Bedtime Rituals

Ritual and routine comfort children in all aspects of their lives. It reassures them to know that the same things happen day in and day out. As we said earlier in this chapter, children under about age three have little concept for "next." Their brains are not yet developed enough for them to recognize that what goes "out of sight" is still there, even though they can't see or hear or touch it. Ritual—absolute repetition of routine—helps them to reach this all-important milestone in development. And bedtime rituals help children to learn that just as everything always is the same when they fall asleep, it always will be the same when they wake up.

In the timeless children's picture-book classic *Goodnight, Moon* by Margaret Wise Brown, first published in 1947, a sleepy little bunny says goodnight, every night, to the same cast of characters that inhabit his waking life—from the toy house on the floor to the moon in the sky. Then and only then, he can fall asleep. Children of all ages (even our ages!) love the soothing calm of this bedtime story.

Research tells us that what's on our minds when we fall asleep is likely to show up in our dreams; it stands to reason that although we know less about the dreams of children than we know about the dreams of adults, the same holds true for children. Bedtime routines help your child transition from waking activity to happy dreams, from the practical (putting on pajamas, brushing teeth) to the comforting (reading stories, a few minutes of talking, prayers). Even adults find routine comforting; we'll talk about creating your own "sweet dream" rituals in Chapter 22.

Oh, Those Teen Years

By the time a child reaches puberty, her sleep patterns and dreaming capability closely match those of an adult. Just like an adult, she spends about 25 percent of her sleep time in REM sleep, and she is biologically and intellectually able to dream the most sophisticated of dreams.

Dream Dictionary

Technically, **adolescence** is the time when secondary sexual characteristics—facial hair for boys, breasts for girls—begin to appear and, eventually, sexual maturity on a physical level is achieved. In our culture, adolescence is also a time of emotional and social development, and extends from about the age of 12 until 18 or 20.

As you may remember, a lot is going on in the life of a teen—many challenges, lots of self-doubt, quite a bit of socializing. A teen might take on an after-school job, be in positions of responsibility at home and at school, and begin to think of the future. While exciting and stimulating, it's the rare teen who doesn't become anxious in the face of such turmoil. We've found that during *adolescence* there's a rise in the frequency of nightmares, but often parents aren't aware of them because the teen doesn't talk about them.

Nightmares Revisited

In some ways, the return of the nightmare during adolescence may signify the re-working of old issues a child faced years ago, specifically issues of autonomy. When adolescence hits, many teens struggle once again with a desire to be independent (just like when they were toddlers) from their parents. This time, though, they want the car keys, which is a scary thought to most parents and, in fact, to the teens themselves. Indeed, the attendant feeling is one of underlying anxiety. Your teen wants to feel independent, but not alone (despite what she says!), and not without support and guidance.

Growing and Changing

At the same time, a teen's sleep patterns might be changing as she grows and develops. Have you noticed that your once sunny morning person of a child is now about as friendly as a hungry bear before 11 A.M.? You can lay this development squarely on the shoulders of biology: A teen's biological clock is rigged later than that of a younger child or older adult. He no doubt wants to stay up later and get up later than he has in the past.

In addition, hormonal changes are taking place that have remarkable consequences. Girls experience a surge in estrogen, boys in testosterone. Melatonin is secreted in a lesser amount and later in the night than in the past. These changes, coupled with the social, intellectual, and emotional demands placed on a teenager, might account for the tendency for teens to go to bed later and get fewer hours of sleep. It's common for teens to repay this sleep debt on the weekends by sleeping late. Experts suggest you let your teen sleep late on the weekends, to counter some of the negative effects of sleep deprivation.

But what are teens dreaming about? Well, we know that their dreaming mind is now mature enough to have dreams where one character morphs into another and where they can be both a participant and observer. People tend to dream about the maturational issues they face in waking life, and teens are no different. Just as the teenager's body is undergoing huge physical changes, the teenager's emotional world is also changing.

> ### Life Is But a Dream
>
> Nocturnal emissions, also known as wet dreams, first begin occurring in males at around puberty with the rise in serum testosterone, and are often—but not necessarily—accompanied by a sexually explicit dream. Similar physiological responses appear to occur in the bodies of girls and women, too, although this is less well studied.

The maturational task at this stage is to begin to form a solid identity. A teenager struggles with who she is sexually and emotionally and how she fits in with her peers and the world at large. She also anticipates her future, which is a way of further sifting through identity possibilities. It is quite common for these issues to appear in dreams. See if you can determine the pertinent themes in these dream fragments:

> *I was in math class. The teacher pointed at me and asked, "Why don't any of the girls want to date David?"*

> *I was in the cockpit, and we hit turbulence. I started to lose control, but managed to right the plane just before we crashed.*

I dreamed I was on TV; I was being interviewed because I'd just invented a new kind of shoe that had wings!

In my dream I was kissing my boyfriend, but then he turned into my best girlfriend.

I was running through dark city streets. Guys were asking me for money and I didn't have any. I ran faster. Suddenly a guy tried to grab me, but then I remembered my mother had put a stone in my pocket. I whipped it at his head and he fell over. I took off.

In these examples we can see the struggles with emerging sexual identity, hopes for the future, and the desire to be totally independent of parental influence. In addition, almost half of all American adolescent dreams involve aggression. Perhaps the high incidence of aggression in adolescent dreams is due to the fact that we live in a very violent society. In fact, Robert Van de Castle reports that there is virtually no incidence of aggression in the dreams of Cuna Indian teenagers, perhaps because of their lower exposure to violence. Or maybe it's because at this stage of life, there are many more internal and external pressures put on teenagers in our society.

Family Dream Time

Dreams can be a window into your child's life. Kids who might be reticent about sharing the challenges they encounter every day at school generally are willing if not eager to talk about their dreams. Such discussions can help you to better understand your child, and may help your child to make sense of the events and feelings that generate concern. Many of the methods you might use to interpret and understand your own dreams also work with kids.

- ◆ For children under age 5 or 6, suggest that they draw their dreams. Then ask your child to tell you the story of the drawing. Ask about the colors and shapes. As we talked about in Chapter 15, these are the most primal representations, and they allow expression of dreams through images, much as dreams themselves take place.

- ◆ Children between ages 7 and 10 or 11 might enjoy more sophisticated artistic explorations of their dreams, such as constructing with Play-Doh and similar products that are easy for small hands to shape and mold. A child who is especially tactile or spatial might like re-creating dream stories with building blocks such as Legos.

- ◆ By age 11 or 12, many kids are developing their abilities to tell stories. If your child enjoys writing, encourage her to write a "book," including pictures if desired, that tells the story of a particularly memorable dream. If this is a scary dream or a nightmare, have the child carry the story far enough to craft solutions (with some guidance from you if necessary) for the scary parts. Or if your child has a flare for the dramatic, suggest that he write and act out a short play, perhaps drafting siblings or friends to play roles from the dream.

◆ Adolescence is a time of self-assessment and introspection. Although teens often are unwilling to let parents in on their musings, your teenager might enjoy keeping a dream journal that records significant dreams and explores possible meanings.

Above all, validate the importance your kids attach to their dreams—even those that feature nonexistent monsters your child just knows lurk under the bed or in the closet. Take your child's dreams seriously, and help your child to understand that everyone has dreams. Encourage your child to use simple methods—such as thinking of something that makes him feel happy or focusing on a favorite memory when falling asleep—to shape dreams that are fun. Share your dreams with your kids, too—filtered for appropriateness and their level of comprehension, of course.

"I Am," I Said

We can see that as the fetus becomes a baby becomes a child becomes a teenager, a major challenge is for the developing individual to become an individual. While this doesn't (hopefully!) mean that we grow up and *away* from our family, it sure does mean that we learn to regard ourselves as separate from our family with a sense of "me-ness." This growing sense is reflected in our dream lives each and every step of the way.

The Least You Need to Know

◆ We probably dream right from the start, but we don't become aware that we're dreaming until we're about two or three years old.

◆ A baby's first dreams likely are centered on basic sensations.

◆ Early childhood dream themes center on waking life concerns: the feeling that the environment is welcoming, that the toddler has some power over her own body, and later, that the small child won't be punished for angry wishes.

◆ As a child develops, dreams begin to include peers and social themes. In the teen years, there is often a resurgence of independence and identity issues that often play out in dreams, commonly even in nightmares.

◆ Encouraging children and teens to communicate about their dreams can help them to open up in communicating about what's going on in their lives.

Chapter 17

Grown-Up Dreams

In This Chapter

- ◆ Early adulthood: Getting started
- ◆ Choosing a dream date and career for a lifetime
- ◆ Responsibilities, with a capital "R"
- ◆ Remodeling the empty nest

So at what age did you finally make the break, cut the cord, leave the nest, strike out on your own? At 18? 21? Or did you find that you never left home, or at least not until you were much older? And do you remember what you dreamed during this age of transition? In this chapter, we explore just that.

The New Beginning

Whether you left home at 18 to go to college, at 21 to join the merchant marines, or at 22 to marry the boy or girl next door, you no doubt struck out on your own at some point. After all, you probably spent the majority of your teen years figuring out who you'd like to be and what you wanted for the future, and felt ready—or almost ready—to put your ideas to the test! Your dreams may well have reflected that urge for independence and new sense of adventure.

There was a huge door at the end of a hall. I walked up to it. I was scared, but pushed it open anyway. My best friend from high school was there—standing at the edge of a town I didn't recognize—and she said, "What took you so long? Let's get going."

This young man's dream wonderfully illustrates the desire—and the fear—many young adults have to strike out on their own. Here, his dream helps him solve the problem by having a comforting friend appear to go with him on his new journey.

Clearly, dreams that occur in your early 20s often reflect the struggle to become as independent as you hoped to be during your teen years. At this point, the theme of your dreams may well center on battles—emotional and physical—that really challenge your strength and tenacity. You're also likely to have more dreams about your ability to perform in school or at work. Characters in these dreams are often out of focus or not quite fully formed, reflecting the incomplete emergence of your adult identity.

> ### Life Is But a Dream
>
> According to Sigmund Freud, the immediate source of adult dreams (and perhaps those of children) are worries about some incomplete or unresolved task from the day before. Freud called these dreams "day residues."

Believe it or not, this time of life is also marked by separation anxiety (which you probably thought you'd left behind at the age of about three!). As you become more independent, you may simultaneously long for the safety of home as, once again, you're conflicted about your independence. In truth, most 20-somethings don't yet have a strong sense of themselves and, for this reason, their dreams often reflect a wish to return home, or to avoid or slow down maturation.

I was back in my old bed, only I was 22, the age I am now. My mother came in to tell me to turn off the light. She didn't seem to think it weird that her grown daughter was in her old bed. I tried to get up, but couldn't move my legs. Then I got really upset because I knew I'd be late for work if I couldn't get my legs to move.

The fact that this young woman couldn't move her legs might represent her wish to be dependent on her parents again. This dream might also serve as a warning to the dreamer about getting enough rest—a warning made all the more urgent because her mother is issuing it. On the other hand, the dreamer actually created the "character" of the mother in this particular dream, which we might view as an attempt for her to fulfill that motherly function herself, in essence, taking care of herself in a responsible, loving way.

Whose House Is It Anyway?

In Gail Sheehy's popular book *Passages* (Bantam, 1976), Sheehy calls the first decade of adulthood the "trying 20s," meaning this is the decade in which we tend to "try on" partners (in relationships sometimes called "starter" relationships) and careers in search of a perfect fit. But sometimes economics, culture, and familial obligation get in the way.

Not only are the 20s a time of moving back and forth psychologically between dependence and independence, it is often a *literal* back-and-forth time. As much as the emerging adult wants to be on her own, and Mom and Dad want her to be on her own, many young adults find it almost impossible to support themselves on entry-level wages. Even with a college education, the ability to pay for living expenses is not a given.

A young woman who has moved back in with her parents after four years of independent college dorm living has this dream, which clearly shows her dismay about being "stalled" on the road to independence:

> *I am in a car. I have turned the motor on and my hands are on the wheel. I look out the rearview mirror and check all around me carefully. It is safe to go forward. All of a sudden I realize that the car has no wheels. Not just no tires, but no wheels. I don't even get upset or cry, I just get out of the car and start walking.*

Life Is But a Dream
In many Latin American and other cultures, young men and women are expected to live at home with their parents until marriage. Most often there *is* no time of moving back and forth. Since the United States still has one of the highest divorce rates in the world, such a tradition might not be such a bad idea!

Getting Started

Sometimes the "starter" relationships that we mentioned earlier in the chapter result in the birth of children. This compounds an already stressful situation. If the young family splits up—or if they can't reliably support themselves—they might move back in with their parents with children in tow.

The young adults are trying to grow into mature relationships, and most grandparents want to spend a lot, but not all, of their time and space with their grandchildren. The house doesn't have enough bathrooms, let alone emotional space. In such instances, *everyone* may end up having distressing dreams, such as the one experienced by this single mother who woke up with tears streaming down her face:

I am on a ship in the ocean, a big cruise ship. My husband is there and so is my daughter. We're all having a wonderful time. I turn to hand my laughing child to my husband so that I can refasten my loose sandal. All of a sudden, I realize that the man clutching my child is a complete stranger and a menacing one at that. I scream for help, but the people around me are unable to help me.

Dreams at this phase for the single parent (who is also thrust back into the role of child) may center on feelings of failure, impotence, and anger at having been put in this position. She might be angry with a partner who is no longer available to her (even if she's the one who gave him the boot!), with her parents (even though they are being loving and supportive!), and with her small daughter (even though she's blameless!). There often seems to be no safe place to let off steam—except in her dreams.

Parents, too, suddenly thrust into the role of live-in grandparents, might find that their resentment is channeled into their dreams. They also might experience a rise in "unpreparedness" dreams—you know, those dreams where you show up for class in your Fruit of the Looms, take a test without a pencil, or find yourself trying to sing an aria without the sheet music. Additionally, there's nothing like becoming a grandparent to drive home the fact of one's mortality. Dreams of being too late or of missed opportunities can occur frequently as parents adjust to their new identity as grandparents.

This is, of course, in addition to all the positive ways the advent of grandkids can make us feel, as this grandfather's dream of flying reveals:

I'm running so fast that I begin to fly. I am with my grown son and he takes my hand. Then I look at my body and I notice that I've turned into my child self!

Often, grandchildren can bring out the child in us and help us reconnect with the part of us that feels free and fun-loving.

Building a Life

Our 30s are often referred to as the "industrious age." We no longer feel that anything is possible; we've accepted the fact that at age 34, we probably won't take up ballet and become a professional dancer. We realize there are some limits, but for the most part we're fit and strong and in control of our faculties. We are more realistic about what we can do in life, and what constitutes the perfect partner.

Gail Sheehy refers to this decade as the "catch 30s," meaning this is the phase of life where we take our shaken illusions (we won't be dancing the lead in *The Nutcracker*, after all), and hopefully turn our efforts into developing some meaningful, deep relationships and endeavors. We choose a life partner, if we desire to do so. We roll up our sleeves and delve into our careers, if that's what we decide we want. We realize our parents aren't as stupid or out of it as we once thought—or that they are and there's no shame in admitting it. And many of us decide to have children, which can stimulate some pretty interesting dreams!

Pregnancy Dreams

If you've ever been pregnant or know someone who has, you probably know that dreams during this period are often vivid and concentrate on specific themes. This may be due to biological factors—certainly the hormonal changes in a woman's body can affect sleep, dreams, and dream recall—psychological factors, or both.

Robert Van de Castle reports that some women have dreams that act as "nocturnal sonograms," or *prodromal dreams.* That is, they can sense and monitor internal biological changes, perhaps even feel the presence of the developing fetus before they've taken a pregnancy test! Some women correctly report a problem with the pregnancy before a formal diagnosis is made. However, these reports are anecdotal and retrospective.

Dream Dictionary

Prodromal dreams may occur when the body and dreaming mind become aware of physiological and biochemical changes and represent them in dreams. This is an area of study that is controversial in the scientific community.

Just as the fetus develops over the course of nine months, so does the expectant mother; she develops the beginnings of an identity as a parent. As reported by Mary A. Carskadon in *The Encyclopedia of Sleep and Dreaming,* first trimester dreams often center on mixed feelings about the body changes a woman is both experiencing and anticipating. Since the bulk of miscarriages occur in the first trimester, there are also many dreams in which fears of losing the baby are prevalent. This is not a harbinger of impending loss; it is a normal fear expressed in the dreaming mind.

> *I am at my doctor's office and I notice there are a group of baby ducklings under the chair. I try to get over to them, but it is so difficult because I've suddenly become enormously pregnant. The ducklings are fine; I just want to be with them. But I realize I have to move very slowly; I have to wait.*

In this dream, the small animals are a symbol of the small human being inside of her. She wants to touch them, be near them, but realizes that she can't do it as quickly and easily as she'd like. This might reflect her excitement over meeting the developing baby and her feeling that she is not quite in control of her body and when she will meet this new person.

Other common dream symbols that tend to crop up during pregnancy include:

- Buildings or houses that are somehow distorted—suggesting the woman's view of her changing body

- The presence of the pregnant woman's mother in some sort of helping capacity, or even as a substitute for the pregnant woman

- Fields of flowers/plants/trees in bloom

- Bodies of water, often with animals swimming in them

During the middle of her pregnancy, a woman's dream content tends to shift, with more dreams about becoming a mother occurring. Often, a woman dreams about her own mother, comparing her care to the care she anticipates giving to the infant. Dreams involving matters of finances, shelter, and the ability to secure health care for her baby are also common.

In the last trimester of pregnancy, images of the baby-to-be increase dramatically. In fact, because of disruptions in sleep (it isn't easy sleeping while your unborn baby seems to be always kicking to get out!), dream recall itself is increased. It's also common to dream of giving birth.

Apart from the discomfort, women may wake more frequently during the last trimester for a more evolutionary biological reason: It could be nature's way of readying the mother for the reduction in sleep she'll suffer once her baby arrives, a problem facing the father-to-be as well.

Indeed, here we are talking about the impending birth of a baby and talking only about the mother. But what about the father-to-be? Good question. Studies show that fathers also undergo predictable changes in dreaming patterns during pregnancy. During his partner's early pregnancy, a man often has dreams with themes of male virility with strongly sexual content. As the pregnancy continues, he may further struggle with his change in identity by dreaming of his own father.

> **Life Is But a Dream**
>
> Third-trimester anxiety dreams about labor might be a good thing, studies show. Researchers at the University of Cincinnati recently found that pregnant women who had threatening, anxiety-filled dreams were more likely to undergo shorter labors due to more efficient uterine contractions and to the mastery, in dream life, of the anticipated event.

Often, his dreams will include themes of abandonment and loss because he feels left out of the pregnancy. As delivery time nears, he, too, begins to dream about it and about his partner and their new baby. Interestingly enough, a large percentage of men dream the unborn baby is male. This may be a way to assuage feelings of being left out and pave the way for father-child bonding.

Dreamy

A father-to-be is more likely than a mother-to-be to dream that his child will be a boy, and images of a future together at baseball games and tossing a football around are common, especially near the end of the pregnancy. Despite our expansion of sex-typed roles, it appears that men during this time retreat into typically masculine father/son fantasies, perhaps to cope with having felt left out of the pregnancy process or as a way to envision themselves in a "hands-on" parenting role.

It would be interesting to look at what sorts of dreams prospective adoptive parents have and at the types of dreams a lesbian couple, with one woman being pregnant, might have. This would further enrich the ways we see and know ourselves. Let's hope scientists and sociologists take up this subject in the near future.

Clearly, these nine months are jam-packed with hopes and fears—probably more so than any other nine-month period—and it makes a lot of sense that they are depicted in dreams in a vivid and telling way.

Nose to the Grindstone

For those with children, the middle adult years are also often the most expensive. The kids need braces, sports equipment, clothes, and many other money-consuming items. And as our children themselves reach toward adulthood, they vocalize their opinions about their needs more loudly and more often. This often translates into us working harder or feeling guilty that we aren't. It can feel that our personal goals get pushed so far aside that they fall off the map altogether! We may experience a host of dreams, like this one, that tells us we're feeling out of control:

> *I was on a business trip, on a plane. From my window I noticed another small plane heading straight for us. I tried to signal the pilot, but he couldn't hear me.*

For more personal reasons, the late 30s and early 40s can be a time when we feel we have to push harder at work. We've realistically accepted who we are and we're working hard to succeed, but perhaps our boss isn't noticing just how tireless we've been. Maybe we're bumping up against a glass ceiling or reaching for a missing rung on the ladder.

Wake Up!

A growing teen may have dreams about issues that parents thought were settled years ago. Remember, development is a spiral, not a straight line. With each step upward, new cognitive abilities necessitate a re-examination of some of the old issues. These issues may well surface in dreams. If your teen looks troubled or pensive in the morning, ask him about his dreams.

Suddenly we notice that our supervisors are getting younger and younger. Dreams during this phase of life can center on acquisition, competition, and last-ditch attempts to grab the brass ring. Sometimes, because we are working so hard and perhaps putting aside our fondest wishes, we tend to recall fewer dreams. We feel we just don't want to know. We feel we don't have time to make our dreams come true, so why even remember them?

Meanwhile, teens are developing distinct personalities and likes and dislikes that may cause clashes or disappointments for Mom and Dad. The problem is heightened when there has been a divorce in the family. If the divorcing parents have not managed to be civil to each other and put their child first, a lot of anger will surface from the young person, who needs good memories of *both* parents to negotiate emerging self-reliance.

Dreamwork _____

Women often come into therapy with vague feelings of unhappiness or unfinished psychological business when their teen daughters begin dating. Many times, they haven't satisfactorily coped with any regrets or disappointments they experienced during their own dating years. Take a look at your own dream journal as your daughter begins dating and see if her development has reawakened memories of yours.

Sometimes a teenager's issues reawaken old issues for his or her parents. Such a confluence of events occurs when parent and child find themselves on the same part of the development spirals but at slightly different levels. Dad may feel blue and not realize that it's because he's worried that his son will have the same kind of devastating injury during football that ended his own promising football career.

As your teenagers begin to separate from you and go out into the world, remember that most likely you've done your job, perhaps not perfectly, but well enough. And remember that as independent as they look, not only will they stay connected, but also they carry a part of you wherever they go. On the other hand, you still have your own life to live and dreams to dream.

Whose Life Is This Anyway?

I am dreaming of a huge diamond. It sparkles so brightly that it would blind Elizabeth Taylor herself. I stand and admire it and bask in the knowledge that it is mine and has been for a long time. Suddenly, I notice flaws that had gone unseen before. I am heartbroken. I have invested all I have in this stone and now it is not worth nearly as much as I thought. Should I sell it and begin again with lesser stones?

As this dream so perfectly illustrates, your middle years are a time for reflection and reevaluation. Are you where you thought you'd be? Does your life have all the shininess and depth of a brilliant diamond? Is your partner the one person in the world you want to spend the rest of your life with? Is this all there is, and if so, is it good enough?

As we've said before, we all change as we age. In midlife, the process of change and the results of the changes we make are especially salient. Often we feel a need to express the polar opposite of our personality traits that have been in evidence before. We might explore our artistic proclivities or return to school. We grow weary of being responsible and fantasize about walking off and leaving it all. We may imagine that a new partner who will resonate with the "new" us is just what we need. And our current partner may be going through the same thing.

Add this developmental stage to the worries about children, money, and work, and it's easy to see where the term "midlife crisis" comes from! Fortunately, most people negotiate this phase of their lives with good sense and good instincts. Maybe a change really *is* needed: a shift in career, an exciting new sport or hobby, new activities with your partner.

As always, our dreams not only tell us that we have new and emerging material to enrich our lives, but if we allow it, our dreams will help us make some of the changes in a positive way.

> **Dreamwork**
>
> If you find yourself craving change—and dreaming about it!—talk with your partner or friends and imagine ways to make the needed changes. The danger comes when we acknowledge the need for change and keep our feelings under wraps until we "blow up" and make hasty decisions that we later may regret.

Where Did Those Darn Kids Go?

Just when you think you have the hang of parenting, the children take off on their own quests. The house is empty of children, for the time being anyway, and now you have time to do what you've been putting off. Research continues to confirm that couples report these years as the happiest of their marriage. This makes sense: The biggest job you have had (rearing your children or establishing your career) is over and now you have a little more money and a lot more time. Those midlife yearnings can be addressed, and you may look at your partner with new eyes, someone to have fun with in new ways—in your dreams and in real life!

> *I am in a warm ocean, swimming at sunset. All at once I am fishing and I catch a huge marlin. I am about to gut it when it looks at me and says, "You don't have to do that." I jump into the ocean with it where I release it, thinking I can go to a restaurant for dinner.*

In this 50-year-old man's dream, we see that he is eschewing his more masculine/ hunting behaviors in favor of a more stereotypically feminine nurturing mode of being. Because of it being "sunset," he seems to be aware of time's passage. Gail Sheehy comments that as men age, as they attain a level of respect and mastery at work, and as their children leave the nest, they are more able to express their "softer" sides. Perhaps they become more expressive.

Women, usually more constricted (especially if children were a part of the partnership), are freer to explore the world in bold new ways at this stage of life. They often feel more confident and full of energy. Dreams in which they find hidden rooms, money, or other valuables are not uncommon.

Sociologists are just beginning to study the growing minority of adults who have chosen not to have children, so it's hard to say how that decision impacts on a "midlife crisis." In our experience, if the decision has been well thought out (for women this usually happens in the late 30s or early 40s), then any attendant period of mourning has been worked through. This mourning period, while not experienced by all women and men, is a natural, transient response to the giving up of societal and internal expectations to have children.

This may also be the time that adults change careers. The familiar workplace becomes monotonous or the irritations that they were able to ignore when they had so much family stuff on the brain now loom front and center. It's time for a change.

Do You Really Want to Spend Your Life Doing This?

I am in a large parking garage. The strange thing is that all of the cars are running. Even stranger, I don't even think of that as odd. In the middle of the garage, there is a beautiful sports car and my wife is in it. She looks beautiful and she is waving to me. As I start toward her, the running cars all begin to move to block my way ... like something out of a horror story. I wake up not knowing if I made it to her or not.

This is a classic dream illustrating the paradox of the desire to change direction and the threat of doing so all being experienced at the same time. This dreamer wants to spend his productive time another way, but has a deep fear of what he will lose if he forges in another direction. His dream is telling him that he is hard at work solving this dilemma.

Way Too Young for Menopause

The way that women look at and experience approaching *menopause* has changed drastically in the last decade—and both the medical and social results of these changes may well have a positive impact on the dreams experienced during this stage of life. Both traditional Western medical treatments and more integrative approaches are available to help alleviate the discomforts women might experience as they make this transition, and women and men alike are now almost expecting the second half of life to be as vital and interesting as the first.

One of the most disturbing of the menopausal symptoms is the hot flash (or flush) that results from the difficulty the body has maintaining even body temperature. During the day, hot flashes are irritating; at night they may prevent good sleep. The discomfort of the hot flash and the resulting wetness of the linens may wake up women more than once during the night. Needless to say, this interferes with the sleep cycle, cutting into both deep, restorative sleep and dream time. Scientists have noted that menopausal women take longer to fall asleep, wake up more frequently, and have somewhat less REM sleep than younger women.

Because the science of both sleep and menopause is complex, there is much to discover about these intricate processes. Still, it is likely that fluctuating hormones and the resulting menopausal symptoms may lead to disturbing dreams or dream fragments. We have seen that the brain doesn't differentiate between somatically experienced events and dreamed events. If you're dreaming of being chased by a tiger, your brain will respond accordingly and, although you are not likely to get up and run, you may start to sweat and not stop until you wake up. The good news is that knowledge about this life stage is growing every day and so are the possibilities for relief, which range from holistic to Western traditional hormone replacement therapy.

Although menopause marks the beginning of the "second half" of life rather dramatically for women, men are also subjected to reminders that time just keeps on ticking—and these reminders may just show up in their dreams.

Dream Dictionary

Menopause refers to the end of a woman's fertility and is marked by the end of her menstrual periods. It typically occurs around the age of 51, but related biological changes can begin in the early 40s (called perimenopause) and continue through the 50s.

Wake Up!

If you're a woman and you're dreaming of being hot, smothered, exhausted, and so on, and you are waking up in a sweat, it may be time to ask your physician for blood tests to see if you are entering perimenopause.

Hair Today, Gone Tomorrow

Just when women are wondering what's going on with their bodies, their partners or husbands or brothers are wondering why it takes so little time to comb their hair in the morning and why their foreheads seem to be growing just a little bit every day!

Anthropologists tell us thinning hair may once have signaled old age to our shorter-lived ancestors. Today, however, the balding process more often comes as a great shock: "I can't possibly be old enough to be losing my hair; that's for those guys in the hair commercials on television!"

Dreams of "losing face" or of one's teeth falling out might reflect a concern with one's changing appearance and of the loss of the "old self." Additionally, dreams with themes of impotence might indicate that, like Samson, a loss of hair (or of a woman's fertility) signals a loss of sexual power. It may take some time and education to realize that reaching menopause or finding a bald spot as large as the moon does not mean you are no longer sexually appealing.

The Sandwich Dilemma

Sometime during the late middle years, the phone call may come. Our parents' accountant is frustrated because Dad can't seem to get all of the needed documents together at tax time. Or Mom has slowed down so much that she seems to have come to a near standstill.

Welcome to the "sandwich" years. Many people have to deal with their parents' failing health at the same time they are paying off the children's college loans or coping with their own needs. With this comes the initially shocking role reversal. This is the first time you realize that you now must parent Mom or Dad or both, rather than them parenting you! The weight of three generations rests on your shoulders.

No surprise here, but dreams experienced in this period often involve themes of escape—part of us wishes to rid ourselves of this enormous responsibility and sad knowledge. In waking life we're probably as dutiful as can be, but in our dreams we're free to run naked through a field, take a plane to nowhere, or pack Mom and Dad off on a never-ending cruise.

> *I am swimming in a crystal-clear lake. It is a lovely day and suddenly I am pulled under the water by a whirlpool. It is terrifying. I don't think that I will make it out alive! I wake soaked in sweat, my heart pounding, and all of my problems rush into my mind. How will I cope with it all?*

This man's dream shows that as we navigate our middle years, we have to envision our lives in new ways so that we won't get sucked down into the whirlpool. Our families, our work, and our bodies change—there is much that is positive in our lives, but it may take different forms than we are used to.

Our dreams are most helpful in accomplishing this task. When the whirlpool dream changes into one in which a friend or partner is there with a boat to rescue us and take us off to Tahiti, we know that we're doing a good job in negotiating this part of our life.

Loving Me, Loving You: Who Cares, and How It Affects Your Dreams

Where are you in life, at what stage? Or are you hovering somewhere between stages as we have described them? Early adulthood, just starting out? Midlife, looking both behind and ahead? Do you depend on others, or do others depend on you? The balance of caring in your life affects your joys and challenges, accomplishments and limitations, plans and worries.

You already know your family tree. So now we're going to craft your caring tree—a visual representation of your life's circle of love and responsibility. All you need is a piece of paper and a pen or pencil.

1. Write your name in the center of your piece of paper.

2. Around your name, write the names of people who are close to you—family and friends. Arrange the names in circles of closeness, with those who are closest to you in the first circle around your name.

3. For each person who cares for you, draw an arrow from that person's name to your name.

4. For each person that you care for, draw an arrow from your name to that person's name.

5. If the person cares for you and you care for the person (in exchange or on balance), draw arrows in both directions.

6. Look at the pattern of relationships in your life that the arrows illustrate. Do you mostly care for, or do others mostly care for you? How interdependent are these relationships?

7. Next to each person's name, note whether he or she shows up regularly in your dreams. In what ways do they make dream appearances? Write some comments about their dream appearances next to their names.

Family (including friends) relationships often are complex and interdependent. It might be difficult for you to determine the direction of caring. The visual representation of this dynamic in your life can lead you to insights with regard to your dreams.

The Least You Need to Know

♦ In our 20s, we try on various identities and partners. Our dreams are often filled with fragments of characters and places, reflecting this not-quite-fully-formed phase.

♦ The dreams of our 30s and 40s reflect our concerns with family and career. Conflicts between what we hoped for and reality are played out in our dreams.

♦ When we enter our 50s our life situations evolve, our dreams often reflect concerns and worries that we have about our family relationships and how they affect us or how we feel about them.

♦ As we move through what psychologists call "young old age" we find that we are freer to explore parts of ourselves that were put on hold due to family and work responsibilities.

Chapter 18

Mixing Memory with Desire: Maturity and Dreams

In This Chapter

- ◆ Sleep changes in late life
- ◆ Setting the stage for restful sleep
- ◆ Body imperfect: Coping with physical and health changes
- ◆ Dreams of renewal and opportunity

Remember your Great Aunt Bessie? How she fell asleep by 8 P.M. in the recliner, but was up and at 'em at 4 A.M. every day? Maybe you're approaching or standing at the threshold of those golden years yourself now, and you find that you're transitioning from night owl to early bird ... just like Great Aunt Bessie. As we'll explore in this chapter, your sleep patterns begin to change as you age and so too will both the amount of time you spend dreaming and the subjects of your dreams.

Early to Bed, Early to Rise ...

All along the span of a lifetime, from infancy to old age, sleep cycles change. By the mid-40s or so, many people begin going to bed a little earlier than they used to, and their sleep tends to be more fragmented. These changes are due in great part to naturally occurring biological and circadian shifts. Other changes of aging also come into play, from the typical aches and discomforts that might make it more challenging to relax and fall asleep to the health conditions that might become more prevalent with advancing age.

> ### Life Is But a Dream
>
> According to the U.S. Administration on Aging, 35 million Americans are age 65 or older— 1 in 8, or 12 percent of the overall population. More people are living longer than any time in history, and demographers project that in less than 30 years 1 in 4 Americans will be age 65 or older.

However, contrary to popular belief, the need for sleep doesn't decrease with age! The pattern of sleep may change, but the need for sleep does not. Brain waves both in sleep and while awake change as you age. The older you are, the more time you spend in Stages 1 and 2 of sleep and the less time you spend in Stages 3 and 4. This means less REM sleep—each REM cycle becomes shorter, and the total number of REM cycles decreases. This means not only that sleep becomes less restorative, but also that it affords less time for dreaming.

Now I Lay Me Down to Sleep

Because deep sleep decreases with age, it makes sense that nighttime awakenings increase. The older you get, the more sensitive you become to nighttime interruptions both from within and outside your body. Aches, discomforts, noises, and even a full bladder can be enough to keep you from falling asleep or rouse you from sleep. And naturally, getting less sleep during the night would lead to increased daytime drowsiness accompanied by a need to nap more. This is one way the body attempts to get the sleep it needs.

You might be tempted to turn to over-the-counter sleep medications to combat sleeplessness. First, though, get a thorough physical exam from your doctor to determine whether there are underlying health issues. It's more effective to treat the cause, and often this is simple to do. Although sleep medications generally are safe when taken as directed or prescribed, they can (like all medications) have undesired side effects. If your doctor gives your health the all clear, try some nonpharmacological remedies to help you fall and stay asleep, such as:

   ◆ Eat your evening meal at least three or four hours before bedtime, so your body isn't quite so busy when you're ready to hit the pillow. If you're hungry right before bed, have a small glass of milk, some cheese, or even some turkey. These foods contain natural substances that induce relaxation. Keep this snack small, though.

◆ Take a short walk an hour or two before you plan to turn in. The fresh air will help you clear your mind, and the gentle activity releases stress in your muscles and your body. Avoid strenuous exercise in the evening, however, as it tends to increase the levels of hormones and other chemicals that stimulate your body's systems. You can make your morning walks brisk and invigorating, but keep the evening ones low-key.

◆ Practice yoga postures or meditations that help you reduce stress and free your thoughts from the busy-ness of the day.

◆ Make sure your sleeping space supports restful sleep and pleasant dreams. Is your mattress comfortable? Are your sheets and bedclothes soothing? Is the environment quiet? Are you warm or cool enough?

◆ Go to bed 30 to 45 minutes earlier to give yourself more time to fall asleep.

> **CAUTION — Wake Up!**
>
> Sleep disorders that become more common with increasing age include sleep apnea (breathing disturbances), restless legs syndrome ("crawling" sensations that cause the person to keep moving the legs), and REM behavior disorder (unknowingly acting out dream activity). There are medical treatments for these problems; see your doctor if you are experiencing any of them.

Can I Trade In This Body for a New Model?

The effects of wear and tear begin to show in chronic health conditions that interfere with sleep such as osteoarthritis, gastroesophageal reflux disorder (GERD), and cardio-vascular disease. Nocturia—frequent nighttime urination that can be caused by weakened pelvic floor muscles in women or enlarged prostate gland in men (as well as by many medications)—can keep you "up and going" and longing for uninterrupted sleep.

Certain medical conditions become more prevalent with increasing age, too, such as heart disease, rheumatoid arthritis, Parkinson's disease, Alzheimer's disease, and cancer. Diseases that affect the brain, such as brain cancer, Alzheimer's, and Parkinson's, have a great impact on sleep disturbance because of the direct effect the diseases have on the areas of the brain that govern sleep.

> **CAUTION — Wake Up!**
>
> As we age, we can be prone to clinical depression due to feelings of isolation, loss of our friends and loved ones, and a loss of independence. But prolonged depression is not a normal part of aging. Please see your doctor and a psychotherapist for help if you feel you are depressed, especially if you have experienced clinical depression earlier in your life.

Often, the medications prescribed for addressing these conditions affect sleep and, consequently, affect dreaming. Levodopa, a medication prescribed to treat Parkinson's disease, can cause especially vivid dreams. The antipsychotic medications sometimes prescribed for people with Alzheimer's disease can have a similar effect or even cause nightmares. Theophylline, a drug used in the treatment of asthma, can disturb and alter sleep patterns. Drugs used for cardiovascular disease can make falling asleep difficult and increase nighttime awakenings.

Pain itself disrupts sleep, but so do the medications to treat it. Narcotic painkillers such as codeine, propoxyphene, and hydrocodone decrease REM sleep and impair daytime performance. Many antidepressants can cause insomnia, while others cause drowsiness. There are some antidepressants that can cause either, depending on the dosage and the individual. Antianxiety medications may cause drowsiness, but interfere with the sleep cycle and tend to reduce REM sleep and dreaming. On the other hand, new research shows that people with fibromyalgia never *enter* stage 3 and 4 sleep. New medications are being tested to help these people cycle through *all* of the sleep stages. Sleep stages 3 and 4 are the stages of muscle replenishment, hence fibromyalgia "muscle knots" that feel like lying on marbles keep the sleeper awake, perpetuating a vicious cycle.

The good news is that if you report your sleep symptoms to your doctor, he or she often can prescribe different medications that may not disturb your sleep as much. New medications that may not have these side effects come onto the market all the time, so it's worth talking with your doctor if you're taking medicine for health conditions and you're having trouble sleeping. After all, if you can't sleep you can't dream!

Dreamwork _____

Light significantly affects the circadian rhythms that regulate our sleep cycles. Yet as we age, we may be prevented from getting enough light either because we become more housebound or because we develop cataracts, which block out much of that light we need. So it's likely that spending more time outdoors and tending to any vision problems can help improve sleep difficulties with few, if any, adverse side effects.

Second Chances

At one time retirement, gray hair, and stiffening joints meant our lives were on the decline. Not so anymore. While we can't put an actual numerical age on when we enter the "second-chances years," we can definitely say that most of us come to a point in our lives when we carefully weigh where we've been and what we've done and decide what, if anything, needs changing. And then we try to do it. But this time around we have the wisdom of our years to guide us, and our dreams often reveal this.

Dream Date for the Renewal Years

For those who remain married to that same guy or girl who swept you off your feet back in your youth, your later life together can be a time of great satisfaction and joy. You've negotiated your differences and found a way to respect and remain loyal to each other and yourselves. You've persevered. You've built a life together, which means you share a history—of pain, of pleasure, of dreams.

> *Daryl was in the garden. I looked out the bedroom window and saw that he'd picked all the flowers. I was very angry because I'd told him to pick the weeds. He came into the house and explained that he wanted to have these in our home. He assured me that new ones would grow the next day! There were bushels of flowers. I began pulling out every vase we had in the house.*

Jim, Daryl's partner of 20 years, had this dream recently. Jim came to believe that the dream was about disagreeing with someone's choices (cutting the flowers) but accepting them anyway. He saw his acceptance of the flowers and the statement that more would grow the next day (such a miracle!) as a metaphor for his overriding trust in his life partner.

Perhaps, though, you and your first partner didn't stay together, due either to a divorce or to death, or you're one of the increasing numbers of single-for-life kind of people. Now, as you're getting older, you're exploring a new relationship (or two), and you have the excitement of romance to help sustain you.

Wake Up!

Don't assume symptoms like mood swings and mild illness are simply side effects of aging. Depression is very common in late life, more common than either doctors or patients often recognize. If you're experiencing symptoms of depression—unexpected weight loss or gain, appetite changes, withdrawal from the people you love, profound sadness over a loss that lasts 6 months or longer, among others—see your doctor and a therapist for help.

> *I am dreaming of a piano. Bart, my new husband, suddenly appears and sits down to play. I tell him, "No, that's my first husband's piano." He protests and begins to play "Fly Me to the Moon," a song my first husband loved. But even though it is the same song, it sounds completely different.*

In this dream, a woman recognizes that change is inevitable, and that to accept those changes along with the also inevitable passage of time will offer new chances to love and to hope.

In the "younger" of the older years—say, 55 to 75—men and women can feel rejuvenated from the changes life brings. A woman who has gone through menopause is no longer on a hormonal roller coaster. She often has the "postmenopausal zest" that author Gail Sheehy speaks about, as well as the opportunity to come to terms with stage-of-life issues. Perhaps she's grown more independent as her need to nurture her children lessens. Perhaps she's made peace with her new role as "older but wiser," and said a healthy farewell to aspects of herself that were more prominent in earlier years.

Men also go through physical changes that prompt psychological ones as they age. Energy levels and sexual urges may lessen, which may be especially troublesome for men if, in heterosexual relationships, their wives are feeling rejuvenated just as they start to slow down.

As men deal with their aches and pains and other physical changes, they may find that they begin to rely more on other aspects of their personality that society had perhaps discouraged in their younger days. Many men become more demonstrative and emotional. A man whose self-concept was largely based on his physical prowess might discover that he has more opinions to share about politics, family, and even the meaning of life than he ever gave himself credit for having.

Looking Ahead

What are the now-aging Baby Boomers looking forward to choosing for themselves? Not usually a rocking chair or knitting needles, that's for sure. Data from the U.S. Bureau of Census and other sources tell us that Americans want to stay busy even after retirement. College enrollment for students 65 and older continues to climb. Many retirement-age people volunteer their time and talents for humanitarian causes, working at childcare centers, schools, homeless shelters, animal shelters, and other community support organizations. Others take part-time jobs in areas they want to learn more about, or do things they've always wanted to do but couldn't afford when supporting a family was the leading priority. And some use retirement as an opportunity to delve into an entirely new career. It seems that, more than ever, retirement promises flexibility.

Dreamwork

Keeping a diary—to track both dreams and daily life events—can be especially rewarding at this time of life. It can become a record of change as well as an opportunity for reflection and assessment.

Mature adults are more fit, more active—and more competitive—than ever before. Masters sports organizations (for serious athletes over 50 years old) are seeing a surge in membership. The fitness industry reports that nearly 1 in 4 health club members today are age 55 and older, up from just 1 in 10 in 1990—and making this the fastest growing segment of the industry. Regular physical exercise has numerous benefits, not the least of which is improved sleep.

Dreams at this stage of life therefore reflect both hope and renewal in addition to the "expected" themes of loss and adjustment. You might dream of a stream drying up (representing a lost opportunity such as the ability to have biological children), but then discover diamonds in the riverbed, which suggests the uncovering of hidden resources and opportunities.

Around the World in 18 Days

Remember when you were a child and a day seemed like *forever* or even longer? Didn't a year seem like an eternity? Have you noticed that after a certain age, the time seems to fly by? The days don't have enough hours in them, the weekend seems like it never happened, the years melt into one another?

As we age, we begin to understand that we are mortal. Our grandparents didn't live forever, our parents don't—and we won't. This is a painful lesson. When we are very young, we lack the ability to grasp this. We are at the center of our universe and believe we have control over it. But as we age, as we turn 55, 60, or 70, we are aware that our time and resources are finite. Hopefully this spurs us to live life to the fullest, to take that whirlwind tour, to try something we've never allowed ourselves to do before.

Life Is But a Dream
It's not just your imagination: Your perception of the passage of time has a biological basis. According to recent research from Clinch Valley College at the University of Virginia, your brain's internal clock actually slows as you age, altering your sense of time and making it seem to pass more quickly. A decline in the production of the neuro-transmitter dopamine, which helps regulate the clock, may be the culprit.

Just as this time in our lives can remind us to take a chance, do something different, or reward ourselves in a way we have not allowed, this phase of life can feel a bit out of control. Certainly it does to this dreamer, a 65-year-old woman struggling with major decisions: to sell the house in which she's reared her family, to move closer to her grown son, or to move far away to a warm climate.

I am playing bridge with my friends, just like we've done on Tuesdays for the last 35 years. But the game has changed; it is now a shell game. The shells, under which there is a gold coin, are moving faster and faster. I want to choose the right one. I really want the coin. I am scared of picking the wrong one, and it is getting harder and harder to remember which shell contains the coin. They are going ever faster. What has happened to my bridge game?

While this dream did not solve the dreamer's particular problem, it did let her know that she was hard at work trying to figure out how she should play her hand.

Taking Stock

As we move through the early older years to the middle older years, we begin to assess our lives in a new way. What have we done? Or not done? How well? How poorly? What have we left out? Author Erik Erikson calls this time "Integrity v. Despair." According to Erikson, it's at this juncture that we replay our decisions and actions and feel regret or happiness, and probably some of both. But because he formulated these thoughts before we started to think of old age as a time of renewal and new opportunity (thanks to modern medicine), he didn't quite focus on the wonderful ability for an older person to correct some of the errors, thus turning regret into satisfaction.

Now, if we see corrections or internal compensations that need to be made, we have some time to make them. We can make amends, even to those who have preceded us in death. That is the spiritual part of us, and it becomes more prominent as we age.

As we become more philosophical and spiritual, issues that we perhaps have not thought about in years may surface. Perhaps you had a falling out with your sister and haven't talked to her in 35 years. You've managed to avoid contacting her because you've been so busy raising kids or working hard. Every so often an uncomfortable twinge overtook you, but you just made yourself that much busier in response.

But in the later years of life, you realize that the time has come to deal with the situation once and for all. If there are feelings of guilt in your life, you must face them and cope with them now. Here's your chance to turn guilt or regret into something positive. As we've mentioned, guilt is functional only as a road map to setting something right.

One opportunity to "put things to right" comes with the arrival of grandchildren. Indeed, it is through relationships with grandchildren that older adults can work through some issues of parenting that have troubled them for years. If you have some regrets about how you related to your children—that you didn't spend enough time with them or failed to support them in certain ways—you have a kind of second chance with their children.

As is true for other times in your life, your dreams can help you explore some of these more philosophical and emotional issues—if you pay attention!

Dreaming of Loved Ones Who Are Gone

Dreams of loved ones who've passed away occur partly as an expression of grief and partly as a way to help us accept our own mortality. Many people don't feel upset about these dreams. In fact, they begin to understand that death is acceptable after—even a reward for—a life well lived. Unless they have unfinished business to attend to with a departed friend or relative, most people feel cheered and touched by dreaming of a loved one who has died. And some dreamers are sure that they are visitations from loved ones rather than dreams.

Dreamy
In Naomi Epel's *Writer's Dreaming* (Carol Southern Books, 1993), the poet Maya Angelou wrote, "There's a phrase in West Africa called 'deep talk.' When a person is informed about a situation, an older person will often use a parable, an axiom, then add to the end of the axiom, 'Take that as deep talk.' Meaning that you will never find the answer. You can continue to go down deeper and deeper. Dreams may be deep talk."

The older years are a complex interaction of our todays, yesterdays, and tomorrows. Our earlier older years afford us the opportunity to shed our fears and try things we've avoided all our lives. In the middle older years, we become very aware of time passing and are given the opportunity to review our lives and change or enhance what we can. In our last years, we can continue to grow and change, but this includes a growing acceptance of our mortality.

Dreaming of our friends and relatives who have died is one very important way that we learn to accept our own passing with grace and strength. In short, there is a lot of time and change between 50 and 90, just as there is a lot of change between birth and 40! We tend to move through this lengthy time in a fairly orderly, somewhat predictable way—barring natural catastrophes or life-threatening illness.

Often it is in the second half of life that we develop our personal philosophy or spirituality. Our deeper questions about the meaning of life and the place a higher being might have in it comes to the fore slowly but surely during these years. We might ask, "What is the meaning or the purpose of my life and how do I want to express it?" Maybe that is why someone who has been an accountant goes to the seminary or volunteers as a wildlife docent.

When the Aches and Pains Come and Don't Go

We all die, and most of us become ill before we die. The quality of the life we've led usually determines the amount of grace that we summon in order to deal with our final illnesses and death. If we are connected with loved ones and mostly satisfied with how we have lived, we are able to look physical death in the face and use our coping skills to negotiate this final passage.

> **CAUTION**
>
> **Wake Up!** _____
>
> Behavioral techniques such as relaxation, meditation, visualization, and biofeedback have been proven to be very effective in treating the anxiety and depression that occurs with chronic pain. The result is improved sleep, which, in turn, improves one's mood.

> **Life Is But a Dream**
>
> People who are struggling with aches and pains may find that they recall fewer dreams. This may be due to the effects of pain medications or reduced sleep secondary to their physical discomfort. It is important to work with your health-care provider to address the pain and the inability to get enough sleep.

People who have terminal illnesses or chronic pain should be *listened* to and respected when it comes to managing their lives. All of us do better in any difficult circumstance when we have a measure of control.

As always, be open to your dreams. It is common to dream of events in your life and people you have loved. Many people who are going through the prelude to death and are able to talk about it tell visitors about those who have died (or religious figures) that they are seeing or hearing or that are waiting for them "on the other side." For those people who believe in some form of life after death, perhaps when we are close to death we drift back and forth across the line. That is, we are living in one dimension part of the time and another at other times.

As we lose some of our physical abilities, we might dream of times when we were younger and able to skydive, dance the rumba, or run fast. Our minds are timeless, and in our dreams we can still do all these things. As you might expect, these dreams can engender both excitement as we perform daring physical feats, and disappointment (once we wake up) over lost prowess.

What's Next?

Is there life after death? Do you believe in heaven? Reincarnation? Do your dreams reflect that belief? In many cultures, dreaming of flying or of unfamiliar places is proof of a past—or future—life. The majority of religions believe that death is a transitory state, a stop on the never-ending road of existence. Our dreams may be glimpses into where we are on that road. They may have much to say about where we've been and what's to come.

Life Passages and Dream Journeys

Try this exercise, no matter what your age. List the major pivotal points in your life. Here are some examples:

- Leaving home

- First job

- Marriage

- Having children

- Loss of relationship, friend, parent

- Career decisions or changes

- Financial booms or busts

- Moving

- Illness

Next, write down how old you were and how you coped with each new stage. How did it feel? Did you have the support of friends and family, or did you isolate yourself? Did you cope by burying your nose in a book, running 100 miles, or crying on your best friend's shoulder? After you have done this, look for any emerging patterns regarding how you deal with life's changes. Pay special attention to the dreams you have as you think about the pivotal points in your life.

The Least You Need to Know

- Sleep patterns change with advancing age, but the amount and quality of sleep that we need remain the same.

- Health conditions as well as the medications taken to treat them can interfere with sleep and with dreams. Often, switching to different medications can mitigate these disturbances.

- Dreams of loved ones who have died are common and often comforting.

- Relaxation techniques and sleep preparation can make it easier to fall, and stay, asleep—and to dream.

- Depression is not *natural* in a person of *any* age. Psychotherapy and possibly medication are important for anyone who is depressed.

Part 5

Dreams and Clairvoyance

Sometimes our dreams defy conventional understanding. How do we explain dreams that seem to predict the future, telepathic dreams, or dreams in which dead friends and relatives stop by to visit? Through the centuries many have tried, yet there is much we still do not know about the functions of the mind and the power of dreaming. Can dreams truly transcend the barriers of physical existence?

In this section, we take a look at some of our most common uncommon dreams. We also explore the world of lucid dreaming—the technique that helps you have "waking" dreams and direct their outcomes with conscious intent!

Chapter 19

ESP, Precognition, and Prophecy

In This Chapter

◆ Paranormal dreams

◆ Sending (and receiving) dream messages

◆ Dreaming of past lives and future events

◆ Applying dream messages in waking life

Can our dreams predict the future? Can we connect to past-life experiences in our dreams? Can we "send" someone images to dream about? Some people say they do all of these things in their dreams; they believe dreaming is a platform for psychic communication. Insomuch as dreams themselves often transcend the boundaries of our tangible senses, these are the kinds of dreams we can categorize as truly extrasensory.

Are You Psychic?

Do you know the doorbell is going to ring 10 minutes before the chimes go off? Can you tell the sex of an unborn baby merely by looking at a pregnant woman's abdomen? Do you often know what people are going to say even before they've opened their mouths to speak? Are you just incredibly perceptive, lucky, or are you tuned into some sort of communication that others aren't?

Psychics have held roles of prominence throughout history. Nearly all indigenous cultures revere the seer, the shaman, the wise man or woman who has this special gift. Perhaps that's because once upon a time, science and magic were more closely related. But as science became more and more rational, the magical aspects of our lives were dismissed or suppressed.

Dreamy

In the fall of 1913, psychoanalyst Carl Jung had a vision in which he saw a massive European flood, complete with the rubble of civilization and massive numbers of people floating by in the muddy water. Then the water turned to blood. In August of the next year, World War I broke out.

American psychic Edgar Cayce, known as "the sleeping prophet," was perhaps a twentieth-century equivalent to an ancient seer. Cayce was noted for slipping into a deep sleep state during which he received messages from the dead through his dreams, many of which gave glimpses of the future. Like the ancient Greeks flocked to the temples of Aesculapius for healing dreams, people swarmed to Cayce for dream insights that would reveal cures for their health ailments. Cayce also believed that a person's own dreams were an abundant source of insight and information for those who could learn to interpret and understand their metaphorical messages.

Beyond the Conventional: Paranormal Dreams

The apparent ability of some people to communicate outside the realm of the five tangible senses has intrigued humankind forever. Husband and wife researchers Joseph B. Rhine and Louisa E. Rhine began using the terms "paranormal" (outside the typical experience or explanation), "parapsychology" (beyond the conventions of established psychology), and "extrasensory perception" or ESP (beyond the realm of the five physical senses) during their research studies at Duke University in the late 1920s to describe this ability. They conducted dozens of experiments over six decades that, although they didn't provide conclusive findings, built the foundation for research that was to follow.

In 1962, psychiatrist Montague Ullman conducted one of the first modern studies of dreams and the paranormal—the Maimonides Project on Paranormal Dreams (named after Maimonides Hospital in Brooklyn, where the study took place). This study became a landmark exploration of ESP, dreams, and the paranormal. After a decade of research, Ullman and colleague Stanley Krippler published their findings in the 1973 classic *Dream Telepathy: Experiments in Nocturnal ESP.* Their conclusions? There is statistically valid evidence to support the existence of paranormal dreams.

No research has yet proved or disproved the existence of psychic dreams. Some scientists believe that what we identify as paranormal dreams actually reflect a dreamer's ability to connect more intensely with his or her memories and subconscious thoughts and to be aware of these connections upon awakening. The dreams that result are not psychic but instead delve more deeply into the brain's data stores. Other scientists believe there is another level of perception—extrasensory—that we can tap into, and that this happens in our dreams because our dreams are less inhibited. However, what is certain is that people do have dreams that they seem to share with others, that appear to foretell events, or in which they communicate with others.

In your waking life, you might experience intuition as those hunches you have every day: The stoplight is about to turn green, your favorite restaurant is closed for plumbing repairs, you call your former college roommate who's just about to leave on a business trip to the city where you live. Paranormal dreams, or psychic dreams, fit into a class of dreams that includes:

◆ Telepathic dreams, in which one dream image is sent to and experienced by another dreamer

◆ Precognitive dreams, which correctly depict a future event (also called prophetic dreams)

◆ Past-life dreams, in which the dreamer experiences living as a different person in another time and place

◆ Clairvoyant dreams, in which the dreamer correctly obtains information about the description or location of an object or a person

Dream Telepathy

Dr. Montague Ullman devised a three-person experiment consisting of a sender, a receiver, and a monitor. The receiver and sender, both monitored on EEGs, went to sleep in separate locked rooms. When the receiver entered into REM sleep, the monitor woke the sender and she tried to transmit an image (usually from a painting) to the receiver by concentrating hard on it during the receiver's REM sleep cycle. After 15 minutes, the monitor woke the receiver and taped the dreams he remembered. This experiment was repeated several times per night. According to Stephen Phillip Policoff in *The Dreamer's Companion*, of the 12 studies completed from 1966 to 1972, 9 showed considerable accuracy between the images sent and received.

In telepathic dreams, dreamers seem to communicate with one another. This communication might occur with intent, as in Dr. Ullman's experiments, or spontaneously.

Generally the two dreamers have a close bond of some sort. It's common for lovers separated by distance and circumstance to feel as though they visit with each other in their dreams—the ultimate dream date, perhaps! Siblings, friends, and parents and children also report experiencing dream communication between them. These dreams might convey messages or information or be shared experiences such as going to a park or to visit a mutual acquaintance.

Shared Dreams

Some people report shared dreams with someone they are close to when they didn't agree beforehand to dream of a specific object or historical period. Instead, they both "just happened" to have a dream about a clay pot that shattered into a thousand pieces or a Ferris wheel that flew through the sky toward the moon. That the meaning behind the specific symbols might indicate how attuned they are to each other is probable, but the fascinating question remains: How on earth was the information communicated?

Who dreams up the dreams? Did both people subliminally register a clay pot while they were having a "shattering" argument that morning? Or were they somehow in contact during REM sleep? This second hypothesis would be considered ESP or paranormal, since it goes beyond what we currently know about our senses.

Dreamwork

Have you and your significant other ever had a shared dream? Did it make you feel even closer? Or … did you feel intruded upon? How do you explain the telepathic dream?

Regardless, the usefulness of dream telepathy can be to alert friends, lovers, or others with whom you are close that there are issues worth talking about while you are awake. Maybe you need to tell one another that the fight you had in the pottery store went too far; you went to sleep feeling a part of you was shattered.

Your Dream Connections

You can attempt to structure telepathic or shared dreams yourself. To experiment with either or both, start by following these steps. As you become more curious about or comfortable with the dream experiences you have as a result, you can craft your own processes that tap into the relationships you have with the others you choose to involve.

1. An hour or so before going to bed, engage in a conscious approach to clearing your mind and body of the day's stresses: Meditate, do yoga, go for a short walk, take a warm bath. If you have an herb pouch, fill it with anise or lavender to encourage restful sleep and with some caraway to help you remember your dreams, and put it under your pillow.

2. Choose a recipient. Who do you want to send a dream message to? Is this person participating (also trying to send you a dream message), or is this person unaware of your plan to send a dream message?

3. Choose a simple message, such as the image of a tangible object. Hold this object in your hands, if you can, and experience it with your physical senses—see it, touch it, smell it, hear it, even taste it (or imagine what it would taste like). Spend about five minutes doing this.

4. Envision the message traveling to your chosen recipient. Experience the message entering the person's dream and becoming part of his or her dream experience. Spend about five minutes doing this.

5. Write your intentions in your dream journal. Describe the message you are trying to send, and how you envision the other person receiving the message.

6. Make yourself comfortable, and try to have images of the object and the recipient in your thoughts as you drift off to sleep.

7. Write in your dream journal immediately upon waking, whether in the middle of the night or in the morning. Write everything you can recall about your dream as well as the circumstances of your awakening.

8. Ask your intended recipient about his or her dreams. If the two of you planned a shared dream, then exchange dream journal notes and observations. If you chose to try sending a message to someone who didn't know you were doing so, ask the person to describe any dreams or dreamlike experiences.

Were you successful? Be alert to dream metaphors, puns, and symbols. If you tried to send an image of a stuffed bunny and your intended recipient dreamed a giant turtle was chasing him (à la the childhood fable "The Tortoise and the Hare"), you might have succeeded. Or perhaps in your recipient's dream everything was yellow and blue—the colors of your stuffed bunny. Try again!

Return to the Past: Previous Lives?

Do you think you've lived before? For a large percentage of the world's population, the answer would be "yes, absolutely. And I will again." In our Western society, reincarnation often isn't taken seriously. It is thought to threaten our more linear belief system, or is considered the sole province of Shirley MacLaine. But there are many people who feel they have re-experienced past lives through their dreams.

It was a long, involved dream about living in a city with cobblestone streets and horses and buggies. The smells, colors, and sounds were all so real. Somehow I knew it was London in the 1740s. I was dressed in a red velvet gown, the corset was very tight. I carried a cloth purse. I opened it to buy some apples from a peasant woman with a dirty face. I felt sorry for her and thought I might give her an extra shilling. But I decided against it.

> **Dream Dictionary**
>
> **Karma** is the Buddhist principle of cosmic rewards or punishments for the things we've done—or left undone—in past lives. It teaches that we can prepare for a fortunate incarnation in the next life by living a good life this time around, and by working to heal mistakes we made in previous lives.

This may or may not be an actual past-life dream. This dreamer believes it is. But here's what's important for our task of understanding dreams: What she takes from the dream are lessons for her current life. If the aim of reincarnation is to improve *karma* and become enlightened, then this dream offers her that opportunity. In her current life she is stingy with herself. She doesn't let herself eat right or take time out to exercise; she's forever working for the benefit of others. This dream message may be that she needs to give aid to the parts of herself that are barely scraping by.

A Chance to Change the Future: Prophetic Dreams

Prophetic dreams are like blockbuster movies, while precognitive dreams are more like small, independent films. Prophetic dreams predict major future events and, if heeded, give us a chance to intervene and change the course of the world's events. Precognitive dreams are usually on a small scale and concern more personal matters.

One challenge in researching dreams that seem to foretell the future is that the only way to label a dream as prophetic is after the fact; the event dreamed of has to occur, and then you can say the dream was a prophecy. But, like all paranormal phenomena, it's hard to prove or disprove, even in retrospect.

If you'd like to explore your precognitive and prophetic dreams, it's important to keep a detailed dream diary to see what, if anything, may have triggered these dreams. If you notice what seems to be a high correlation between your dreams and events that happen days, weeks, or months later, perhaps you have precognitive ability that manifests through your dreams.

Harbingers of Future Events

In ancient times, dreams were important divining rods for the future—remember Joseph's interpretation of the Pharaoh's dreams? Nowadays we tend to seek out the symbolic meaning of our dreams for clues to our emotional state, rather than predictions of what's to come. *Oneiromancers* are people who divine things from dreams.

Let's say you dream of a house on fire. The flames are hot and fiery red. A few days later there's a huge fire in the center of town. Was this a precognitive dream? Could be. Did you have any connection to the house that burned? Did you know the people who lived there (at present or previously), drive past on your way to the grocery store, consider buying it at one time? Does the house remind you of the house you grew up in? Such connections strengthen the dream's prophetic potential.

Even when a dream seems clearly precognitive, there often is value in exploring its symbols and messages using the conventional methods you apply to other dreams. Dreams present multiple layers of meaning; even a precognitive dream can have messages that are relevant to you in the here and now of your everyday life.

It's also important to look at how common the events are that show up in your dreams. There's nothing unusual about a house catching on fire; in a moderately sized city, this could happen several times in a night. But if in your dream you see a shadowy figure throw something through the window and run away, and three days later the newspaper reports an arson ... well, that could be a different story.

Dream Dictionary

Oneiromancy, the activity of divining future events from one's dreams, comes from the Greek *oneiros* (dream) and *mants* (diviner). As we've said in Chapter 2, in the second century B.C.E., Artemidorus of Daldis wrote a book, *Oneirocritica,* that catalogued thousands of dream symbols and their portent.

Dreamy

In 1865, Abraham Lincoln had a dream in which he heard people sobbing. He followed the sound downstairs. His eyes landed upon a coffin, but he couldn't see who was inside. He asked a nearby soldier the identity of the deceased. "It's the president," Lincoln was told, "killed by an assassin." A few weeks later President Lincoln was murdered.

Perhaps, as you are writing in your dream journal, you'll recall that you also received an irate e-mail (known as an e-mail flame), or your old flame came to town unexpectedly. As many dream researchers and theorists will concur, a fire in the center of town (or other "prophetic" event) is not more significant than the other events that could have either triggered or explained your dream.

If we took to heart each dream in which some disaster befalls our loved ones or society in general, we'd be emotional wrecks. Most, if not all, of our dreams about crisis and disaster are symbolic ways of representing some conflict we're facing in life and have nothing to do with bona-fide earthquakes, tidal waves, or plane crashes.

Sometimes, what appear to be precognitive dreams are really self-fulfilling prophecies. For instance, you might dream that you get accepted into graduate school ... yet you have no intentions of going back to school. Then three weeks later your boss calls you into her office and says the company is starting an employee-retention initiative that includes paying for college tuition, and tells you that were you to enroll in graduate school you would meet the requirement for the new management position she is creating. Was your dream giving you a heads-up that this opportunity was coming? Or was your mind surfacing a desire to improve your job situation?

Warnings from Within

> *I dreamed that my brother was in the hospital. I rushed to see him, but the doctors told me that he was locked in ICU. They refused to let me see him because he would infect me. No matter how much I argued, they would not budge.*

The next morning this dreamer received word that her brother was in the hospital after having been seriously wounded by the police in a drug raid. Her brother had been manufacturing drugs in his basement.

Was this a psychic dream? Perhaps. And it may have also been a warning dream from the dreamer's subconscious. Clearly, she may have picked up on the fact that her brother had fallen in with the wrong crowd. And maybe this dream was a way of letting the dreamer know she had to distance herself from her brother (she wasn't allowed to get near him in the hospital) unless she, too, wanted to end up in trouble with the law.

Ann Faraday thinks that psychic dreams can usually be traced to the subtle vibes and small impressions we pick up on during the day. Psychologists call the act of our unconscious picking up on nonverbal warnings or messages, "fine cueing." Often our premonitions, either dreamed or experienced while awake, can be the result of our mind putting the pieces of the puzzle together rather than literally seeing the future. However, a good number of people have precognitive dreams or dreams that are psychic in some other way that are verifiable.

I Can See Clearly Now: Clairvoyant Dreams

In clairvoyant dreams, people report that they see other people, places, and objects. Such dream sightings might involve the familiar or the unfamiliar and are similar to waking experiences of clairvoyant intuition or psychic ability. The word *clairvoyant* means "clear vision." Clairvoyant dreams differ from telepathic dreams in that there is no communication between dreamers … this is a dream solo experience. Generally, clairvoyant experiences (waking or dreaming) involve events that have already occurred. You might have a clairvoyant dream in which you see your best friend arranging a bouquet of flowers, then go to her house for dinner and see the bouquet on her table.

Been There, Done That … Dream Déjà Vu

Have you ever dreamed of being somewhere, then going to a place in your waking life that's where you were in your dream—even though you *know* you've never been there? Déjà vu strikes again—it's that odd feeling that a situation, a person, a conversation, or an action is utterly familiar and has already been experienced.

But how do you explain it? Well, there's no definitive answer. Some scientists think that there's a lag time in our perception of things and what we think of as déjà vu is really our mind catching up with ourselves, so to speak. Some believe that we recognize events in daily life from precognitive or telepathic dreams.

Others think of déjà vu as the result of collective unconscious memories (or even past-life experiences) resonating with current experiences. In any event, the feeling that your current life is somehow connected to past events can be a strong indication that you are connecting closely with deeply buried feelings—extrasensory or not.

> **Life Is But a Dream**
>
> According to James R. Lewis, author of *The Dream Encyclopedia*, a 1986 poll showed that 67 percent of Americans have experienced déjà vu. Other studies have shown that more women than men experience déjà vu and younger people experience the phenomenon more often than older people.

Subconscious Memories Surface

It's not easy to figure out if our dreams are psychic, prophetic, or deep messages from our psyche. If your dream feels like it is in some way paranormal, what does that say about who is creating the dream? What does that say about how and what we perceive? Is the dream coming from within, or are we picking it up on a kind of paranormal radio frequency? Or perhaps a time warp? After all, scientists tell us that time is a human construct.

These questions are fascinating and exciting because we don't know the answers, not definitively. In an age where we can decode large sequences of DNA and predict the rate at which the universe is expanding, it's almost a relief to know that the many mysteries of how we dream and think are yet to be solved.

Wake Up!

Are you attributing the content of all your dreams to psychic phenomena? Are you far along the road of thinking your dreams have nothing to do with you? Think again. In our experience, many prophetic, telepathic, and precognitive dreams are primarily related to the dreamer's current internal struggles.

But if we take the view that dreams can be a very useful tool in leading fuller, richer lives, then we should regard dream messages—whether they come from within or without—as ways to illuminate our daily lives.

Sometimes our dreams contain bits of information that we cannot account for. Dreaming of a long-dead aunt's childhood stuffed animal—an item we'd never seen and could not possibly describe, yet in our dream, we did—might very well be a psychic perception. But the question that's important to our waking life in the here and now is: Why is the tan and black one-eyed doggie in our dream? And why now?

Remember that in our Western, modern culture, we're pretty strict about what is considered reality. In other cultures, the idea that the boundaries between past and present are permeable is acknowledged. And it is accepted that all sorts of (what we would consider strange) things occur in dreams.

Tuning In

What are your dreams telling you about your hopes and fears and wishes? Are they telling you about paranormal experiences as well? How do you feel about this? Do you tune them out, hoping they'll leave you alone? Or do you seek them out, feeling that your ESP capacity is a special awareness you possess? If you have had prophetic dreams, do you talk about it? Or do you think it's just too weird?

It's important to think about your attitudes toward your own powers of psychic intuition. Whatever it is you feel and experience—either in your dreams or while awake—should be accepted and understood as part of the whole amazing package: you.

Are you in tune with your intuition? Do you trust your own "sixth sense"? Have you ever had your astrological birth chart done, been to a Tarot reader, or had a session with a psychic? Even the most die-hard skeptics have expressed curiosity about the paranormal at some point.

When was the last time you had a waking experience or a dream experience that you'd call psychic? Write down the dream content in your dream journal. Does recalling this experience make you feel

- Exhilarated?

- Frightened?

- Curious?

- Uncertain?

- All of the above?

Ask yourself the following questions about your paranormal experience:

- Are you eager to explore the experience further? Or would you rather just put it behind you and forget all about it?

- What about the experience causes you to describe it as psychic?

- Through which of the senses did you receive your psychic message: hearing, taste, touch, smell, vision?

- Did your experience change your conscious viewpoints in any way?

If you desire to, ask your dreams to elaborate upon the experience by clarifying the psychic experience for you, or by revealing more about the psychic message intended for your receipt. Remember, the experience you had is unique to you and to your own individual psyche. Whether you believe in the paranormal or not, exploring your out-of-the-ordinary dream or experience may yield a rich terrain of self-knowledge if you summon the courage to access it.

So you've *never* had a psychic experience or dream intuition? Why not? Write your feelings about this in your dream journal. In the spirit of open-mindedness, write down what kind of paranormal dream or experience you'd like to have, if you believe that, indeed, such things do occur …. For example, imagine who you were in a past life, or that you are able to see events at which you're not present. (Remember, keep an open mind.) Now, meditate on this before falling asleep. Record the dream that results.

You may create or receive dreams that give you rich insights into your life and relationships.

The Least You Need to Know

- ESP, precognition, telepathy, and prophecy are paranormal experiences. Their existence has neither been wholly proved or disproved.

- Many prophetic dreams may be attributed to "fine cueing," or the process by which our unconscious picks up nonverbal warnings, subtle vibes, or small impressions.

- People who have close relationships with each other, such as lovers or siblings, often report similar dreams or common dream elements.

- Even if our dreams contain psychic aspects, the goal of understanding them remains the same: to apply the message to our waking life.

Chapter 20

Spirit Communication in Dreams

In This Chapter

- ◆ Who's sending the message?
- ◆ What is the message?
- ◆ The stages of grief
- ◆ Healing dreams

How many of us have had dreams—or heard of others' dreams—about loved ones who've died? This is a very common experience, and a very powerful one. Whether it's reassuring, frightening, joyous, or agonizing, it's surely moving in the deepest of ways.

Is This a Dream or a Visitation?

On several occasions, we've had friends and patients tell us of visual, auditory, or emotive contact with deceased loved ones while they were dreaming—a deep "knowing" feeling that someone was there.

When people talk about seeing departed friends and family, they speak of somehow knowing that it really is the person. "It's not a dream," they insist, "it's a visitation." What's the difference? It's hard for them to explain. Often there is more connection with the dead visitor, a deep and emotional understanding about the purpose of the visit. "My mother is here to tell me that she's fine," or "My sister wants me to know that she did love me, even though she had a hard time showing it."

It's impossible to pinpoint what differentiates a dream from a visitation. And no one has been able to prove that dream visits from those who have passed on do or do not occur. To a great extent, it doesn't really matter. What does matter is how you feel about the dreams. What messages do you feel they are bringing you, and are those messages leading you toward healing your grief?

Messages from Beyond

So why is the feeling so prevalent that we have been visited by someone in our dreams who has died? Here are a few snippets of common experiences:

- **Dreaming that someone you know visits you and says "good-bye."** It is only later that you learn this person has died. Was his spirit saying good-bye? Or were you preoccupied with your friend's state of ill health, and the dream material reflected these fears?

- **Dreaming that a deceased loved one comforts you while you're very ill or close to death.** Was this a true, soothing visit? Or an awareness of and preparation for dying?

- **Dreaming that someone who died of a disfiguring disease appears to you looking whole and healthy.** Is this her way of letting you know she is now all right? Or is it your attempt to move beyond what her pain and suffering did to her physically?

Dreamwork

The Dalai Lama recommends a meditative visualization exercise in which you imagine a cord of cloud descending from the heart of Buddha or God to connect you to someone who is special to you who has passed on. The cord evokes birth imagery and comforting renewal. Use this visualization before falling asleep.

In *The Dream Game*, Ann Faraday says the real question is, why would a spirit want to visit a dreamer? By and large, the purpose would be to reassure the dreamer that he or she is still around and all right. Once that message is conveyed, any other visitations should be regarded the same way we regard all other dreams: They bring messages about our lives to our waking attention. And as with other types of dreams, our aim is to understand the message.

Are we dreaming, or is someone we love coming to us in spirit form in our dreams? We don't know what's true. What we do believe to be absolutely true are the feelings the dream/visit brings up in us and leaves us with. We also believe that these dreams are so prevalent because they are an important way to work through the grieving process.

Messages from Within

When someone we care about dies, we have to get used to the simple but totally mind-bending fact that they are no longer in our physical world. We won't see them at Thanksgiving. We can't call them on the phone. We won't run into them at the Shriner's Club meeting. This is extremely hard to comprehend, to say the least, and it brings up so many feelings in us.

Not only can these emotions be confusing and painful to sort out, but we often can't or don't give ourselves the time and space to do just that. We've got to get back to work, prepare for little Suzie's Sweet Sixteen, train for the marathon, complete our dissertation. In other words—we have to go on living our full lives at our typical breakneck pace. But in our dreams, we continue to go through the process of coming to terms with what we've lost. Paying attention to our dreams helps us pay attention to the process of grieving a loss.

Inviting Dream Visits

Whether spirit or memory, dream visits from loved ones who have died can provide a safe forum for resolving, or at least accepting, unsettled issues. Do you feel you could have done more for an ailing parent? Should you have kept a biting comment to yourself? (Perhaps it was the last thing, as it turned out, that you said to the person before he or she died.) Would you have handled a situation differently had you known then what you know now? Of course you can't use your dreams to turn back the clock, but you can ask questions and offer explanations.

Use your dream journal to write an invitation to your loved one. You can be open-ended: "Please join me in my dream tonight." Or you can target a specific focus: "Please come to my dream tonight so I can explain why I was so upset with you when you left." Then, establish the setting and atmosphere to encourage the dream visitation:

1. An hour before you plan to go to bed, take a relaxing bath. Add essential oils such as lavender or sandalwood to the water. Light the bathroom with candles. As your body soaks in the warm, fragrant water, let the tension ease from your body and the worries and thoughts of the day slip from your mind. Envision your concerns dissolving in the water.

2. When you get out of the water, dry your body and put on your most comforting pajamas. (Remember to blow out the candles.) Get into bed with your dream journal and write at the top of the page what you want your dream to achieve.

3. Set your dream journal aside (but within easy reach should you awaken during the night). Close your eyes and focus your thoughts on your dream. Ask that your dream, or your dream visitor, come in goodness and healing. Then let yourself fall asleep, calm and relaxed.

4. When you wake up, write in your dream journal before you do anything else. Write as much as you can remember about the dream—when it started, whether you knew during the dream that you were dreaming, who was in the dream, what actions and conversations took place, any elements of the dream that seemed out of context. Did the person you invited to your dream make an appearance? Did he or she look or sound as you expected? Do any "aha!" reactions strike you?

Take some time to mull over the messages and insights from your dream visit. Do you now have the answers you needed or do you have more questions? Do you feel calmer, more at ease, about your loved one? Or do you feel new anxiety about what your dream messages seem to be telling you? Sometimes extending an invitation in this way gives your mind permission to release the inhibitions it has long maintained about certain events or circumstances, opening the floodgates to painful memories and emotions.

You should never feel threatened or endangered by dream visitations. Sometimes the information that surfaces during times of intense emotional stress is surprising or alarming, resulting in dream events that you find frightening. These images might be completely true (representing memories you have repressed), a mix of truth and mistruth, or completely false. Consult with family members to determine whether there is any truth to information that disturbs you, or talk with a therapist.

Coping with the Death of Someone Close to Us

How close were you to the person who died? Was it expected (and your sadness is tinged with relief that the person is no longer suffering) or was it sudden? Was it so sudden that you didn't have a chance to say good-bye? Were you on good terms or was your relationship strained? Was it a young person or an elderly one? Was it your life partner of 54 years or your significant other of 4 months? Did he or she die peacefully or was violence involved? Is this the first person you're close to who died or have there already been many, many losses in your life?

Your relationship to and the circumstances under which this person died will affect you in different ways, to be sure. How much support you have in your life and your spiritual beliefs will also color how you feel. And no two people will have the exact same reaction to a person's death because we all have individual histories, temperaments, and resources. But despite these many variations, there is a common process that we all go through in order to grieve the loss of someone close to us.

Elisabeth Kübler-Ross, author of *On Death and Dying* (Macmillan, 1969), wrote that grief consists of five stages. While she specifically wrote about these stages as they applied to the dying person, they also describe what the surviving person feels:

1. Denial

2. Anger

3. Bargaining

4. Depression

5. Acceptance

> **Life Is But a Dream**
>
> John Quincy Adams once stated that he himself was very well but the house he was living in (that is, his body) was becoming decrepit and he might have to move out soon and find another abode.

As we go through each stage of the mourning process (and these stages don't all have to occur in exact order and can be revisited), our dreams tend to reflect where we are in processing our loss.

Feelings That Linger

Coping with death, from the first shocking realization to the point where you can pick up the pieces of your life, has been compared to being pregnant in that both are natural processes that have their own rhythm, starting point, and endpoint, and both have excellent odds for a positive outcome. Jane A. Kamm, D.S.W., says in her article "Grief and Therapy: Two Processes in Interaction," which appeared in the journal *Psychotherapy and the Grieving Patient* (Harrington Park Press, 1985), that like pregnancy, grief is accompanied by suffering but is time-limited.

Often the dreams that focus on the initial phase of the mourning process are dreams in which the dead person is alive and well, continuing to participate in your relationship.

> *Margaret and I were sitting at the breakfast table. She read the front section of the paper and remarked—as usual—that I shouldn't feed table scraps to the dog.*

When this dreamer woke up, she was filled with despair because she realized it was only a dream. Our dreaming minds, at this point, haven't computed or accepted the person's departure from our lives. This is a natural and healthy type of dream to have in the beginning phases of mourning. It's as if the dreaming mind escapes the painful waking reality. We all need momentary escapes. Others have described having these dreams not as an escape into denial (Kübler-Ross's first stage), but as a cataloging of all the memories the survivor has of the person who died.

We're taught that it's not "nice" to be angry at the person who died; after all, they may have suffered during their illness. But along with feelings of deep sadness, there are also feelings of fury that the person you cared about has left you.

> *James kept appearing at my windows, and I kept pulling down the blinds, yelling "Go away, you're dead!"*

There can be angry feelings that this person took the best years of your life and then up and died on you before you reaped the rewards of your sacrifices. Homemakers or primary caretakers are especially prone to these feelings. It doesn't matter a bit that this doesn't make a whole lot of sense; after all, except in cases of suicide, the person didn't want to die. If we don't recognize what is emotionally true—resentment, fear, anger at being left to deal with feeling deserted—then we can't hope to someday move beyond our anger and make new lives.

As we begin to realize that we are angry (Stage 2 in Kübler-Ross's book), even just on the dream level, we can also begin to have dreams that express how guilty we feel for having these powerfully negative thoughts about someone we loved. Maybe we nursed a sick parent through a long and debilitating illness. Maybe it took all our emotional and financial resources. We may very well have dreams in which we are tending to our sick parent once again. But in our dream we cannot make our parent comfortable, or our attention to her is spotty. Here we can see both the anger (we create a dream scene in which our parent is uncomfortable or our attention is less that perfect) and the guilt (we keep dreaming of tending to this parent).

Dreamwork

Are there other stages that you pass through when you recover from a loved one's death? Do you go through a phase of worrying about your own or others' mortality? Do you wear a piece of jewelry or assume a certain mannerism that belonged to the person who died? Does that make you feel comforted and connected?

We also might have dreams in which we become sick, or give items away in an attempt to stop the death from happening. This is bargaining in its most powerful form (Stage 3). Perhaps you have a dream in which you are frantically giving away all the flowers growing in your garden. You demand that everyone take some. What do you suppose you're hoping to get in return?

Nurturing Acceptance

At some point, your dreams may reflect the *grief* and awareness that your loved one has died. Perhaps you dream you are at the movies and you suddenly realize that you should not hold the seat open next to you; your mate is not delayed in the concessions line. You realize with a horrible thud that he is dead. These dreams are often characterized by deep sadness and tears. It's normal to feel quite depressed (Stage 4).

As we work through feelings of denial, anger, guilt, and depression, in all likelihood we will come to a point where we begin to feel these emotions less intensely. We will begin to feel that we've accepted the reality and enormity of our loss and begin to move beyond it. Even as we are accepting the loss (Stage 5), we often find ourselves revisiting earlier stages for short periods of time. In this stage, it is very common for the dead person to come to us in our dreams and let us know it's time to stop the deepest grieving.

Dream Dictionary

Grieve has a Latin root, *gravare* (to burden), and a French root, *gravis* (heavy). Indeed, grieving is a heavy burden; it weighs heavily upon the heart and pulls us down, especially if we don't find ways to express it.

Dreamy

Author Amy Tan relates a series of dreams after the murder of a close friend. She dreamed of him all during the killer's trial. At the end of the trial, Pete—her friend—came to her in a dream and told her that she should go on with her life as he now had to go on with his. She was angry, but he told her that he was leaving her a friend. Indeed she did meet a new friend, a fiction writer who encouraged her to begin to write fiction herself.

Stopping or Completing the Process

Even if our spiritual beliefs lead us to trust that the person who has died is fundamentally still with us, we have to go through the healing process that acknowledges all the good and bad feelings we had for this person and what the person's death has meant to us.

Putting On the Brakes

Pain hurts. Who needs it? And aren't most of us just a bit scared of death, anyway? Could that be why our culture is so youth-oriented?

Sometimes our grief is not healthy. Sometimes we feel it too much for too long, and sometimes we don't feel it at all.

While there's no set time limit for how long the grieving process takes, we believe it takes roughly two years to fully pass through the grief stages. But what if it's been five years and you're still having frequent dreams in which the dead person is alive but caught in a perilous, dangerous struggle? It's possible that you're still holding on to ambivalent feelings of love and anger. Maybe you are "stuck" in your grief, having difficulty acknowledging that it's okay to be furious that this terrible event has happened to you. Perhaps you should ask yourself what you're scared will happen if you express your anger: Are you afraid you'll be seen as or feel

- ◆ Selfish?

- ◆ Too dramatic?

- ◆ Petty?

There are other beliefs we carry that can make it hard to move through the grief stages. Our dreams can reflect this. We can dream that our dead mother keeps turning up just as we're about to take a glitzy job in Paris. She makes us feel really guilty about getting on that Air France jet and looking forward to sipping wine on the Left Bank.

> **Wake Up!**
>
> Many people feel better and less alone if they can talk in a group with others who are going through a similar experience. Check with your doctor, therapist, or local hospital for grief and loss support groups.

What may be expressed in this dream is a belief that if you are a good and faithful person, you will honor the memory of the dead. You will not move on with your life. You will uphold the notion of honoring the dead to an exaggerated degree. This will keep you in a perpetual frozen state of mourning.

Perhaps another dreamer reports that his recently deceased brother shows up in his dreams to yell at him. The dreamer's brother shouts for him to give him some privacy. The dreamer turns away with dry eyes. In this example the dreamer has been taught that he needs to be strong in the face of death. He may feel that it's a sign of weakness to cry (even when he's being yelled at!), that he needs to "act like a man." Yet these harmful and narrow stereotypes also keep a dreamer from getting over the loss.

In both cases, the dreamers are experiencing "unfinished business" or "incomplete mourning" dreams. These are dreams that attempt to depict where and what the dreamer is stuck on that make it hard to accept the loved one's death. Other "unfinished business" dreams can concern our guilt over not having treated the person nicely while he or she was alive or a more general regret about the relationship.

Completing the Process

Time doesn't heal all wounds. Accepting your feelings and paying attention to your emotional needs as you are exploring your grief through your dreams does.

At a certain point, a middle-aged widow might find herself ready to take a cruise that she'd planned to go on with her husband. She has realized that he would want her to enjoy herself and resume her life. Perhaps in her dreams her husband's presence feels welcome and natural. Maybe she dreams of him when she needs a pep talk in order to rejoin the world. But now there is room for other sorts of dreams, too, dreams in which other hopes and feelings are expressed about what might lie ahead for her.

Dreamy

In *Paula* (HarperCollins, 1994), Isabel Allende writes about letting go of her daughter, who died after a long illness. After her death, her daughter repeatedly visited her mother at night, dressed in her nightgown and slippers, asking her mother to let her go. She says it's because her mother is holding on to her with her grief. One night, Allende is woken out of her sleep, crying, and sees her daughter, smiling from the doorway and waving good-bye. She vanishes down the hallway, her nightgown floating like wings. That's when Allende notices her daughter's rabbit-fur slippers left by her bedside.

A man in his 30s suffered the loss of his father a few years ago. Lately, when he dreams of his father he is able to understand that his father, whom he considered to be very compassionate, is his personal symbol that tells him he's accessing the compassion in himself. The qualities of the father now live on in the son.

A woman in her 40s has lost her mother. But there is a catch: The mother abused her daughter terribly when she was a child. In a dream visit the mother came to her looking as she looked in her 30s. But there was no pain or anger on her mother's face; on the contrary, there was a peaceful glow about her. For the first time the woman felt she saw her mother as she was without life's burdens. Her grief and anger were much alleviated because she understood what had happened to both herself and her mother and that now her mother was at peace.

These dreamers have been able to feel pain, sadness, anger, denial, desperation, and hope. And each of us must accept it as an undeniable and natural unfolding of events: We live, we mourn, we strive, we love, we celebrate, we die—and we dream.

Let Your Dreams Help You Move Beyond Grief

Are you mourning someone or something? What we mourn is not restricted to our friends and family or even our pets. We grieve for what we have lost. We can grieve for important objects such as a home that has burned to the ground or a lost heirloom. We can also mourn the intangibles: our sense of trust after being the victim of a violent crime, our fantasized expected future that a divorce took from us, or our giving up of a professional or artistic dream. Make note of what you have mourned. Try to ascertain which stage of grief you were or are in. Do your dreams reflect this ... and do they give you suggestions for how you might begin to accept the loss?

The Least You Need to Know

- Many people have had the feeling they've been visited by a deceased loved one.

- The message the dead person—whether a spirit visitor or a creation from your imagination—brings is of primary importance to your waking life.

- Getting over the death of someone we care about is a process with distinct phases. It's likely that each phase will play out in our dreams just as it will in waking life.

- For us to go on with our lives unencumbered, it is important to complete the grieving process.

- If you are unable to resolve "unfinished business" and move beyond feeling stuck in the grief process, consulting a therapist could be helpful.

Chapter 21

Going Out of Your Body: Lucid Dreams

In This Chapter

- ◆ Being your own dream driver
- ◆ What's your destination?
- ◆ Out-of-body and astral body experiences
- ◆ Lucid dreaming: Getting started

As you learned in Chapter 13, Green, Yellow, and Red signal dreams help us understand the road map of our lives. Lucid dreams stand at the intersection of conscious and unconscious territory. Almost everyone has had a dream in which they recognized that, hey, they were dreaming! It's as if one part of the self is driving the car while another part is cheering from the stands. With mindful practice, the cheering fan can also become the director and change the course or outcome of the race. Taking an active part in the dream is a skill that psychologist Stephen La Berge says you can learn. So let the race begin!

The Power to Manipulate Your Dreams

As your dream journal begins to fill up, you might notice that there are moments in your dreams where you realize that you're in the midst of a dream. This is particularly likely to happen when you take the time to concentrate on a certain kind of dream you wish to have and to prepare yourself for sleeping and dreaming, as we talk about in earlier chapters and in Chapter 22. This preparation is the launching pad for learning how to manipulate your dreams.

Embarking on an Odyssey of the Mind

In his book *On Dreams*, Aristotle wrote that "often when one is asleep, there is something in his consciousness which declares that what then presents itself is but a dream." On the other hand, Freud thought that lucid dreaming wasn't an actual state, but a partial awakening. It turns out Aristotle was right. But that scientific proof didn't come until much, much later.

Today, researchers know that lucid dream time is much the same as waking clock time—events unfold at the same rate as they would if the dreamer were awake. Scientists postulate that the paralyzing effect of REM sleep may be the only thing keeping dreamers from actually performing the actions of their lucid dreams!

The Dalai Lama describes "dream yoga" as the ability to distinguish between dreamless sleep, dreaming, and waking. The practice of meditation in waking consciousness prepares you for learning how to be aware that you are dreaming. Once you are able to focus your mind as a lucid dreamer, you are ready to enter the more subtle awareness of dreamless sleep, non-REM sleep, or "the clear light of sleep." This, according to the Dalai Lama, is a high form of consciousness that prepares practitioners for smooth entry to the next life upon death.

Dreamwork

Did you have OBEs when you were a kid? What were they like and how did you feel about them? Where did you go? Does your child have them now? Do you talk about them? Why or why not?

It's an Out-of-Body Experience

Have you ever been dreaming that you were floating and then when you looked down you saw yourself fast asleep in your bed? While this could be merely part of your dream, many people think that this is an out-of-body experience, or OBE.

Children, who don't have very firm boundaries yet, often have this sort of experience. Many people who are ill, coming out of anesthesia, or experiencing periods of severe trauma report OBEs. While the OBEs are often extraordinarily pleasant, even euphoric, there are people who create an OBE because they need to escape an abusive situation. This type of OBE usually occurs while awake. When it occurs while we are awake and in response to a trauma, it's called a *dissociative* state.

OBEs can begin in dreams with the sensation of pressure on the feet, head, or abdomen because that is a reasonable exit point for the person's spirit/other being/consciousness. Often OBEs take the form of flying dreams. (Well, if you leave your legs behind, you'd better be able to fly!)

> *I looked down at my feet and saw that a foggy mist surrounded them. The mist turned into a white rope, and then I knew that it was me, my spirit, that was leaving my body. I felt light and floated about 20 feet into the air, at which time I turned and saw myself sitting in a field. That's when I knew I was dreaming.*

Dream Dictionary

Dissociation is a psychological term that describes ways in which we detach from ourselves. While awake, we may "leave" our body or even feel that other people, things, and our emotions don't seem real. In either case, the person isn't able to react normally in his environment for a set period of time.

Life Is But a Dream

Researchers in both the United States and England have confirmed that subjects experiencing lucid dreams can "signal" it to researchers by making prearranged eye movements during their dreams. Lucid dreams tend to occur during periods of high brain activity, usually during long, uninterrupted REM periods occurring late in the sleep cycle.

Such dreams tend to be described in (literally) glowing terms. There's often much light and atmospheric shimmering. Dreamers generally report positive feelings associated with their OBEs. This makes sense; if OBEs are starting to happen to those of us who're paying closer attention to our dreams, it's likely we're becoming more aware of various dreams and dream states.

In Eastern, ancient, and indigenous traditions, there has been much written (or talked about) on astral projections and OBEs. In terms of scientific proof, however, the ability of humans to leave their bodies hasn't been demonstrated. Some dream experts believe that OBEs are simply part of the dream itself and should be understood as such.

But OBEs while dreaming are felt to be real occurrences by many people, and it may very well be that they are one experience on the unconscious-conscious continuum that we don't have the capacity to truly understand—yet. Perhaps what OBEs point to are questions about the very nature of what is real. Who can say? After all, yesterday's "magic" can become today's science!

Getting to Know Your Astral Body

Although it has many more religious and spiritual connotations, for our purposes, the term *astral body* can be best understood as a less modern term for OBE.

Dreamy

Nerys Dee, author of *The Dreamer's Workbook* (Sterling, 1989), reports a dream that archaeologist Tudor Pole had in the 1930s while taken sick in Egypt: A doctor entered his cabin wearing a top hat, striped trousers, and a black coat. He prescribed a cure and then told him that he was a British physician who often left his sleeping body to heal the sick. Upon Tudor Pole's return to Britain, he appealed over BBC radio for the doctor to come forward. A Scottish doctor confirmed that he traveled by astral projection and that his daily attire was as Tudor Pole described.

As always, the questions to focus on in terms of out-of-body or astral dreams are, what do I need to learn or to understand about my waking life? How may I use this gift as a lesson or a launch pad to growth? Or do I want to "fly above" my problem and watch from a safe place?

Most often, people who experience a state of astral or out-of-body travel have arrived at that place within a dream, by intense self-instruction that's a form of light self-hypnosis. So when you're lying in bed at night, telling yourself over and over that you wish to "fly out of your body," you're putting yourself in a state of relaxed awareness, or mild hypnosis. It might take a long while for you to achieve this, but keep trying.

So what is your dream-flying self like? Do you soar, do you explore your immediate environment, do you visit people in your dreamland that you love or want to love you? How does your astral body feel? Are you strong, supple, smaller, larger? And what does this tell you about the desires, needs, or issues in your waking life?

Dropping In for a Visit

Taken a step further, OBE can take the form of actually "meeting up with others" who are also having an OBE!

I was feeling sad and lonely—my husband was stationed in Saudi during the Gulf War. And I was angry, too, that he wasn't here to help with the kids. What if he never came home? One night I woke up to find him standing at the edge of the bed. He put his hand on my foot and told me that he was there for me. It felt different from a dream because his hand was so warm. I woke up and a few weeks later a letter came from him where he told me that he "visited" me while he slept. He described his dream just as I did mine. He even described the brand new alarm clock I had by the side of the bed!

Sure, people sharing similar concerns would have similar dreams. Perhaps this can be seen more easily as dream sharing rather than an astral projection of one's consciousness to a different plane. In Chapter 19, we talked about dream sharing as happening when two (or more) people have the same dream at the same time. It would make sense that the soldier and his wife, both concerned about family and safety, would dream identical dreams. But just as we can't prove or disprove telepathic dreams, we can neither prove nor disprove astral projection dreams. This may be a very good thing, because it forces us to keep an open mind and closely examine all of our dreams and dream messages.

The Science of Lucid Dreaming

Lucid dreaming describes those experiences we have when we become consciously aware *in our dream* that we're dreaming. The most striking feature of lucid dreaming is the ability of the dreamer to alter the content and outcome of his or her dream.

When we are experiencing lucid dreaming, we experience the dream as reality, and yet we know that we are dreaming—a startling condition.

Does this happen all at once? Maybe yes, but probably no; like all other learned skills, it comes in stages. Some researchers liken it to playing a musical instrument: for those who have natural aptitude it comes easy, but others have to work at it and might never become all that good at it.

Dream researcher Dr. Stephen LaBerge says the first step is to learn to identify that you are in a dream, to notice in the dream that something is weird. Maybe we ask ourselves, "Oh, I wonder what that dancing pear is doing there?" but then we lapse back into our full dream state. Later, we realize that there's a dancing pear in our dream and we say, "Hey, there's a dancing pear in my dream. That's not real; I must be dreaming!"

Still later, with practice, we may happen upon the dancing pear, realize we're having a lucid dream, and then slice the pear up to make a nice tart; or we may dance with the pear or make it as big as a truck or as small as a gnat. In this ultimate state of lucid dreaming, we've become aware that we manipulate the dream's contents and outcome.

> **CAUTION** **Wake Up!**
>
> How conscious do you really want to be? Some people decide that they really want to tune out when they sleep; it's their only escape from their busy minds. What do you think?

Dr. LaBerge, who founded Stanford University's dream research center, the Lucidity Institute, has spent much of his professional life researching lucid dreams. As a child he experienced lucid dreams frequently. His experiments in the 1980s pointed toward ways to increase a person's incidence of lucid dreaming (tips on that later in the chapter!) that were published in his book *Exploring the World of Lucid Dreaming*.

The Usefulness of Lucid Dreaming

So now you want to take the scenic route to lucid dreaming, but you're not sure what your destination should or could be!

Would you like to turn around and punch the eighth-grade bully in the nose? Would you like to give your speech successfully and hear the applause and not be sweating bullets before it's over? Would you like to have one more conversation with a loved one you lost and be able to say the things that you want to say? And listen to what you need to hear?

Most of us have, at one time or another, awakened from a nightmare and found ourselves holding our breath from fear or with an elevated heartbeat. It may have taken us a while to realize that we were safe in our own beds. The nightmare looks, feels, and sometimes smells or sounds real because our brain has processed it as real, and the realness has manifested somewhat in our body. Dr. Stephen LaBerge says that the mind processes dreaming and waking knowledge in the same way in that both are equally real.

Controlled lucid dreaming can be a very powerful tool for healing, dealing with recurring nightmares, moving into new ways of experiencing and living life, and, sometimes, just for fun! So something that most of us have experienced at least once in our lives can be experienced almost at will if we "train" ourselves to do it.

Dr. LaBerge believes lucid dreaming is evidence that the body and the mind are most closely connected during REM sleep. This connection, he and other scientists think, holds promise for mind/body healing, although as yet scientific evidence for this is scant. Dreams that suggest there is an illness or problem in your body are common; lucid dreaming might offer a way for your mind to get more information about health matters as well as to direct the body's own healing mechanisms when illness has been diagnosed.

How to Notice When You're Dreaming

So how do we step into our dreams, to guide their direction and content? We don't usually have conscious control over our dream material, let alone the ability to put ourselves in the director's chair. It's hard enough to be aware of what we're doing when we're awake!

Some dream theorists suggest that you begin to prepare for a lucid dream during waking hours. When you're first getting started in lucid dreaming, choose a common object to invite into your dream, like a tree. Tell yourself that when you see a tree in your dreams, it will be a signal to let you know that you're dreaming. What other common items (things you're likely to come across in dreams) can you pick as your trigger?

◆ Dog

◆ House

◆ Car

◆ Sun

◆ Lamp

◆ Shoes

You've picked a trigger that will let you know that you're dreaming. What next? Practice, choosing more relevant dream content as you get better at it. Let's talk about other important things to practice to help you begin to recognize lucid dreaming:

◆ During the day, tell yourself that you will have a lucid dream that night. Do this several times. If you know what you want to dream about, tell this to yourself also.

◆ At night before you go to bed, select your lucid dream goal ("Show me how to fly in my dreams," "Show me how to feel confident," "Help me win at chess").

◆ Write down your goal in your dream journal. Choose only one! Repeat this goal, out loud or in writing, blocking out all other thoughts. Concentrate on images your goal brings up. What will it look like to give that speech without sweating? Can you imagine it? Repeat the goal, imagine it, repeat it.

◆ If you awaken from the dream during the night or when you wake up in the morning, write in your dream journal before doing anything else. Can you recall the moment in the dream when you recognized you were dreaming and began to guide the dream's path toward your goal? How successful were you? What messages did your dream have for you? Did you get what you expected? Sometimes what we believe we want isn't really the answer, and our dreams will reveal this.

Any time we concentrate on something, we're telling our mind to keep outside interference to a minimum and focus on a task. When we work on a term paper or a business project, we are moving along on a definable task, and we give our brain a message about staying in a continuing state of progressive work. The same holds true with lucid dreaming. You might continue a particular focus in your lucid dreams over a period of time, probing deeper with each dream session as your dreams disclose new information.

When we drive a car and get to where we were going without really being aware of the journey, we've given our minds permission to drift to a certain degree. We may gather roses along the mountain path, but we still maintain a certain observational quality, hopefully. Or, if we're gazing out the window of a fast-moving plane or train, someone else is doing the work, and it's safe for us to zone out to the movie we can't get out of our head, the person we're dating, or the idea for a novel or invention. Or perhaps we land three hours later and we realize we haven't been thinking of anything much at all!

Guess what? When we do this, we're turning toward a meditative state. We're moving into a process of letting our mind take us where it wants to. We may be giving it suggestions to focus on a word or phrase, to be spiritually open in a communal worship time, or to listen to music and let go of mental control. During a focused time of letting go, we may even fall asleep for a while or think that we are asleep but really hear everything that's going on.

Perhaps you are familiar with the process of hypnosis. With someone else's help, you have gone into a state of being deeply relaxed and aware at the same time. Or you understand light trance or self-hypnosis, where you focus on a signal thought or object and accomplish whatever it is you wish to do.

All of these examples tell us how remarkably flexible our mind is. Just as we direct our mind and thoughts in our waking life, we can direct our mind in our dreams. As we focus on giving ourselves suggestions to have a particular lucid dream, we are delving into a meditative and light hypnotic state.

Some people have lucid dreams just by reading about them or hearing someone talk about them. The level of self-suggestion varies with the individual. If you want to be awake in your dreams, ask for it. And once you're dreaming and realize that you're dreaming, let your imagination soar and direct the experience the way that you want or need to. As you progress and gain proficiency, you'll probably have longer and more frequent lucid dreams. You will also develop more finely tuned control over the process.

Life Is But a Dream

People who meditate regularly are continually moving between the early stages of non-REM sleep and waking, descending from and ascending to a state of waking consciousness in an effort to focus and concentrate the mind. Is there a state that perfectly blends sleeping and waking in a seamless experience of conscious awareness? Well, maybe that's nirvana, or the Buddha's perfect bliss state!

Life Is But a Dream

In his book *Adventures Beyond the Body* (HarperCollins, 1996), William Buhlman talks about gaining control of his out-of-body experiences by shouting brief commands such as "Control now!" or "Clarity now!" He says that the controlling part of his mind functions in a concrete manner and he must be precise about what he asks for.

Remember, also, that your psyche may have a message to get to you. If an issue needs or wants attention, you may *ask* for a lucid dream about your grandmother and *get* a lucid dream about finalizing the choice of your new car, or the color of the bridesmaid dresses, or whatever needs to be attended to in order to reduce unwanted mental (or physical) tension.

Exercises to Sharpen Your Lucid Dream Skills

Are you starting to have lucid dreams yet? Maybe you're just having them for a few moments, but then you lapse back into your regular old dreams. That is a common occurrence for beginning lucid dreamers. What needs to be practiced, practiced, practiced is a constant conscious awareness that this is your dream and you can change it at any moment. You have to be aware of this during the lucid dream. Again, some people have trained themselves to use that common trigger object as a reminder throughout the dream that it's a lucid dream.

As you begin to explore your lucid dreams, you might become more aware of "false awakenings," or those times you think you wake up from a dream only to discover after your alarm blares in your ear that the first "awakening" occurred within a dream!

The next time you think you've woken up from a dream, check out the other possibilities. Are you in your bed, do the sheets and the environment feel normal? If so, then you're probably truly awake. But if you find yourself looking down at your sleeping figure, then you may be having an OBE. Becoming aware of it turns it into a lucid dream! Finally, if you check out your surroundings and find that George Clooney, Sarah Jessica Parker, or the cast of *The Producers* is in your bed with you, then we'd bet you're still dreaming—only now in a lucid state.

Putting Your Lucid Dreams to Work

So what are you going to do in your lucid state? If you're flying, you might try soaring or doing acrobatics. Maybe take a quick trip to Paris for a croissant? If you're playing soccer, how about making a few goals in the finals of the World Cup? Or perhaps you want to have a heart-to-heart with your long-dead grandfather.

For many years, sports psychologists have used visualization techniques to help athletes with performance. This visualization often crosses over into an athlete's dream. In dreams, a person can create a reality that includes the opponent, the crowd, and feelings of nervous concentration—all the elements found in the waking competition. In lucid dreams, athletes can rehearse all aspects of the event without courting the danger of overtraining and overuse injuries!

Dreamy

Pro golfer Jack Nicklaus used a dream to get out of a rather protracted golf slump. For quite some time his game was off. He was able to concentrate on correcting his problem through dreaming. One night, he had a dream in which he used a new grip. The next time he played, he tried out his dream grip; his game was much improved and the slump was history.

Learning to Become Mindful

Being mindful, in a healthy, positive way, is almost a foreign concept to us because of our fast-paced way of life. For most of us, the ethic is *doing*, and if we have any time left, we may think about *being*. Doing is important and we have much to be proud of, as a nation and a people, in what we have accomplished. But enough is enough; mindful awareness is a practice whose time has come.

Practicing mindfulness is simple yet complex—simple to do, but complex to maintain. Here are some ideas to help you along the way:

- Allow some time during the day to sit in a quiet place and notice all that your senses take in, dwelling on anything that especially interests you. The smell of a flower, the sound of lapping waves, the sight of midcity traffic at dusk, the asphalt patterns seen from a tall building.

- Visit a museum or art gallery. Be aware of the brush strokes in the paintings, the carvings of the frames, the time-etching on the bones of the displayed animal fossils ... or maybe the view of city traffic with no sound from inside the quiet of the museum. Try to experience them through all of your senses.

- Concentrate on your breathing. In yoga, the breath is called prana and represents the life force that animates all living beings. Breathe deeply; feel your breath move through your body into your fingers and toes. If there's an area of discomfort in your body, direct the breath to fill that place and alleviate the pain or stress. As you breathe in, concentrate on gathering up all of your tension and stress. Hold the breath for a second or two. Slowly breathe out. As you breathe out, concentrate on releasing that stress into the world as joy and peacefulness. Contemplate a *mantra*, such as Om, shanti, shanti, shanti ... (All is peace, peace, peace ...).

Dream Dictionary

Mantras are repeated words or phrases with special meaning to those meditating. By focusing on the mantra primarily with sound and breath, the person encourages a desired mental state or emotional response. The increased power of concentration that using mantras creates can be useful to lucid dreamers!

♦ Watch your sleeping child or lover. Notice the peacefulness of the person's in-and-out breathing, the subtle shift in position as the sleeper adjusts for comfort.

♦ Listen to music and pick out the various instruments.

♦ View an interesting scene through the lens of a camera and notice all of the detail.

♦ Watch moving animals; pay attention to their muscles, stride, time at rest.

♦ Go to a library or bookstore and look at the titles related to meditation or relaxation. If something interests you, check it out. Try *The Complete Idiot's Guide to Yoga, Third Edition, Illustrated* (Alpha Books, 2003), and *The Complete Idiot's Guide to Massage* (Alpha Books, 1998).

♦ Set aside a time each week to go to a film that you might not otherwise choose to see or that your family, friends, or partner wouldn't want to see.

♦ Consider taking a tai chi, yoga, or meditation class. Or get a wonderful stress-reducing massage.

See how good it feels just to read these descriptions? For a few seconds, your body relaxed and you became mindfully aware, possibly drifting through a series of scenes in your mind.

It's nice to have the same time during each day for growing mindful. Your mind and body will quickly learn to expect this experience at this time just as it expects sleep and meals at a certain time. During your time of mindful awareness or focused meditation, ask for what you need to accomplish in your lucid dream. This may take the form of a prayer, a repeated thought, or just a notion as you begin your quiet time. As you begin to experience lucid dreams, congratulate yourself. Remember there is a part of your mind that needs to hear that it's doing a good job, especially from yourself.

Set the Stage for a Lucid Dream

Go back through your dream journal and choose several recurring dream images. Categorize the images by their appearance in Green, Yellow, or Red signal dreams. If you already understand (or think you do!) the significance of the dream image or symbol, write that down as well. If you don't have a clue yet what that symbol might mean, enter a question mark next to it in your journal.

Now, before falling asleep, concentrate on one of the images. Repeat a mantra to yourself that you will recognize the image and interact with it in your dream. Invite a lucid dream!

Record the resulting dreams in your dream journal. At first, you might find that it's a significant step simply to be able to summon the desired dream symbol. Over time, you may be able to have lucid dreams involving that symbol: You become aware that you're dreaming about the image you're consciously attempting to evoke.

That's when the fun begins! Especially if the dream symbol is one whose meaning has been troubling or puzzling you, interacting with it in a lucid dream will be an exciting journey toward self-awareness as you discover something new about your dreaming landscape. Ah ... nirvana!

The Least You Need to Know

- Some people believe that astral projection/out-of-body experiences in dreams are actual events in which some level of our being leaves our corporeal body and travels.

- We have the power to manipulate and guide our dreams. This is important in trying to come to terms with nightmares.

- You enter lucid dreaming when you become fully aware in a dream that you are dreaming. After this realization, it's possible to alter the content, course, and outcome of the dream.

- The process by which we work toward giving ourselves lucid dreams has a lot in common with meditation, mild hypnosis, and mindful awareness.

Part 6

Recalling and Recording Your Dreams

There's much that your dreams can reveal to you. But first you must remember them. How often do you wake up after a particularly vivid dream and say, "Wow! No way I'll forget *that* by morning!"? Yet when the alarm clock goes off, what do you remember? Maybe that you *had* a dream ....

So get your pen and paper ready! It's time to write your own Book of Dreams. It's time to train yourself to remember and write the details of your dreams, so you can learn to identify their meanings and messages. Over time, you can look at your entries and see patterns emerging, patterns that illuminate some of your deepest thoughts and feelings.

In these chapters, we help you set up your dream journal, give you suggestions on capturing your dreams on paper, and tell you how to make sense of those confusing dream images and story lines.

Chapter 22

Dream Time!

In This Chapter

◆ Creating a comfortable sleeping space

◆ Soothing your senses for restful sleep

◆ How to make your own herb pouch

◆ Ground yourself through yoga's corpse pose

Take a look around your bedroom. Does it present an environment that invites and supports restful sleep and peaceful dreams? How do you feel when you walk in? Do you anticipate a sense of retreat when you get ready to turn in for the night? Or does your sleeping space share multiple functions that are difficult for you to separate from when you climb into bed?

Our sleeping arrangements are as individual as we are. Yet often we don't think much about whether those arrangements are really conducive to sleep. Your "bedroom" might be a suite of several rooms or a futon in the corner that doubles as your sofa during the day. How many other activities share the setting? Even when you have a dedicated bedroom, you might use it for other things such as folding the laundry or paying your bills. How do you transition from these "awake" tasks to the state of relaxation good sleep and good dreaming require?

Clearing Space

Most sleep experts recommend establishing a sleeping space dedicated solely to sleep and sleep-related activities (as do we in Chapter 3). This encourages your mind and body to separate from the hectic pace of your waking life, leaving behind the stress and activity so you can fall asleep. It also trains you, so to speak, to enter a sleep-oriented mind-set when you enter the space.

Childhood habits tend to follow most of us into adulthood. When we're kids, our bedrooms are our kingdoms. Everything that's important to us is on, around, or under our beds (especially when we share bedrooms with siblings), and we become quite territorial about this small space we can call our own. Many of us move from child-hood homes into other group living arrangements as we transition to adulthood, such as college dormitories or apartments we share with roommates. By the time we're in homes we can call our own, we're well established in the patterns of how we structure our sleep spaces.

Depending on your living arrangements, you may or may not have the luxury of physically isolating your sleeping space from the rest of your household. The optimal setting is a room you can close off, that contains just a bed and other accoutrements that help you feel comfortable. Some people like a sense of spaciousness, while others prefer cozy closeness. If your layout allows it, consider putting dressers, desks, and other items in a space that is physically separated from your bed. This shapes your focus on going to bed rather than getting up from bed. You can also create this sepa-ration with curtains or screens.

Life Is But a Dream

Use your imagination when it comes to crafting your dream space! Color, furnishings, bed linens, lighting, and sounds all contribute to the environment in which you'll spend a third of your day. Even though you have little conscious awareness of the time you spend in your bed, that time is one of the most important influences on your quality of life. Put planning and conscious effort into making your sleeping space comfortable—it's an investment you'll appreciate during your waking time as well as when it's time for bed.

Do you live in a studio apartment or other setting in which you don't have a clearly defined bedroom? This can present more of a challenge, but again you can use your creativity to establish boundaries to separate waking and sleeping functions. If physi-cal boundaries are not very practical, you might use a certain lamp only when it's time to go to bed, turn on a particular music CD, or turn on an aromatherapy infuser containing sleep-inducing essential oils. (We discuss essential oils, herbs, and aroma-therapy later in this chapter.) If you sleep on a sofa bed or a futon, pull it into its intended sleeping position to help your body and mind perceive it as a place for rest.

The Art of Arrangement: Feng Shui

Have you ever walked into a room and felt immediately calm and relaxed? Or the opposite—agitated and anxious? Some rooms just feel "right," while others feel out of sorts, somehow. You credit (or blame) the room's furnishings and their arrangements; the goal of interior design, after all, is to create living spaces that are compatible with their intended uses. You might walk into a living room that feels awkward and notice immediately that the furniture is placed such that it blocks the smooth flow of traffic through the room.

Feng shui is a centuries-old tradition that originated in Japan. Its goal is to arrange one's physical environment to allow an open and supportive flow of life energy (called chi). Feng shui views this flow as similar to the flow of water or wind, with environmental objects either impeding or facilitating its movement.

Dream Dictionary

Feng shui (pronounced "fung shway") is an ancient Japanese art of placement that strives to create balance and harmony in a physical environment.

There are some simple basics of feng shui that you can implement yourself. Much of what we consider "good design" inherently applies these basics; although there is a method to its practice, feng shui also is highly intuitive. A room that feels right when you walk in is a room that is in balance … and harmony is the foundation of feng shui. You can read more about feng shui in *The Complete Idiot's Guide to Feng Shui, Second Edition*, by Elizabeth Moran, Master Joseph Yu, and Master Val Biktashev (Alpha Books, 2002).

When you stand in the doorway of your bedroom or entrance to your sleeping space and close your eyes, what do you feel? Do you feel drawn into the space, or apprehensive about bumping into things should you take more than a few steps? When you open your eyes, do you see anything that strikes you as an impediment? If it looks out of place, chances are it feels that way, too. And it's hard to be comfortable, to feel that you yourself are in place, when the room's arrangement is awkward.

Here are some general feng shui methods you can implement in your sleeping space to encourage peaceful sleep and fertile dreams:

◆ Round the room's corners. Feng shui holds that just as water bounces abruptly from sharp edges, so does the energy of a space. You can place furnishings at angles across corners (even your bed), or use corners for plants or to showcase sculptures or other artwork.

♦ Place your bed so it is sheltered from any cross flow of energy such as might occur in the path between two windows or the room's door and a window. If you can lie on your bed and feel a literal breeze blow across you, this is not a good placement from a feng shui perspective; energy will "blow" across you in the same way, keeping you agitated and disturbing your sleep.

♦ Place furnishings and objects so you can walk without stepping around them. If water were to flow through your room, would it bounce from the items in your room like a stream bounces from rocks that are in its path?

♦ Clear clutter (even from under the bed and in the closets). Clutter creates obstacles and represents stagnation. From a feng shui perspective, stagnant energy can cause you to feel restless and stuck.

♦ Keep books and magazines in another room, or at least distanced from your bed. Some bedframe designs have bookcase headboards that are very attractive, but filling them with books draws the energy of mental stimulation to your bed. If you have such a headboard, you might instead use the shelves for objects that you find calming, crystals, or a potpourri bowl filled with herbs to facilitate sound sleep and pleasant dreams.

♦ Choose colors that support the space's purpose. (We discuss color in more detail later in this chapter.) White, a common wall color because it goes with everything, is what feng shui views as a very "yang" or action-oriented color. You might look at white and see it as an absence of color, but technically it is the presence of all colors. (Black is the absence of color.) White might let you accessorize in any color scheme you choose, but when it is the color of your walls it creates an energy environment of harshness and activity. Intense patterns are also yang.

Dreamwork

In feng shui, every room has stations, called *guas*, that represent the key areas of life. Your relationship gua is always located in a room's far- or back-right corner (viewed from the room's primary entrance). In your bedroom, you might want to place your bed in this location to create supportive energy for intimate relationships such as with your spouse or significant other. This is also a good location to place personal mementos and photos that represent happiness and love, and a candle to spark the flame of romance!

The principles of feng shui are compatible with, and often integrated within, conventional approaches to room design. You might be surprised at what a major difference a few minor changes can make in how your bedroom or sleeping space looks and feels.

Now I Lay Me Down to Sleep ...

Is your bed someplace you can't wait to crawl into, a nest that welcomes you? Or do you let out a deep breath of resignation as you slip between the sheets to begin a nightly ritual of tossing and turning to find just the right spot? Because we tend to view a bed as an item of necessity, it's easy to overlook the importance of making the right choice for comfort.

If you've been shopping for a bed lately, you might be reeling from sticker shock. For a piece of furniture that seems fairly straightforward, a bed can cost a pretty penny! Do you *really* have to spend hundreds or even thousands of dollars for a good night's sleep? Well, consider that you're going to spend a third of your life occupying this piece of furniture. What is that worth to you? (No, we're not mattress sales reps!) As hard as it might be to put a price tag on the value of a good night's sleep, we all know the costs of not getting one.

Sleep experts recommend that you buy a mattress that provides firm, even support for your entire body. Of course this is a subjective judgment; what feels firm to you might feel soft and saggy to someone else. Shop around. Here are some tips for finding the right bed:

- ◆ Test various mattresses before making your decision. Lie on the mattress in the positions you sleep in. If you share a bed with a significant other, make sure both of you go bed shopping—and testing—together.

- ◆ When you narrow your selection to two or three mattresses, go back to the store several times, at different times of the day, to see how the mattress feels. Try to lie on the mattress for 20 minutes or so each time, to let your body settle into it. (Don't worry, mattress salespeople are used to this.)

- ◆ Do you feel any pressure points when lying on the mattress? If so, try another model or brand; anything that's uncomfortable after just 20 minutes could prove to be pure agony after a few hours.

- ◆ If you stay in a hotel and really like the bed, look at the mattress label or ask at the front desk what brand of mattress the hotel uses. Then go to a store that sells the brand, and give it a test.

◆ What about your pillow? You might like a firm, flat pillow or a fluffy, sink-into pillow … feathers or foam … one or several. Like a mattress, this is a matter of personal preference and comfort. Most stores that sell mattresses will let you test pillows, too.

◆ Bed linens are important for restful comfort, too. Most people prefer fabrics that feel soft against their skin. You might need to try several brands of sheets before you find what you like. Generally, higher thread counts are smoother and softer, and last longer.

What about alternatives, such as futons, air beds, and waterbeds? Again, this is personal preference. Go with what makes you feel comfortable, and what makes sense for your living arrangements. The main objective is to have a place you want to retreat to when it's time to go to bed, something you can view as inviting rather than punishing.

Environmental Control

The environment of your sleeping space is an important factor in how easily you fall and stay asleep. Is your room too hot, too cold, too dry, too humid? These elements affect your body temperature and physical comfort. Some people like a room that's on the warm side, with minimal bed covers. Others like to snuggle under layers of blankets in a room that is cool. Other environmental factors include what you can see, hear, and smell.

The Color of Calm

Colors strongly influence our perceptions and moods. Schools use bold, bright primary colors to stimulate creativity and focus. Businesses use certain colors to establish authority and professionalism. From military uniforms to beachwear, color elicits certain responses and expectations.

What are the main colors in your bedroom or sleeping space? Are they bright and bold, or subdued and calm? Is there contrast between the wall colors and other items in the room, or is everything a variation on the same shade? When your sleeping space is in a room that has multiple functions, you can use color as another method to establish a sense of separation. These are some common color associations:

Color	Representation
Red	Excitation, agitation, aggression
Yellow	Concentration, focus, personal power

Blue	Calm, fidelity, trust
Green	Healing
Orange	Mental stimulation
Purple	Intimacy, passion
Brown	Security, stability
Gray	Neutrality

If you like bright, bold colors, it's fine to use them as accents in your sleeping space. (We suggest you go very light on the red.) But the room's dominant colors should be those that support a sense of calm and relaxation: greens, blues, and grays. You might want to add some lilac (light purple) to enhance your bedroom's relationship gua, as this is the color of intimacy. Using mixed colors brings the attributes of both (or all) in combination. For example purple, the color of intimacy and passion, blends red (excitation) and blue (fidelity). Many people like shades of color that blend greens and blues, such as teal and turquoise, combinations that evoke both calm and healing.

If you're stuck with the colors on the walls because you can't paint or otherwise change them, you can use window dressings (blinds or curtains), standing or hanging screens, furniture slipcovers, and other approaches to bring a balance and blend of colors into the room that are conducive to sleep.

> **Life Is But a Dream**
>
> Color research conducted in the 1960s and 1970s showed that of all the colors, pink had the strongest calming effect. This was tested by painting the walls of prisons pink. Pink symbolizes peace and unity. Red, not surprisingly, encourages aggression and agitation (and actually causes blood pressure to rise). Blue is also soothing, and causes blood pressure to drop.

Sounds to Soothe

Whether you prefer Brahms or a rock 'n' roll lullaby, music can help calm the busy thoughts of your waking mind so you can drift into restful asleep. You might have a certain style of music that you like to listen to when you go to bed, or even a recording of sounds such as ocean waves or nighttime nature noises like crickets and frogs. Some people prefer "white noise," sounds that really have no purpose but that mask other sounds. Fans make good white noise, and also keep the room cool if you like that.

Sleep Scents: Aromatherapy

Aromatherapy uses fragrances to change the way you feel. Scented candles and herbs are among the most popular aromatherapy methods. Candles, of course, put out fragrances as they burn. (Make sure to blow them out before you fall asleep.) Herbs are fragrant in fresh and dried forms, which you can use in an herb pillow, drink as tea, or mix as potpourri. You also can put a few drops of *essential oils* into your bath, on a cloth under your pillow, or in an *aromatherapy diffuser*.

> **Dream Dictionary**
>
> **Aromatherapy** is a method of influencing your mood and energy level through fragrances. **Essential oils** are concentrated extracts from plants and flowers that intensify the fragrance. An **aromatherapy diffuser** heats water containing essential oils to carry their fragrances into the air.

You can buy herbs, essential oils, and aromatherapy candles at natural food stores as well as specialty "New Age" shops. Many regular department stores also carry a limited selection of aromatherapy products in the bath supplies section. Here is a table of common herbs and fragrances that can ease your transition to relaxation and sleep.

Common Herbs and Fragrances for Sleep and Dreams

Herb or Essential Oil	Application	Form
Anise	Restful sleep	Seed
Bay laurel	Sound sleep	Fresh, dried, oil
Birch	Peaceful sleep, end nightmares	Fresh, dried, leaf, bark, tea, tincture
Caraway	Remember dreams	Seed
Citrus	Calming, relaxing	Fresh, dried, oil
Chamomile	Restful sleep	Fresh, dried, leaf, flower, tea
Hop	Relaxation, restful sleep	Fresh, dried, powder, tincture
Jasmine	Soothing, can be mild aphrodisiac	Fresh, dried, oil, leaf, flower
Lavender	Calming, mild sedative, restful sleep	Fresh, dried, leaf, flower, tincture
Marjoram	Restful sleep	Fresh, dried, oil
Rose	Calming, restful sleep	Fresh, dried, oil, flower, tincture
Sandalwood	Calm, relaxing, restful sleep, can be mild aphrodisiac	Oil

Herb or Essential Oil	Application	Form
Valerian	Mild sedative, restful sleep	Fresh, dried, root, leaf, tincture, powder (capsule)
Ylang ylang	Relaxation, peaceful sleep	Oil

You can make your own herb pillow, blending the herbs you want to use for the effects you wish to encourage. Here's how you can create your own herb pillow:

1. Buy a yard of muslin at a fabric store. Cut 2 pieces from it that are about 8 inches by 10 inches.

2. Pin the muslin pieces together at the edges on three sides, and sew along the pins.

3. Turn the pouch you've made right-side out, so the seams are now on the inside.

4. Fill the pouch with the herb blend you want to use. Use fresh herbs if possible. Lavender, hop, birch, chamomile, jasmine, and marjoram are usually easy to find and go well together.

5. Turn the edges of the open end under to form a smooth edge and stitch it loosely together.

6. Place your herb pouch under your pillow at night. When the herbs lose their fragrance, you can cut your loose stitching, empty the old herbs, and refill your pouch with fresh herbs. Sweet dreams!

CAUTION **Wake Up!**

If it's going in your mouth, make sure you know what's in it. Read labels carefully on herbal products sold for ingestion (such as teas and capsules). If you are taking any prescription medications, check with your doctor before consuming any herbal products promoted as sleep aids, such as valerian root. Some herbal products can interact with medications to cause unexpected (and sometimes unpleasant) side effects.

Quiet Your Mind, Calm Your Body

With the busy and sometimes frantic pace of our hectic lifestyles, our minds often are still racing when it's time for our bodies to rest and sleep. Mind-body methods such as meditation and yoga help to ground and relax us in preparation for restful sleep. Yoga's corpse pose (called shavasana) is an effective way to achieve total relaxation. The challenge for most of us with this pose is *not* to fall asleep while doing it! *The Complete*

Idiot's Guide to Yoga, Third Edition Illustrated, by Joan Budilovsky and Eve Adamson (Alpha Books, 2003), can introduce you to the basics of shavasana and other yoga poses.

To do shavasana, lie down on a hard surface (like a yoga mat or carpet on the floor), *not* your bed. It's okay, though, to be wearing your pajamas or comfortable loose clothing. Put yourself in somewhat of a spread-eagle posture, lying on your back with your hands at your sides, palms up, and your legs straight out in front of you with your feet about shoulder-width apart. Starting with your head and neck, relax your muscles all the way down your body, one muscle group at a time, until you reach your toes. Focus on your breath, breathing into tight or stressed areas and breathing out release and restoration. Continue until your body and your mind feel completely relaxed. Allow your body to sink back into the ground beneath it, rooted and calm. After 20 minutes, rise and transition into bed. You're ready for … sleep … dreams!

The Least You Need to Know

- The physical environment of your sleeping space is a significant influence over the quality of your sleep and dreams.

- The basic principles of feng shui are largely intuitive and can help you arrange your sleeping space to facilitate restful sleep and peaceful dreams.

- Aromatherapy, use of colors, and music are all ways you can make your bedroom or sleeping space more conducive to sleep.

- Yoga, meditation, and other mind-body methods help you to relax and clear your thoughts so you're ready for sound sleep and pleasant dreams.

Chapter **23**

Keeping a Dream Journal

In This Chapter

- ◆ Setting up your dream journal
- ◆ Boosting dream recall
- ◆ Looking for key dream concepts
- ◆ When dream recall runs dry

You've done the reading. You've thought about your own dream symbols and themes. You're ready for your own journey into your dreams. Maybe one part of this book has really sparked your interest; maybe you've always wondered why you have that recurring nightmare about monsters under the bed or dream of long-dead cousin Tim. There's one way to find out—are you ready to begin keeping your own dream journal?

In Your Book of Dreams

Starting your dream journal should be a lot of fun but can also feel a bit overwhelming. How much should you write? What if you can't remember a single dream or you remember five or six dreams each night? What if you have no idea what those bizarre images mean? What should you write about, exactly?

What Is a Dream Journal?

A dream journal is an ongoing written (and even pictorial!) account of your dreams that, over time, gives you insights into your dreaming mind's messages. People organize their dream journals in all sorts of ways, but the key here is to find some way to set up your dream journal that makes sense to you.

Setting Up Your Dream Journal

In Chapter 1, we gave you some suggestions for keeping a journal. Here are the two most important features:

◆ Choose a journal that appeals to you but is easy to use—using it will become part of your daily ritual.

◆ Purchase a loose-leaf notebook so you can add to or rearrange important dream-thoughts. It should have a pocket on the inside cover to hold those dream realizations you have written on scraps of paper at the office, on the train, on your blind date, at lunch, wherever you happen to be when they strike you. Keeping these tidbits in one place until you can add them to the body of your journal will serve as a great *dream catcher.*

You'll also need ...

◆ A pen or pencil—again, pick one that feels good in your hand so you'll enjoy writing with it.

◆ A flashlight, book light, or a small bedside lamp.

Always be sure to keep your journal-writing supplies next to your bed. We've found that one of the major reasons people stop keeping a journal is because they don't have easy access to pen and paper. By the time they locate their journals, they've forgotten their dreams!

Some people find it easier, especially when dreams awaken them in the middle of the night, to speak their feelings and thoughts into a tape recorder and then transcribe their comments into their dream journals later. If you want to try this, just make sure you keep up with the transcribing. It's easy to collect recorded tapes, but you lose out on the messages and learnings of your dreams unless you take the next steps of identifying common or significant symbols, story lines, and characters that populate your dreams. Remember, too, to keep fresh replacement batteries and empty tapes at the ready!

Dream Dictionary

According to Native American legend, all dreams are caught and held by a wooden, feathered and threaded web called a **dream catcher.** These Native American craft objects hang over the sleeper's bed or just inside their bedroom window. Captured dreams are destroyed by the first ray of sunlight. All except the good dreams, that is; only good dreams find their way through the web and enter the dreamer's life.

You should actually begin writing in your dream journal *before* you go to sleep. Start on a fresh page by writing the date. As we've discussed, some of our dreams can be sparked by special anniversaries and holidays, and noting the date will alert us to dreams that are reminding us of these yearly events.

Draw a line about halfway down the center of the page. The left side of the page will be used for the actual dream entry, and the right side of the page will be used for the associations you have to the dream.

On the left side of the page, simply note how you feel as you lie in bed. Don't spend a lot of time on this. The goal here is to write just enough so that you begin to focus on your feelings, especially your bodily sensations. Some people prefer to create a numbered scale to rate their physical and emotional mood (for example, a continuum from 1 to 10, with 1 being very relaxed and 10 being totally tense!) and leave it at that.

Then, on a separate line, write down the next morning's date. This will send a message to your unconscious that you are expecting to awaken with dreams and that you are ready for them.

Next, try to relax. Concentrate on your breathing; imagine the tension leaving your toes, your ankles, your legs—all the way up to the top of your head. If you practice meditation, you might think or speak your mantra. You might even count sheep if that clears your mind of the day's clutter. Be open to whatever thoughts and emotional/corporeal feelings come to you.

Some dreamers find unexpected thoughts crossing their minds, such as: "Why haven't I ever seen a bird asleep?" or "What movies has Shelly Winters been in lately?" Whatever thoughts pass through your mind probably have a direct relation to something that you experienced during the day or some issue, however deeply buried or disguised, that might be ready to surface.

Other dreamers find that they have no thoughts at all. They notice colors or shapes in their mind's eye. Or perhaps they hear bits of music.

Finally, some dreamers find that important questions or thoughts pop into their heads as they are relaxing into the presleep state. If this happens to you, you might try asking your dream to help you solve the issue. For instance, a thought like, "Should I fly home for my sister's birthday even though I always feel like I give her more than I get?" could be a good question to ask your dreaming mind.

Getting It All Down

If you awaken in the middle of the night with a dream fresh in your mind, do not, under any circumstances, tell yourself you'll remember it in the morning. You won't! Those extra few minutes of sleep will cost you your dream. According to Ann Faraday's *The Dream Game*, as much as 50 percent of dream information you recall in the middle of the night is lost by the morning. The time to write down your dream is when you wake up with it fresh in your thoughts, when its details are as vivid as if you were still dreaming.

With practice, it won't feel like a superhuman effort to jot down the gist of your dream at 3 A.M. In fact, the effort you put into *not* writing down the dream by arguing with yourself or promising that you will remember this and that detail can be far greater than the few minutes it takes to wake up and record the dream.

When you wake up in the morning (assuming you didn't bolt awake at 3 A.M. with a dream to record), begin by recording your dream. Do this while you're still in bed. Even routine movements like getting up, brushing your teeth, and feeding the cat can drive the dream afterimages from your mind.

Record as much of your dream as you can. Include actions, characters, symbols, colors, puns, and most important, how you felt about these things. If your dream sparks associations, jot them down in the right-hand column. Maybe a part of your dream reminds you of an old *I Love Lucy* episode, or a painting your best friend is working on. Pay attention to any outstanding images in the dream and write down in the margin two or three adjectives for that image.

So if there's a red sports car that feels key in your dream, you might write "sexy, dangerous, fast." You also might have a more personal association to the image, in which case you'll write "the kind of car Rachel had when we broke up." So the feelings about that image on a more intimate level might be "angry, hurt, shocked." You can figure out if an image is key by how much emotion you feel toward it either in the dream or upon waking.

You might also wish to sketch an image in the actual dream entry or sketch an association to an image in the margin.

Once you've recorded the body of your dream, think of a title for it and write that above the dream entry. Choose a title that captures both the action and general feeling of the dream. Giving dreams titles like "Playing Basketball Naked and Loving It" or "Frenetic Journey to Paris and Back" will help you spot trends in your dream journal over time and also help you crystallize what the dream feels like to you.

At first, this can be difficult; but with practice, you should have little trouble finding titles for your dreams. A good way to begin getting used to capturing the essence of a dream in 15 words or less is to do this first with movies (or even books). In Hollywood, they call summing up the gist of the movie the "high concept." To test your summing-up skills, mix and match the following movies with their description. And don't be afraid to improve upon our summaries!

The High Concept Matching Quiz

Movie Title	Movie Theme
1. *Funny Girl* _____	a. Modern NYC love story between neurotic Jewish guy and WASP girl
2. *Annie Hall* _____	b. Talented singer/actress from the wrong side of the tracks makes it big, gets heart broken
3. *Gone With the Wind* _____	c. Mobster enters psychotherapy and discovers his softer, gentler side
4. *Analyze This* _____	d. Cockney girl transformed into a real lady by uptight Svengali, ends up taming him
5. *The Matrix* _____	e. Southern belle cut down to size by Civil War despite man who loves her
6. *My Fair Lady* _____	f. Is it real or is it cyberspace?

Answers: (1-b, 2-a, 3-e, 4-c, 5-f, 6-d)

How did you do? Get the idea? Remember to use titles that sum up the main dream action and dream feeling. This will help you look at patterns over time when you review your dream journal.

In the beginning you might have difficulty remembering any dreams, or you might only be able to write down dream fragments. That's fine. If you keep up with your dream journal, eventually more and more dreams will come to you.

Dreamwork

If you record more than one dream per night in your dream journal, be sure to number them or otherwise indicate that they are different dreams.

You should also record the type of dream it is. A Dream in a Series, Signal Dream, Nightmare, Anxiety Dream, or Fear-of-Losing-Control Dream are some classifications you can use.

We're ready to look at the dream with an eye toward connecting it to three different categories of past events. First, what recent events (the last 24 hours) might have sparked this dream? Second, what events in the last year might have led to such a dream? And finally, what events in the distant past (from your childhood, from Grandpa's stories of life in rural Nova Scotia, from age-old cultural myth) does your dream draw upon?

Wake Up!

Don't overdo it on your dream journal! If writing down every single dream and commenting at length feels taxing, pick one or two dreams per night. Keeping a dream journal should be something you enjoy, not a task!

For each category of past events, consider what the dream message might be. If something occurs to you, take note of it.

Don't be discouraged if you don't know what to make of your dream. If the message was important, it will repeat itself.

To illustrate the basic dream journal blueprint, we've chosen to present an entry from a friend's dream journal:

June 19, 2003

I'm tired, both in my head and body. There's tension in my shoulders. My mood's sort of blah.

June 20, 2003

Dream Title: Jimmy Carter flies the plane

Dream Category: Dream in a Series

Dream: *I'm flying to NYC on an old plane that is filled with people, none of whom I know.*

Thought: I'm not in the driver's seat = out of control.

Dream Element: *Suddenly, a baby starts to cry and it's all I can do not to yell at the poor mother to shut the kid up!*

Thought: This really aggravates me!

Dream Element: *The flight attendant appears—I recognize her; she's one of my clients—and yells that there's something wrong with the pilot. She looks at me to fly the plane. I can't move, my limbs won't budge. We start to crash.*

Thought: This is scary. Why do I feel so responsible? Why is she picking on me? The plane: rickety, untrustworthy, about to break apart.

Dream Element: *I turn to the person next to me to ask if he can help me to the cockpit—and it's Jimmy Carter! He tells me he'll fly the plane. He goes into the cockpit and the plane levels off.*

Thought: Him again! Adjectives for Jimmy: capable, kind, heroic. I'm so happy to see him, but hide this. I think I shouldn't need him!

Associations (recent past), Category 1: Yesterday was such a busy day! Took on a new and exciting project. Wondered how I'd juggle it with all the others. Went out for a quick dinner with Joe. Got home around 10 P.M. and did a few more hours of work. At first I felt good that I'd gotten so much done, but then worried that I couldn't keep the pace up. Worked some more and fell into bed exhausted.

Dream Message, Category 1: I'm feeling stressed out and overly responsible for keeping the plane from crashing. I feel out of control in my dream. Seems that's how I've been feeling at work.

Associations (in the last year), Category 2: I've had a Jimmy Carter series dream only one other time this year. It was when Joe wanted me to move in with him. I ended up telling him that it wasn't a good time to sell my condo. He asked out of the blue and it really freaked me out. The commitment made me feel overwhelmed, and my dream told me that I needed Jimmy Carter to come rescue me. Last night, Joe hinted at me moving in with him again. I can feel myself caving in, even though I'm not ready!

Dream Message, Category 2: I'm starting to feel pressured by Joe.

Associations (distant past), Category 3: I was 14 when Jimmy Carter was president. First year of high school. I felt: pressured, stressed, out of control.

Dream Message, Category 3: I need to feel better about setting limits with my personal and professional life. I don't protect myself, so I rely on Jimmy Carter to come to the rescue.

Dreamwork

Don't forget your mood: When we ask how you *feel*, do you answer with what you *think*, instead? This is a common area of difficulty. Keep working on it!

Exercises to Help You Remember Your Dreams

We've warned against the biggest threat to dream recall: procrastination. But what if you are diligent about writing down your dreams as soon as you have them (no matter what the ungodly hour), and you are still having difficulty recalling dreams?

Everyone experiences a dream dry spell. It can be due to medication, alcohol, or some other disruption in the REM cycle. (You might want to review Chapter 3 for sleep hygiene tips.) Assuming our difficulty remembering dreams isn't due to a sleep problem, here are some ideas for getting back on the dreaming track:

◆ **Sleep in a different location.** Sometimes a change can sharpen our senses. Have a sleepover at a friend's place, take your blanket out under the stars, or splurge for a room at the Four Seasons. And be sure to take your dream journal.

◆ **Lie in bed for a few moments after you wake up.** Dreams can sometimes come back to us slowly. If you still draw a blank, write down how you feel when you wake up. Often this jogs the memory, even if it is only a fragment of a dream that is recalled.

Life Is But a Dream
Author Susan Sontag once wrote, "I was not looking for my dreams to interpret my life, but rather for my life to interpret my dreams."

◆ **Don't try to police your dreams.** Sometimes we judge our dreams and try to forget the ones that paint us in a bad light or contain upsetting material. Remember, everyone has violent and sexual dreams. Also, don't judge a dream as too trivial. In order to get to know all parts of yourself, try to welcome all types of dreams.

◆ **Talk to a trusted friend about her dreams.** Sometimes when we're treated to someone else's dream stories, they not only spark our own, but also rekindle our interest in remembering them.

◆ **Allow yourself to get swept up in poetry, literature, a great movie, or play.** Experiencing (on a gut level) others' creativity can often spark a desire to experience our own in waking—and dreaming—life.

◆ **Work backward, step by step, to remember your dreams.** Often we remember just the end of a dream—especially if an alarm clock jolts us awake. If this happens to you, ask yourself what happened just before that last image.

Your Dream Journal Is Your Creation

We've offered a dream journal template that we've found to be helpful. But be sure to add your own personal touch. Maybe what works best for you is to keep it neat and clean and totally focused on dreams and feelings written in a certain blue ink pen.

But then again, you may find your creativity flowing in more ways than you anticipated. Go ahead and paste a particularly telling fortune you got at the Chinese restaurant in your journal. Look for cartoons about dreams or anything else that has meaning for you and paste them in, too. Have fun with it—make a list of the 10 people you most want to dream about.

If you're really industrious, in addition to the dream journal, cross-reference your dreams by theme; keep them in a file box with colored index cards. Let the blue ones stand for nightmares, the green ones for Green Signal dreams, the purple ones for sex dreams, and so on.

Keep paints or crayons on hand. Some dreams beg to be drawn. Use a different color of ink each day. Imagine what other people whom you admire or feel you have nothing in common with are dreaming about. Write down song lyrics that you just can't get out of your head. Make a list of people whose dreams you wish you could have:

- Norah Jones
- Matt Damon
- Ella Fitzgerald
- Alexander the Great
- Michael Jordan
- Albert Einstein
- Madeleine Albright
- Steven Spielberg
- Maya Angelou

In short, express yourself.

Dreamy

Novelist William Burroughs recorded this dream in his dream journal shortly after the publication of his classic novel *Naked Lunch*:

Airport. Like a high school play, attempting to convey a spectral atmosphere. One desk onstage, a gray woman behind the desk with the cold waxen face of an intergalactic bureaucrat … Standing to one side of the desk are three men, grinning with joy at their prospective destinations. When I present myself at the desk, the woman says: "You haven't had your education yet."

Dream Journal Practice

For the next week, record your dreams as suggested in this chapter. Write in your dream journal every night before you fall asleep and each morning when you wake up—even if you can't recall any dreams. For the dreams and dream fragments you can remember, take note of any recurring symbols, images, or feelings. Go easy on yourself; this is only the beginning. In the next chapter, we'll examine how to look for patterns over time.

The Least You Need to Know

- A dream journal is an ongoing, personal chronicle of dream images and feelings that we try to relate to waking events.

- It's important to have a basic dream journal because journaling will make it easier to spot trends and themes.

- Keep your dream journal and a pen near your bed at all times and write down the dream as soon as you can—procrastination will steal your dream!

- We all have times where dream recall is difficult. Try to keep writing in the journal even if it is only to record how you feel when you wake up.

- Relaxation exercises, checking your sleep hygiene, and sleeping in a different place can all boost dream recall.

Chapter **24**

Asking Your Dreams
to Help You

In This Chapter

◆ Unlocking dream solutions: Your dream journal is the key

◆ Identifying and interpreting dream patterns

◆ Conversing with dream characters

◆ Dream review: Revisiting your dream journal

Like most worthwhile things we do in life, keeping a dream journal has both short-term and long-term benefits. In the short run, your daily dream journal can help you remember more dream details and become more aware of your day-to-day struggles.

Over the long haul, your dream journal can be the richest chronicle of your personal growth. Big statement, right? Over time, and with the right tools, you can track changes in symbols, images, and types of dreams. In addition to the instructions we've talked about so far, there are a few more tools you can use to get the most out of your dream journal.

Asking Your Dreaming Mind Questions

As you make dream journal entries, your dream deciphering skills will sharpen. You'll develop a sense for the details that are important to record, and your conscious mind will start to make connections right away when it comes to the personal dream symbols and patterns that are significant to you. In the following sections, we discuss some ways to focus your dreaming mind on uncovering deeper dream meanings.

Elaborating on a Confusing Dream

How many times have you woken up and asked yourself, "What the heck did *that* mean?" Did your dream take you on a confusing odyssey—one that makes absolutely no sense to you? Or perhaps there was one element in your dream that puzzled you. You can't understand why on earth Bob Barker was in your dream last night. He has nothing to do with your day residue, you don't know a soul named Bob, and there's no linguistic meaning for you (no associations with bobbing for apples or bobbing in the water).

> ### Dreamy
>
> According to James R. Lewis, author of *The Dream Encyclopedia*, in one dream study one group of participants was instructed to call for local weather information immediately upon awakening and write down a few items about the weather before recording their dreams. The participants in the other group were directed to document their dreams before doing anything else after awakening. Those who dealt with weather matters first recalled far fewer dreams than participants who immediately wrote down their dreams.

When you wake up with a confusing dream, it is important to write down both the content of the dream and the source of your confusion. Be sure to use the right-hand column of your dream journal pages to record any and all associations, no matter how minimal or "out there." Here's why: As you go about your day, your unconscious is doing what you asked by mulling over the confusing dream.

> ### Life Is But a Dream
>
> The phrase "let me sleep on it" might not be about procrastination so much as about realizing that we can solve problems in our dreams.

You might want to ask your dream to elaborate on the puzzling message when you set up your dream journal for the next night. Sometimes you will get rapid clarification; other times you will get even more confusing symbols that only make sense days, months, or even years later. Again, remember that if the message is important, it will come back to you over and over again. Here's an example:

June 3, 2003:

I feel sort of restless, a little out of sorts. Jittery.

June 4, 2003:

Dream Title: Bob Barker Keeps Popping Up

Dream Category: Confusing Dream

Dream: *I'm happily doing my Saturday errands until I see him. What is Bob Barker doing in my dream? He seems so serious.*

Thought: I feel annoyed that he wants my attention.

Dream Element: *I'm doing errands. I notice Bob Barker arranging teddy bears in a children's shop window. He waves to me, but I ignore him.*

Thought: I don't want to be bothered!

Dream Element: *In the parking lot outside the store, a car pulls up. Bob Barker is driving the car. I ask him what he wants from me. He shrugs and says, "Don't you want to get into the car?" I tell him to leave me alone. Then I wake up.*

Thought: I'm feeling harassed.

Associations (recent past), Category 1: Yesterday Ray and I met for tennis and relaxed in the park—teeming with kids, dogs, families … I felt free (it was Saturday, after all!), happy, but also a little frustrated with Ray.

Dream Message, Category 1: I'm not sure what the dream is telling me. But I'd like to figure out why Ray (and Bob Barker) frustrate me so much!

Associations (in the last year), Category 2: I've had a number of dreams where it seems I'm dragging Ray to things (parties, weekend trips) he's not really interested in. But in waking life, he couldn't be more enthusiastic about doing things together.

Dream Message, Category 2: Still not sure. But it's becoming clear that part of me is concerned about Ray's level of participation in this relationship.

Associations (distant past), Category 3: Can't imagine! Bob Barker is a game-show host; I used to watch him on *The Price Is Right*. He gave out prizes, or withheld them. In fact, I was addicted to the show; my mother would yell at me to do my chores. This annoyed me because I didn't want to be bothered with doing what I was supposed to do.

Dream Message, Category 3: Bob Barker symbolizes something important about my feelings for Ray. But what? The overwhelming feeling is that he represents something I don't want to bother with (like I didn't want to do my chores and shut the TV off), but what? Tonight I'll try to dream on it.

The next night, our dreamer did just that:

June 4, 1998: I feel sad.

June 5, 1998: A pit in my stomach. Nothing too terrible, just aware of it.

Dream Title: Bob Barker Gives Me a Message About Ray

Dream Category: Signal Dream?

Dream: *I'm in my car with Bob Barker. We are going to the movies. I'm thrilled. Suddenly we're surrounded by dogs. We get to the movie theater, but it's really filled with people.*

Thought: This reminds me of the large playground by the tennis court—the one Ray and I went to on Saturday. Why isn't Ray with me?

Dream Element: *But Bob Barker turns to me and says, "You can't have something so precious!" I feel terribly sad. I start to cry. Then I wake up.*

Thought: Why is Bob Barker telling me I can't have this?

Associations (recent past), Category 1: Yesterday I read the Sunday paper. Did laundry. Met up with Ray at Joan's BBQ—played with her kids. I felt relaxed and happy with my friends. Ray seemed distant. Bugged me.

Dream Message, Category 1: Maybe Ray's seeming distance felt like he was telling me I can't have this: kids (or maybe what they symbolize: fun, freedom, spontaneity).

Associations, (in the last year), Category 2: I haven't felt that sad (when Bob Barker told me I couldn't have the something) in waking life in quite a while. Dogs = barking = Bob *Barker?* Now when I think about it, when Ray and I were in the park the other day amid all those dogs, kids, and parents, I remember feeling frustrated with him.

Dream Message, Category 2: I guess I really do want that: marriage, kids, pets. I sense that Ray doesn't want those things, at least not now. I'm afraid if I stick with Ray, I won't get those things I want.

Associations, (distant past), Category 3:
I tend to avoid confrontations with people; I'd rather play along than risk losing them or hurting them. This is a pretty old pattern.

Dream Message, Category 3: I've been avoiding talking to Ray about my desires. Bob Barker had to get up in my face and bark at me to pay attention!

Talking Back to Dream Characters

In Chapters 12 and 21, we suggested ways to get to know what the bogeyman or wicked witch wants from you. Instead of yelling at them to beat it, we suggested asking them what they're doing in your dream. More often than not, such an approach turns them into a friend, or at least into a character that isn't so horrific.

You don't have to restrict your conversations to only the frightening dream characters. Since these are your dreams, you are free to chat with anyone or anything in your dream. You can try to do it in the dream itself as it is occurring. This approach requires a certain proficiency with lucid dreaming, and that might take a good deal of practice.

There are two other ways to converse with dream characters. First, suggest to yourself in your dream journal that you will do just that. Simply jot down a sentence such as, "Ask the lifeguard why he keeps telling me to do a swan dive." Very often the lifeguard's purpose will be revealed, but often in a cryptic form—remember Bob Barker?

The second way to converse with dream characters is to do so in your dream journal by continuing your dream on the page. Many people find this really helpful, especially if they write it in a movie script form. Here is an example:

> **Life Is But a Dream**
>
> During one period in ancient Mesopotamia, it was common practice to have a professional dreamer (usually a priest) seek the answer to your dream questions for you. And in ancient Greece, if it was too far for you to travel to the temple of Aesculapius to incubate your dream solutions, you could have someone make the journey—and dream—on your behalf.

> **Wake Up!**
>
> The sample journal we presented is merely one of hundreds of ways of setting up a dream journal. There's no right way to record dreams. Explore all different formats for constructing the most captivating and useful journal you can.

You: So, why do you keep telling me I should do a swan dive? I don't even know how to do the backstroke.

Lifeguard: I think you can. Just try.

You: Do you just want to make a fool of me? Don't you know I'll do a belly flop?

Lifeguard: You have me confused with other people in your life who want to see you fail.

You: Why are you telling me this?

Lifeguard: I'm a *lifeguard*—I'm here to protect you. You have been living too long as the ugly duckling, refusing to recognize you're a beautiful *swan*. And you can do more than you think. Just try.

Looking for Advice

Who hasn't consulted the Magic Eight Ball, the crack in the sidewalk, or the daisy (petal by petal) in hopes of getting the right advice? Why is it that we are less likely to consult ourselves than something or someone outside ourselves? Relying on our intuition may be a process of primal *mentation*—of listening to the messages of our inner selves.

Dream Dictionary

Many researchers postulate that **mentation,** a term used to refer to the process of mental activity thought to be one step below actual thinking, continues even in non-REM sleep. This might account for our ability to problem-solve while we sleep.

Our dreams are filled with advice. When we meet with career counselors, wondering if we'd find more meaning in our lives if we left the corporate world, we are most likely already dreaming the answer. As we trust our dreaming mind to reveal what we really feel and really want and are really concerned about, the more we will be able to rely on ourselves for advice.

Using Your Dream Journal for Self-Discovery

Periodic rereading of your dream journal is just as important as writing in it. It's the difference between looking at something close up and from far away. Both perspectives are important and give you different information about the same subject; one gives you the details and the other gives you the scope of how those details fit into the larger picture. Recording your dream documents the details of what happened in the dream, who the dream's cast of characters were, how you were feeling, and how the dream relates to daily events. Rereading your dream journal gives you the distance, like looking at the dream from far away, that lets you recognize repetitive symbols and patterns, and overlapping themes and concerns.

Uncovering Patterns

So why do you always dream that you're in the kitchen, or why are you always walking down the same path in your dreams? Or haven't you noticed that these common settings are actually patterns?

We suggest that after you've used your dream journal for two or three months, go back to its beginning pages. Read what you wrote about each dream. Underline any recurring images or symbols in different colors of ink. Get the flavor of the journal in its entirety. Then write a summary—a dream review—of your dream themes and daily events. Did you have many dreams about being chased? How did you respond? What has been going on in your waking life? And how have you been responding to that?

Gayle Delaney, Ph.D., notes that in her dream seminars students who rewrite and review an entire eight weeks' worth of dreams almost always notice a new level of clarity. Maybe you will notice that a dream or theme that you thought was meaningless wasn't. Or maybe you'll notice, like one of Dr. Delaney's students, that you feel stuck in a rut. Your dreams express this and so does your waking life. Is it time for you to do something new and truly wake up?

When you review your dream journal, you can often see that your dreaming mind remembers anniversaries and important dates. Ten years after your divorce and three years after your remarriage, you might still dream of walking out on Harry (or something more disguised) each April 9th or thereabouts.

It is also common for American adults of all ages to have dreams during the late spring when the theme of freedom and celebration prevails. It seems like part of us still celebrates the end of the school year, even if we don't get three months of summer vacation anymore.

When you write a dream review, try to give your mind room to roam when considering what your patterns might mean. There's a good chance that you might not be able to figure out why you seem to be in a dream kitchen so often, but take note of it. At the next review, the answer might be revealed.

> **Dreamwork** _____
>
> Just as we're supposed to change the batteries in our smoke alarms twice a year, at the beginning and end of daylight saving time (spring and fall, for those who live in areas that don't adhere to this clock-switching ritual), we should reread and review our dream diaries at least twice a year. Pick two important dates (like your birthday and New Year's) to do this so that you don't forget.

"Why Do I Always Dream About Jimmy Carter?"

In Chapter 23, we shared a dreamer's Jimmy Carter series dreams. We decided this dreamer called upon Jimmy Carter when she needed to be rescued. Period, end of story. Right? Wrong.

When we look at our dream diaries over time, we begin to notice not only patterns, but also changes in patterns. We change over time, so why shouldn't our dreams?

A dreamer in college might dream she's in the kitchen because she misses home and her mother—things she associates with the kitchen. As she climbs into her 30s, dreaming about the kitchen might cease or it might mean something different. It might still symbolize home, but refer to her feeling captive. She might be spending great amounts of time feeding her family of four. It might symbolize conflict over her husband's reluctance to help her out more with child-rearing chores. And once she's well into her 50s, the kitchen might stand for her feelings of missing her own children who've just packed up and gone to college, or her own youth. Or the empty, immaculate kitchen in her dreams could symbolize liberation from the 300,000 meals she cooked!

In the same vein, Jimmy Carter might not always play the role of rescuer. As this dreamer matures and faces new challenges in life, Jimmy Carter might disappear from her dreams altogether or make fewer appearances. Perhaps she's able to rescue herself more often in her waking life. If so, then maybe Jimmy's appearances indicate that she's done it again, and she should congratulate herself for coming to her own rescue!

Crafting a View to the Inner You

One way to keep track of repetitive dream symbols and images is to keep a personalized dream dictionary. You might find it helpful to review Chapter 5, in which we gave suggestions for starting a dream dictionary. Set this up in a separate section of your journal. The associations you have in your dictionary may change over time—either as you grow and change or as new facets of your personality are revealed to you—so don't hesitate to add to it. The dictionary, like you, is a work in progress.

Time for a Dream Review

After you've kept your journal for a month or two, do a review of your entries. If you can, choose one strong repeating symbol. Use three adjectives to describe it the first time it appears in your journal and the last time it appears. Is there any shift in the symbol's meaning?

The Least You Need to Know

♦ Your dream journal can help you ask focused questions of dream characters in confusing dreams, to gain understanding about the patterns and symbolism such dreams present for you.

♦ Often the advice you seek about concerns or problems in your life appears to you within your dreams.

♦ It is just as important to periodically review your dream journal as it is to write in it on a daily basis.

♦ Dream patterns and symbols can change or cease over time. This might be because we've grown out of them.

Chapter 25

Dream Groups and Role-Playing: All the World's a Stage

In This Chapter

- ◆ Sharing your dreams
- ◆ Starting your own dream group
- ◆ Exercises for your dream group
- ◆ To boldly go where no dreamer has gone before

Remember that really wonderful dream you had last week? Did you keep it to yourself, or did you tell someone about it? Was that person interested or did she keep looking at the clock? Did she seem preoccupied or did she somehow manage to make *your* dream about *her?* Imagine if you had a group of friends you met with to talk about dreams, and nothing but dreams.

"I'll Let You Be in My Dream If I Can Be in Yours"

These lyrics from the Bob Dylan song put into words the feelings you might have when you decide to share your dreams. It's human nature to want to communicate and to be curious about what makes other people tick. But telling someone your dreams can make you feel vulnerable. After all, when we begin to explore our dreams, we're often exposing parts of ourselves that we're just getting to know.

Yet it can be helpful to get someone else's take on our dreams. Especially if it's someone who knows us well. Sometimes just putting the dream into words can be clarifying. Other times, we may be in the mood to talk about what the whole bizarre dream meant.

Sharing Your Dreams

In many indigenous cultures, dream sharing is an important part of daily life. The day's events are often determined by the content of the prior night's dreams. But in our society, sharing dreams and dreaming itself isn't given much of a soapbox. So it's up to you to find a way to have your dreams heard. Plenty of people have formed all manner of dream groups; others feel more comfortable sharing their dreams with a close friend or partner.

Somewhere along the line, lots of folks got the idea that dreams are either to be kept private or told only to a therapist. Maybe, in part, this has to do with the Freudian stereotype that our dreams contain all sorts of dangerous impulses that would make polite society blush.

> **CAUTION**
> ### Wake Up!
> If you find that, over a period of time, the content of your dreams significantly interferes with your daily functioning, then it probably *is* a good idea to consult a mental health professional.

So you've decided that you want to talk about your dreams. But if you have a disturbing dream about your mother, you might not want to pick up the phone and discuss it with her. And if you have an erotic dream about your next-door neighbor, you might not feel comfortable about telling your partner—nor do you want to greet your neighbor with "Guess what I dreamed about you!"

So whom do you talk to? Generally speaking, share your dreams with people you feel you can trust, who can keep a confidence, who respect that dreams have meaning, and who are interested in hearing about you and your dreams.

We know of a group of friends who go for a walk every morning before work. They've been doing this for five years. In their sleepy state they share what they dreamed the night before in much the same way that other groups of friends might talk about what they did on Saturday afternoon. But this group focuses on what they "did" the previous night while they slept.

Learning That There Are No Right or Wrong Dreams

We have all learned too well that it's important to get an "A" in class, write the most brilliant term paper, say the funniest thing at the dinner party. And when we begin to look at our dreams, the tendency to "do it right" kicks in. We may feel frustrated when our dreams don't make sense or when they seem silly. We imagine that other people have better dreams that reflect, in fact, that they are actually better people than we are!

Try not to compare your dreams to other people's dreams. Forget about what your more successful, prettier, luckier, smarter co-worker must dream about. Focus on yourself. In truth, you don't know what goes on deep inside another person, and even if you did, you've still got to deal with your own life.

So do it. Deal with your own life by learning that there are no right or wrong dreams. Dreams full of grief and loss aren't pleasant, but they're not "wrong." Likewise, dreams full of sports cars and expensive champagne aren't "right." (Granted, they're pretty fun.) If you don't understand your dreams, that doesn't mean they are worse than other dreams in which the meaning seems apparent.

> **Dreamwork**
>
> Try noticing what words you use when labeling your dreams. Are you using judgmental words (stupid, foolish, obscene)? Practice not doing that. Try to understand the dream for what it is, not denigrate it—and yourself— by putting negative labels on it.

Starting Your Own Dream Group

Okay, so maybe you've decided you don't want to tell your best friend about your dreams because he always lets you know his are far more fascinating. Maybe your second-best friend tends to analyze your dreams—and you—to death. It's time to start thinking of branching out.

As you begin to think about starting a dream group, it's important to know there are lots of ways to structure it. The first thing you should explore is if you're the kind of person who'll be comfortable in a group and in what kind.

- ◆ Do you prefer the intensity of a one-on-one situation? Or is that too close for comfort?

- ◆ Would you prefer sharing your dreams with a therapist—and only a therapist?

- ◆ When the workday is over, do you like to socialize with people in your profession? Or does the idea of sitting in a circle with other dentists, teachers, or accountants make you feel like running the other way?

Life Is But a Dream

Dream groups are great ways to puzzle through the changes that come during life's many passages. Researchers Montague Ullman and Gayle Delaney believe that the impartial insights other group members have into your dreams can help you develop an intuitive perspective that's unbiased by your own emotional closeness to your situation. Plus, you get to see how other people deal with the changes in *their* lives.

- ◆ Do you like to be in the company of people of all ages, or do you prefer a more homogenous group?

- ◆ Do you tend to make long-term commitments to groups or projects (like, were you in Girl Scouts for 46 years)? Or do you feel better about having an end date to your projects? (Little League is only for 12 weeks and that's quite enough, thank you.)

What Are the Rules?

Ultimately, that's for the group to decide. We can provide you with a few guidelines for getting your group off the ground. There are many kinds of dream groups. Some are single-sex groups, others mixed. Some are just for artists, others are for new mothers, philosophers, accountants, or any other type of person or group that you can think of.

Once you've figured out what type of group you'd like, decide if you want it to be *ongoing* or *time limited*. A first-time dream group explorer might like to begin with less of a commitment.

Dream Dictionary

Time-limited groups, unlike **ongoing** groups, are groups with a preset end date that everyone agrees upon before the group gets underway.

In our experience, groups of four to six people seem to work best; there are enough folks to spice things up but not so many that you'd feel you don't get enough room to participate. Once you've found your group members, have a first meeting in which you discuss and agree upon some ground rules. We've found that the three most important ones are:

♦ **Focus on the nitty-gritty.** Establish a meeting time, meeting place, how often you'll meet, and for how long.

♦ **Maintain confidentiality.** It's vital to be clear that what's shared in the group isn't talked about outside the group. This will allow people to feel safe and respected.

♦ **Agree on a structure.** For example, do you want people to take predetermined turns? Or will the understanding be that at the beginning of each meeting you'll discuss who'd like to share a dream that day and take it from there? Is there someone who would like to be a discussion leader (maybe someone who has experience with dream groups), or would the group prefer to have no leader at all?

Dreaming Together

Because you don't want your experience in your dream group to be a nightmare, it's a good idea to remember that sharing dreams is a tricky business. We tend to feel exposed, and the last thing we want to feel is judged, dismissed, or ridiculed. A crucial safeguard against feeling those things is the explicit understanding that the dreamer is in control of her dream and in the presentation of it.

Many of the most widely used dream group formats are based on the work of Montague Ullman, a psychoanalyst and author. As a result of his extensive experience with setting up dream groups, he has found that issues of safety and discovery are key; the dream group members need to feel that their needs are respected and their inner selves protected so that they can discover what their dreams convey.

Here's a sample dream we can use to illustrate a possible dream group format, relying on some of Montague Ullman's suggestions, that you may wish to use in part or whole:

> *I'm on a boat. It's calm and the sun is out. I'm too hot. I'm hungry and thirsty. Then other people come join me on the bow. The wind picks up and we capsize. I fall into the water, which is warm and full of bubbles. It's a bubble bath. Suddenly I am plucked out of the water by a sea gull.*

The first phase of sharing a dream is ... sharing a dream. Remember to put it in the present tense. Often the next phase is to invite questions that clarify the dream. But if you want, you can ask the group not to comment at all; maybe it's a painful dream and the act of verbalizing it is all you can tolerate at the moment. If you wish to go on, invite questions.

At this point, no opinions/feelings about the dream may be given. (For example, "Gee, I thought it was so cool when the boat began to capsize!" isn't, in fact, cool.)

Clarifying questions answer *who, what, when, where, why* (sometimes), and *how*. More appropriate questions might be: What kind of boat was it? A sailboat? How big was it? Who was on it?

Often the next phase focuses on responding to the dream from the listener's experience while at the same time remembering that the point of doing this is to help the dreamer, not shift the spotlight onto the listener. As a listener, you might share three adjectives for how the dream made you feel ("I felt *scared, out of control,* and *surprised* when the boat capsized"; another person might relate feeling "*relieved, excited,* and *free*" instead). Your group may decide to associate to the dream by recasting it as if it were their own dream. The hope is that the group's associations will inspire the dreamer's own associations. During this phase, the dreamer is a sponge: She should soak up the group's impressions.

Next, the group offers associations to the dream that focus on metaphors. For example, the member who felt that the boat capsizing was freeing might regard the big waves that crashed over the bow as "sweeping him off his feet." Another member may take up that association, adding that getting swept off your feet reminds her of romance. Another member may offer that it reminds her of dancing with Fred Astaire. These metaphorical associations will, hopefully, feed the dreamer's imagination and associations.

Once the dreamer has taken in all the group has to offer, she can respond (if she wants—remember, the dreamer is in control of the dream and the dream-sharing process). She can talk about the ways in which the dream-storming session has helped her think about her dream.

As a final step, at the beginning of the next meeting the dreamer might share whether she "slept on" her previous experience with the group and if that affected her understanding of the dream.

Exercises for Your Dream Group

Some groups, as author Stephen Phillip Policoff points out in *The Dreamer's Companion* (Chicago Review Press, 1997), experiment with "shared dreaming." That is, the group decides to "incubate" a particular dream. The goal is to agree on a dream image—a party at the Waldorf, a carnival in 1890s Coney Island—or a phrase or theme, like "snowmen" or "look for the silver lining." At the next meeting, group members compare how closely their dreams resembled each other's!

Role-Playing: Bringing Your Dreams to Life

When your group stages a dream play, it affords the opportunity not only to bring your dream to life, but also to change or enhance the content of your dream. In so doing, the hope is that conflicts you face might be clarified and resolved. The dreamer is the director of the dream play and can also be an actor.

In 1920s Vienna, J. L. Moreno began to practice and teach a form of group therapy called psychodrama. Developed as a way to recognize and alter the "life scripts" we reenact unconsciously, he focused on assigning roles in dreams to others and acting the dreams out. This form of therapy has many critics because it is quite easy for powerful emotions to emerge in a way that does not feel "safe" to the group members. Still, used in a careful, more playful way, this type of exercise can be really informative.

Just remember, your dream group is not a therapy group engaging in psychodrama, like Moreno's groups, but is instead a discovery group. So have fun with it, but be sure to stop the scene if you or any group member feels too uncomfortable in any way. Perhaps the exercise has brought up new emotions, and these might be better explored in depth with a mental health professional. Dreams that are intensely troubling or disturbing in nature are best discussed in therapy and are not appropriate for dream group role-playing.

To use some basic role-playing concepts in your dream group, first, tell the group your dream, paying special attention to detail and character—after all, you've got to entice your actors! The "actors" should clarify the dream, without attaching interpretation or judgment. The goal here should be to understand the dreamer's experience and get excited about the dream play.

You can either assign parts or ask for volunteers. You don't have to limit the cast to human or even animate characters. In the short dream example we gave in the preceding section, you could cast someone as the wind! That person would decide how to play it (under your expert direction, of course!): as a ferocious force, a playful power, or a saving grace.

Often the dreamer will switch actors' roles in the middle of the enactment in order to experience a unique twist on the character's motivation. Another interesting idea is to cast a person (or persons) in the role of "assistant." That person can come to the aid of the director and be a sounding board for the director.

For example, in the boat dream we mentioned earlier, the dreamer might ask the assistant how to stage the action differently so that she could get cooled off without tipping the boat over! Maybe the suggestion would be that the other people onboard could steer the boat north, to cooler waters. The helper's suggestion would certainly change the outcome of the dream.

By switching roles and playing with the dream, all the aspects of the dreamer's personality encoded in the various characters and symbols crystallize, making it easier for the dreamer to recognize and acknowledge part of herself or conflicts within her she hadn't been aware of.

Artistic Creativity and Dream Expression

Often our dreams inspire us to write, dance, paint, or sculpt. The fact that most of us can't hold a candle to Picasso or Twyla Tharp tends to stop us dead in our tracks. We're lucky if we allow ourselves to paint by number. But here's the truth: The desire to express ourselves creatively is not the sole domain of the super-talented; we all feel those urges, and they're ours for the taking.

Your dreams are creative expressions, so it's natural that you'd want to express them in creative ways from time to time. Sometimes it's hard to find the words to describe a dream. Try sharing a drawing you made after a particularly vivid dream, instead of relating your dream to others in the usual, narrative way.

> **CAUTION**
>
> **Wake Up!**
>
> It is never recommended that you engage in violence—physical or verbal—during your dream play (or any time, for that matter), despite its centrality to your dream. Recurring troubling dreams containing physical violence or extreme emotions are best discussed with a mental health professional.

> **Dreamy**
>
> The philosopher Friedrich Nietzsche once said, "Every man creating the beautiful appearance of the dream world is a perfect artist."

Remember to curb any desire to be your own or another's art critic, art teacher, or art therapist. Chances are you are none of the above. And anyway, that's not why the sculpture or painting is being shared. Respond to the dreamer's needs and listen to the emotions the artwork brings up in you. By the same token, don't heap praise on someone's piece. This tends to set up a feeling of competition in the rest of the group. Above all, remember that the piece being shown is an *expression of a dream*. And since we don't judge dreams as right or wrong, we similarly don't judge the work they inspire.

If you present a poem, for instance, try to talk about how it felt to engage in your project. Maybe your dream was troubling and it was through writing that you began to feel soothed. Or maybe that came later when you read the poem to the group.

More Exercises for Your Dream Group

Just as you can enlist members of your dream group to be actors in your dream, you can enlist them to help paint your dream. Why not create a mural of one member's dream? Or have everyone contribute his or her own dream to a mural?

Make flash cards with different words, such as "mother," "blue," and "convertible." Ask group members to free-associate to them. Just maybe it will remind someone of a recent dream.

If you tend to either relate your dreams in words or paint a picture of them, try something different. Write lyrics (and have a member who plays piano compose a tune), or compose a poem or a limerick. Write lyrics and set them to the theme from *The Beverly Hillbillies.*

Is your dream group in the dumps? Suffering from dreamer's block? Can't associate to a symbol of a yellow cup? Well, maybe the thing your group needs to get those creative juices flowing is The Backward Dream Game. Here's how it works.

Have everyone write a scenario on a piece of paper. In the first round, choose scenarios that are simple and straightforward. In later rounds you can get more complicated, silly, or outlandish. Some possible scenario ideas are …

> **Life Is But a Dream**
>
> Many indigenous cultures have and do practice some form of public dream interpretation. The Zuni of New Mexico, for example, share and explore certain dreams at certain times with maternal relatives. Good dreams are not discussed until the event has come true, while bad dreams are reported and discussed right away.

- ◆ A package arrives for you.

- ◆ Your dog can speak.

- ◆ An elderly couple walking in front of you won't let you pass, even though you have a baby in each arm.

- ◆ You realize there are 20 people tap dancing on the moon with your mother.

- ◆ A cow climbs to the top of the Empire State building.

Place the pieces of paper in a bag or cup and have everyone pick one (but not their own). Construct a dream around the scenario you chose. Have the other members guess what your scenario was.

In the first scenario, a dream group member might supply details, such as what the package looked, felt, and smelled like. Another member might add that it arrived in the middle of the night, and so he was startled. Still another member might ascribe a metaphorical meaning to the (small) package: "Good things come in small packages." Hopefully, at the end of the exercise the creative juices will be flowing enough to stimulate a dream memory.

To Boldly Go Where No One Has Gone Before

The right group of people can help you learn more about yourself than you thought possible. They can help shed light on what seemed hopelessly murky and indecipherable. So go ahead and fling open the window that separates you from your dreams, and take flight. Chances are, you and your dream partners will discover whole new flight patterns together.

The Least You Need to Know

- We have an urge to share dreams, but sharing them makes us feel vulnerable.

- There are no right and wrong dreams!

- Dream groups should adhere to a structure that everyone agrees to that should include maintaining confidentiality and the dream sharer's control over the presentation of the dream.

- Dream groups come in all shapes and sizes and can help you understand your dreams and yourself. Sometimes dream groups act out dreams or use other creative outlets such as painting, drawing, and poetry.

Chapter **26**

Unleashing the Creative Power of Dreams

In This Chapter

- ◆ Leonardo and you: More in common than you think

- ◆ The many presentations of creativity

- ◆ Charting the course of your dreams

- ◆ Which way will you let your dreams take you?

If you're a human being, you are creative. Even if you're a major couch potato, you still have more in common with Leonardo or Michelangelo than with a spud.

Creativity and You (Yes, *You!*)

No one else conceives ideas, arranges surroundings, experiences conversations, or even feels about the Ferris wheel exactly as you do. Even the most sedentary and regimented among us has a unique and particular routine that's an individual creation.

Have you ever watched Cub Scouts gluing pumpkin seeds on a wooden spoon? No two designs are ever alike. Or if you've sat with a roomful of young children and watched as they drew houses, no two pictures were exactly the same (nor their explanations). And identical twins don't describe their childhoods in identical ways, nor do people married for half a century remember their wedding day in just the same way.

To create means to bring into being. Any set of behaviors or rituals you exhibit are your creations. Even on a mundane level you are creating a system for living your life. Think about how you perform daily tasks: Do you do them in the same order, one at a time, or all at once? Do you tackle them starting from left to right or pick up what's nearest? Do you organize your routine in terms of what you enjoy the most or make your way using a visual or audio pattern? Take a moment to think about how you do the following things:

Dreamwork _____

Ask your spouse, significant other, or oldest friend to describe your first meeting or date. How does it differ from the version you remember?

- ◆ Your system for paying bills (even if it's haphazard!)

- ◆ The first seven things you do when you get up in the morning

- ◆ Cooking dinner

- ◆ Mowing the lawn

- ◆ Leafing through the Sunday paper

Life Is But a Dream

According to Jill Mellick, author of *The Natural Artistry of Dreams* (Conari, 1996), the Native American Tewa people have no word for "art" in their language because art is not seen as a separate activity from any other in life; it is intrinsic, like breathing. The Tewa are always creating, even in dreams.

Those mental health professionals that we've been talking about all through this book have a saying that goes something like this: You can line up three identical crystal goblets and strike each of them lightly with a tuning fork. One will ring, one will clink, and one will shatter.

Each of us is unique, even in our couch potato-ness. Even in how we tackle that task of brushing our teeth. We are creative. By now you've realized that in our dreams we are often at our most creative.

We're Not in Kansas Anymore

Have you ever watched a child on a playground? How she builds imaginary cities in the sandbox, how she pumps her legs on the swing and begins singing a song? She doesn't know or care that she's off-key or that her lyrics make sense only to her!

Maybe then a group of kids playing tag catches her attention and she leaps from the swing to join them. Perhaps she dashes off to explore another part of the playground, or to follow a young robin's wobbly flight back to its nest. She practically dances with excitement. In fact, as it turns out, she *is* dancing. And loving it.

You've probably heard this so many times that it sounds like a cliché, but it's worth repeating: Kids don't worry about how they are being perceived; they're too busy *being*. They don't put a cork in their expressions of creativity. But can you imagine your uptight boss doing the happy dance when someone brings in a cake for his birthday? Those feelings and the expression of them have been bottled up in the name of maturity and propriety.

But even the most "behaved" among us experience a fantastical, expressive world when we dream. When you dream, your imagination breaks free from the constraints of everyday life.

> **Wake Up!**
>
> Reminder: Don't judge your dreams as bad or good or _____ (fill in the adjective). If you do, you will miss messages from your unconscious.

Inspiration That Comes from an Inner Knowledge

What about all those creative types in our world? Those artists, dancers, scientists (yup, they're creative, too), sculptors, actors, writers, and musicians very often get their *inspiration* from their dreams.

Consider this example: Chemist Friedrich Kekule had been working to understand the structure of the benzene molecule, a fundamental component of organic compounds. One night in 1865, he fell asleep and dreamed of the atoms dancing. In his dream the atoms formed a snake, and before he knew it, the head of the snake bit its own tail, forming a ring.

Professor Kekule, *inspired* by his dream of the circular snake-ring, hypothesized that the benzene molecule was a ring. He was correct, and this discovery was a huge leap for organic chemistry.

Here are some well-known artists who have been inspired by their dreams:

> **Dream Dictionary**
>
> The word **inspiration** is derived from the French language, meaning "to breathe in." We think of it as the action or power of moving the intellect or emotions, usually toward a wish for or an actual expression.

- Salvador Dali
- Orson Welles
- Amy Tan
- Steve Allen
- William Blake
- William Butler Yeats
- William S. Burroughs
- Graham Greene
- Barbra Streisand
- Robert Louis Stevenson
- Jasper Johns
- René Magritte
- C. S. Lewis
- Emily Brontë
- Edgar Allen Poe

- D. H. Lawrence
- T. S. Eliot
- Percy Bysshe Shelley
- Mary Shelley
- Ludwig van Beethoven
- Wolfgang Amadeus Mozart
- Ann Sexton
- Isabel Allende
- Norman Mailer
- E. M. Forster
- May Sarton
- Anne Rice
- Maya Angelou
- Henry David Thoreau
- Dante

Dreamy

Novelist Stephen King recalls a vivid childhood dream in which he sees a dead man hanging from a scaffold surrounded by circling birds. Suddenly, the man opens his eyes and grabs him! King awoke screaming and was afraid of the dark for a long time. Many years later, he used the dream as the basis for a particularly malevolent character in one of his books.

And the list goes on. In fact, we'd bet that if you asked other prominent artists—and scientists—if they've been inspired by their dreams, almost all, if not all, would say yes.

Then there are those of us who don't have the creative brilliance of Stephen Hawking or Twyla Tharp. Some people, in this vast majority, measure themselves against these prolific and accomplished artists. And frankly, they don't quite meet the bar. Unfortunately, this causes them to stop expressing their creativity, to stop looking to their dreams and to nature and to their relationships for inspiration.

Some tried-and-true advice comes in handy here: There will always be someone who can do it faster, more often, or better in some way. So stop comparing yourself! Trust yourself to try something. Dream a big dream, and make it *your* dream. The prize is the experience of it.

We know a writer who worked for four years on a mystery novel. She just couldn't make the ending work—we always guessed who did it. Turns out, she was trying to be "as good as Sir Arthur Conan Doyle." Then one night she dreamed of a different plot twist (very un-Doyle-like). Guess what? She had her book.

Creativity comes in many shapes and styles, and not all of them are conventional. Yours might be teaching, developing databases, establishing accounting systems, answering customer service questions, repairing lawnmowers—the spectrum truly is unlimited.

Dream Maps

Even if we don't come up with the theory of relativity in our dreams, or write a bestseller based on Frankenstein's monster that appears in our dreams, we certainly can take what our dreams give us and either simply appreciate the creation of it or do more: Take the dream and do something with it.

As we pay more attention to our dreams, keeping a dream journal and reviewing it from time to time, we can begin to see patterns. These patterns are like a road map to our deepest feelings. This is our dream map.

Our dreams are an ever-flowing guide. Imagine a road map that unfolds over time, displaying each new place you come to. Once we have established some of our dream patterns, our road map's common symbols can stay the same for long periods of time. Let's say that every time you dream of your childhood home you know that this indicates you are feeling a bit insecure about a new opportunity in your life. The house is your signpost for a detour, a pothole, or a speed zone up ahead. You can use your dream map to pinpoint where you are emotionally and to anticipate what challenges are around the next bend.

Just as a road map guides us along the twists and turns of our journey, so does the dream map. When looked upon as a whole, our dream map captures the entirety of our life experiences. What a wonderful resource!

So how will you choose to use this resource? (Here's the part where you get to take your dream, decipher it, and do something with it!) If you've realized that your dreams tell you to get out of a certain relationship, will you? Will you face your dream demons? Will you take heed of a dream message telling you that you should choose one life path over another? In other words, how will you choose to let your dreams inspire you?

Mapping Your Dreams

You can make your dream map a tangible tool for working with your dreams. You can create a map for a specific dream or a cluster of dreams with common themes, or map the journey of your dreams over a particular period of time (like six months or a year). Here's how you might structure a dream map for a group of dreams that seem to be conveying different messages around common themes:

1. You'll need a piece of poster board and colored markers or pens, and your choice of pictures that you cut out of magazines, poster paints, finger paints, or dimensional structures that you create from construction paper (and anything else you want to use to make your map more creative).

2. Choose a starting point on the poster board and place there a symbol that represents what you feel is the core that links these dreams—you can draw it, paint it, or glue a picture or an object. (This might be that childhood house that shows up in your dreams when your life presents you with insecurities.)

3. Place key symbols in other locations on the board. Is there always a dog in these dreams, or the color red? Let your intuition, rather than your conscious thoughts, guide where you place these symbols.

4. When you have the major dream symbols in place, study your map for a few minutes. Then begin to draw connecting lines between the symbols. Do they follow a mostly linear progression, like a highway? Are they scattered here and there, so getting from one to the other involves zigzagging back and forth like driving a rural road between small towns? Mark your lines as to whether they lead *from* or *to* a symbol.

5. Add any final details that you feel belong on your dream map. Don't worry whether they make logical sense; again, follow your intuition.

6. When you're finished, look at your dream map. Do you get any "aha" reactions, or come to a different understanding of what these dreams might be trying to tell you? Are there obvious messages? Does your dream map seem complete, finished? Write your initial thoughts and comments here:

_____

_____

You can come back to your dream map as often as you like, to add to it or to glean additional insights from the course it plots out.

Dreams Really Can Come True

Understanding our dream messages is only half the equation. What we do with that understanding is the other half. We can take a cue from the list of artists who allowed their dreams to come true. What are your dreams telling you? What can you create from them?

We've talked throughout this book about looking to your dreams for the solutions and answers to the problems and questions you confront in your daily life. The path to greater satisfaction—to what Jung defined as self-actualization—might start with your dreams, as well. When you read your dream journal, what themes jump out at you? Choose three and write them across the top of a sheet of paper. Read through the dreams that represent each theme. How might you translate the ideas of these dreams to your waking life? Write these ideas—tangible actions—below the theme. Now, how can you apply those ideas to your waking life?

We tend to get stuck in the routines of our daily lives, even to the extent that we believe change, at least the change we want in our heart of hearts to make, is impossible. Is it? What keeps you from implementing some of those action-oriented ideas that keep surfacing in your dreams? Maybe your dreams are telling you that it's time to break through your self-imposed boundaries!

This isn't a call to irrationality ... just a call to action. Take small, single steps. Do you want to paint? Stop by an art supply store on your way home from work and just look. Do you love to sing? Join a holiday-season choir, sign up for voice lessons, sing along with the radio even when someone else is in the car with you. Make a list of all the reasons you *can't* indulge your creative desires ... and then fill in the blanks in these sentences for each one of them:

"The worst that could happen if I did _____ is _____."

"The best that could happen if I did _____ is _____."

Still uncertain? Sleep on it! Ask your dreams to help you find a way to fulfill your wishes.

The World Is a Circle

"Two steps forward, one step back." How many times has that adage applied to you? Once we decide to learn to play the piano, for example, it rarely happens that the path to Carnegie Hall is straight and rapid. No, we learn a few dazzling scales, become all thumbs, stop practicing, and then slowly start over again.

Psychoanalyst Carl Jung once said that all his works, his creative activity, came from his initial fantasies and dreams. He returned to their messages again and again over 50 years. Each time they told him something new and important. This ongoing process is what we might think of as his personal mandala.

Mandala means "circle" or "magic circle" in Sanskrit. Originally used as a common aid in Eastern meditation, the mandala (a visual representation of a pattern of geometric forms contained within a circle) was adopted by Jung to express our movement toward self-realization. He believed that the presence of circles (from the most ornate spheres to the rudimentary bagel) in dreams denoted an inner struggle toward wholeness.

We introduced the concept of the mandala in Chapter 4 and in Chapter 11. Mandalas, like the one you created in Chapter 11, can become literal metaphors for our physical and our spiritual journeys through life. The Chartres labyrinth, another form of mandala, has been reconstructed on the floor of Grace Cathedral in San Francisco. Visitors use the labyrinth for personal reflection and meditative stress relief.

As we begin to put our dream messages into action, we should expect that there will be days when the boss still intimidates us and other days when we feel we can squeak out a minor protest. Over time, this process of change will ebb and flow until, hopefully, we begin to have solid, confident feelings about our worth as an employee. This is an example of the mandala principle.

Just as nature is cyclical, so are our lives. We might approach something, begin it, back off, and then return to it. This applies to the process of change—of putting our dreams into action—as well as to a more straightforward creative process. Remember that book your friend gave you two years ago? It's been sitting on the shelf collecting dust, right? Maybe that's not all there is to it, though. Just maybe you aren't yet ready to read it and be moved by it. Chances are, though, one day you'll notice it and pick it up! Like tracing the circular pattern of a mandala, you'll circle back to the book. And it just might inspire you to write a story, paint a picture, make up a song … or have a dream.

Going For Our Heart's Desire

What is your creative mandala? What desires have you approached or wanted to approach in your life? This is really another way of asking what your dream map is. Can you begin to see the rhythms in your emotional life? What have you been stopping, going toward, and stopping again? What seem to be the central themes in your dreams and in your life? How would attaining them make you feel? When do your dreams tell you to stop or go or take heed? Do you?

Go back to the dream mandala you constructed in Chapter 11. Can you remember the dream it represents? What do you think of when you look at your mandala? Does it seem now to represent a broader interpretation, perhaps across several dreams? Now, look at your dream mandala and your dream map together. Do they present any common themes or evoke similar responses from you?

A way that the mandala principle and the dream map differ is that the former also takes into account outside forces that influence us. Remember, this is a Jungian concept and, as such, focuses on the collective unconscious. So inasmuch as we strive to express ourselves in the fullest way possible, some of those strivings can be affected by syncronicity, chance, coincidence, or serendipity.

But even though there are forces beyond our control, our dream map can still guide us. We just need to keep in mind that life is full of changes and chances that we can't anticipate. Sometimes we don't know what the cycles will bring, much in the same way that we expect snow in winter, but can't predict 32 blizzards in a row. The same holds true for our dreaming mind: While we can still know what a cat with one eye, a burning house, or a beautiful lake tends to signify, we must leave room for the idea that these things might not always mean exactly that over time.

It is precisely this mix of tendencies and propensity toward change in us that makes each of us a unique dreamer, human being, and creation.

Sweet Dreams!

Now you try it. Try going to sleep and remembering your dreams. What are the recognizable signposts? What are the expressions that urge you to take note or take action? What can you learn about your world from them? Most important, what will you do with them?

The Least You Need to Know

- We are all creative; our dreams represent creativity unleashed.
- Most artists find inspiration in their dreams.
- Our dreams give us a guide for understanding the twists and turns of life that we can represent in tangible ways, such as with a dream mandala or a dream map.
- Dreams can help us view our lives more creatively so we can bring about desired changes.

Glossary

anorexia nervosa   A disorder characterized by refusal to eat resulting in emaciation, emotional disturbance concerning body image, and abnormal fear of becoming obese. Eating disorders affect sleep and dream quality, and may result in dreams about food and eating.

archetype   A primitive, universal representation. Common archetypes are the nurturing mother, the wise old man, the authoritarian father. Archetypes are the basis of mythology.

aromatherapy   Pleasing, relaxing, and healing fragrances that can come from essential oils, herbs, and candles.

astral body   Believed to be an aspect of the self surrounded by an aura of flashing colors and composed of matter finer than that of physical matter. Feelings, passions, desires, and emotions are expressed and act as a bridge between the physical brain and the mind.

bruxism   Grinding the teeth during sleep. *See also* parasomnia.

bulimia   Insatiable craving for food often resulting in binge eating and followed by purging, depression, and self-deprivation. Eating disorders affect sleep and dream quality, and may result in dreams of food.

Cayce, Edgar   Twentieth-century American psychic called "the sleeping prophet" who received messages through his dreams, and also believed that a person's dreams provide a connection between the conscious self and the higher self.

chakra   According to Eastern practices, the body's seven energy centers that are roughly aligned along the spinal column.

chronobiology   The study of the natural rhythms of all living things.

circadian rhythm   The synchronized action, on a 24-hour cycle, that regulates our body's impulse to sleep or stay awake.

compulsive eating   Uncontrolled eating despite satiation or knowledge that it is abnormal behavior. Eating disorders affect sleep and dream quality, and often result in dreams about eating and food.

dissociation   A psychiatric term that describes ways in which we detach ourselves from our normal, functioning conscious state while awake. We may "leave" our body or even feel that other people, things, and our emotions don't seem real. In either case, the person isn't able to react normally in his environment for a set period of time.

dream catcher   A device crafted by Native Americans. According to legend, all dreams are caught and held by the web until they are destroyed by the first ray of sunlight. Only good dreams find their way through the hoop and enter the dreamer's life.

dream incubation   The practice that originated in the ancient world of seeking out dreams to answer specific and general questions. Greeks believed the closer you were to a deity, the easier to "catch" the dream sent, so sleeping in a temple was the surest way to produce a divine dream. The Greeks used dream incubation for healing; the Egyptians, mainly for prophecy.

dreamlet   A term coined by author and dream expert Ann Faraday; this is another term for a dream fragment—a piece of dream belonging to a larger dream.

ego   Defined by Freud as that part of our psyche that moderates between instinctual (id) drives and our sense of prohibition against their expression (superego). The ego has many capabilities; it is the seat of our defense mechanisms and reasoning mechanisms, to name a few.

essential oils   The highly concentrated "essence" of a plant or flower, which contains its healing energies.

fear of success   The feeling, often illogical, that success will cause us pain or be to our detriment in some way. This is a common concern and shows up in our dreams.

feng shui   The ancient Chinese art of placement. In contemporary Western culture, feng shui has become a system of design that accommodates the comfort and function of a space.

Freud, Sigmund   Twentieth-century psychoanalyst whose extensive work with dream analysis gave therapeutic credibility to dream content and interpretation. Freud believed many dream metaphors had sexual connotations.

healthy narcissism   Refers first to a small child's tendency to think of all relationships, events, and objects as somehow emanating from him and under his control. As he grows, he learns his proper, more realistic place in the world, but retains a positive sense of self and what that self can accomplish.

herbs   Plants with medicinal or healing qualities.

homeostasis   Self-regulation, either autonomic or deliberate, aimed at maintaining a constant environment.

hypnagogic hallucinations   Images that overcome us as we drift off to NREM Stage 1 sleep. Characterized by vivid colors, these images have much to do with our day experiences. During this state, we are apt to have involuntary limb movements.

hypnopompic   The complement to the hypnagogic state and accompanying hallucinations is this state, in which we experience the same things, but as we pass from sleeping to wakefulness.

Icarus   The Greek youth whose attempt to escape from emprisonment by flying away with wings made of feathers and wax took him too close to the sun. The wax melted, the wings came apart, and Icarus fell to the earth.

inspiration   Derived from the French language, meaning "to breathe in." We think of it as the action or power of moving the intellect or emotions, usually toward a wish for or actual expression.

Jung, Carl   Twentieth-century psychoanalyst who initially studied with Sigmund Freud and then took his work with dreams in the direction of archetypes.

labyrinth   A life-size mandala that people walk as a form of meditation, prayer, and spiritual seeking. One of the most famous labyrinths is in the Chartres Cathedral.

light   The portion of the electromagnetic spectrum that's visible to the human eye. Light varies in wavelength and so appears as different colors to our eye. From the longest wave to the shortest, the colors in the spectrum are red, orange, yellow, green, blue, indigo, and violet.

lucid dreaming   The technique developed by scientist and author Stephen LaBerge, Ph.D., who scientifically demonstrated the dreamer's ability to consciously alter the content of his or her own dreams. Dr. LaBerge's findings are used by sleep researchers to treat nightmares, and many laypeople use his work to solve their problems in dreams.

mandala   In Sanskrit, a circle or magic circle. Originally used as a common aid in Eastern meditation, the mandala was adopted by Jung to express our movement toward self-realization. He believed that the presence of circles (from the most ornate spheres to the rudimentary bagel) in dreams denoted an inner struggle toward wholeness.

melatonin   A human hormone that is often taken as a supplement because it creates longer REM phases of sleep.

mentation   The process of mental activity thought to be one step below actual thinking. Some people hypothesize that it continues even in non-REM sleep, accounting for our ability to problem-solve while we sleep.

metaphysics   The philosophical exploration of the nature of reality and being.

Morpheus   In Greek mythology, Morpheus is the god of dreams. He's the son of Hypnos, the god of sleep. Morpheus formed the dreams that came to those asleep. He also represented human beings in dreams. The name Morpheus is derived from the Greek word for shape or form.

near-death experience (NDE)   Strong anecdotal evidence characterized by one's heart stopping secondary to accident or illness; one's spirit, soul, or nonphysical body pleasantly floating away from the scene and viewing it from a distance; the movement toward a path or tunnel where friends, loved ones, or some religious guide awaits; and a sudden, often reluctant return to the corporeal body.

night terrors   Partial awakenings during the first deep sleep cycle, accompanied by rapid heartbeat and pulse and increased perspiration. Night terrors often begin with a shout or a yell and are common in children under the age of seven. Scientists aren't quite sure what causes them.

nightmare   From an Old High German phrase, *mara incubus*. An incubus is an evil, fiendish spirit of the night that descends while we sleep—especially to seek sex with women! Modern-day nightmares are frightening dreams with clear story lines that occur mainly during REM-phase sleep.

nocturia   A medical condition referring to excessive nighttime urination. In the elderly, this can be caused by diuretics or an alteration in hormones that results in the kidneys producing more urine at night; in men, this condition may be tied to problems with the prostate gland.

nocturnal emissions   These so-called "wet dreams" first begin occurring in males at around puberty with the rise in serum testosterone, and are not necessarily accompanied by a sexually explicit dream.

nymphomania   Defined as "excessive sexual desire by a female," originally referred to nubile, unmarried, young women. During the Middle Ages, they were represented by fairies or sprites. Because of their reputed orgies during seasons of the moon, their sexual connotations were preserved.

out-of-body experience (OBE)   The paranormal experience or feeling that one's nonphysical being is separated from the physical body for a period of time. Some people believe that flying dreams are examples of this. Those who have had near-death experiences relate OBEs as an integral aspect of the experience.

paranormal dreams   Products of extrasensory perception (ESP). They are psychic dreams, a class of dreams including precognitive (dreams that correctly depict a future event), telepathic (dreams in which one dream image is sent to and experienced by a dreamer), and clairvoyant (dreams in which the dreamer correctly obtains information about the description or location of an object).

parasomnia   Episodic physiological occurrences during sleep. They include night terrors, bruxism, sleeptalking, and sleepwalking.

perimenopause   Term commonly used to denote the span of time before the cessation of menstruation, marked by shifting hormonal levels. Other symptoms that may emerge are difficulty sleeping, hot flashes, erratic menstrual bleeding and cycle, night sweats, and changes in mood and/or appetite.

Perls, Frederick "Fritz" Twentieth-century psychologist who developed the Gestalt approach to therapy and dream interpretation, which relates parts to the wholeness. Perls believed dreams represented disowned parts of the self, and understanding dreams could restore those parts to conscious awareness.

phoenix A mythological Egyptian bird that after 500 years consumed itself by fire and rose, renewed, from its ashes.

phoneme A linguistic term referring to the smallest units of sound.

pineal gland Located deep inside the brain, thought to participate in the regulation of the internal human body clock, secreting more melatonin in darkness and less as light increases.

posttraumatic stress disorder A psychiatric condition triggered by an overwhelming, out-of-the-ordinary event or stress. Common symptoms include nightmares, uncontrollable flashbacks, fight-or-flight response, and irritability. This condition very often impairs daily life.

prodromal dreams May occur when the dreaming mind becomes aware of physiological and biochemical changes and represents them in dreams. This is an area of study that is controversial in the scientific community.

puns The humorous usage of words and images to suggest associated meanings or applications of words having similar sounds but different definitions.

rapid eye movement (REM) In the 1950s, scientists proved that the stage of sleep in which our eyes move rapidly back and forth is when the bulk of our dreaming occurs. Scientists refer to REM sleep as "paradoxical sleep" because the nerve center during this busy phase holds the body in near paralysis.

REM-Sleep Behavior Disorder (RBD) A sleep disorder in which the paralysis mechanisms that prevent the body from acting out the events and actions of dreams fail, allowing the person to physically enact his or her dreams. People with RBD typically thrash around in bed, and often get out of bed and walk through the actions of their dreams. This can be dangerous for the dreamer, who might get hurt, and for the significant other with whom the dreamer shares a bed.

repetition compulsion The act of repeating past behaviors, in particular ones that aren't healthy, as defined by Freud. It's our mind's flawed but best-guess way of trying to go back and replay events, hoping to reduce anxiety and bring about a better outcome.

representational intelligence Refers to the developmental ability to recall conscious events—to symbolize them—when those same events aren't present in the child's environment.

restless leg syndrome (RLS) An uncomfortable, pins-and-needles sensation in the legs resulting in a strong desire to move the limbs. Often these sensations occur just as you're falling asleep. This condition is frequently seen in pregnant women (as well as patients with kidney failure or rheumatoid arthritis). It's aggravated by caffeine, being overly tired, or exposure to extreme cold or warmth.

sandwich years   A generational term describing the double burden—emotional and financial—of caring for aging parents and growing children at the same time.

separation anxiety   Refers to the stress a child feels when not in the presence of his parent. Very young children lack the ability to understand that they will be reunited with their parent, so they can feel that the parent has gone away forever. Separation anxiety abates as the child develops the ability to "keep his parent in mind," but even as adults we can experience this feeling.

signal dream   A dream that tells us that something important is happening within ourself or our life. This type of dream usually occurs when we need validation of a new direction.

sleep satchet   A small pouch filled with herbs that encourage restful sleep and pleasant dreams when placed under the pillow.

slip of the tongue   A common expression referring to our unconscious partial inability to repress an anxiety-producing thought.

time-limited groups   Usually contain four to eight members and focus on support or psychotherapy issues. Unlike ongoing groups, time-limited groups have a preset end date that everyone agrees upon before the group gets underway.

walkabout   The journey upon which aboriginal people embark, retracing familial ancestral paths and following songlines, the trail of words and music scattered along with the ancestor's footprints. By traveling in these dreaming tracks, singing the same notes from long ago, the creation of the planet and all living things is re-created. The modern walkabout involves using trains or the family truck, but sacred ceremonies that no outsider is allowed to see are still practiced.

Suggested Reading

Allende, Isabel. *Paula*. New York: HarperCollins, 1994.

Alvarez, A. *Night*. New York: W.W. Norton & Company, 1995.

American Psychiatric Association. *Diagnostic and Statistical Manual of Mental Disorders, Fourth Edition*. Washington, D.C.: American Psychiatric Association, 1994.

Ancoli-Israel, Sonia. *All I Want Is a Good Night's Sleep*. St. Louis: Mosby-Year Book, Inc., 1996.

Anderson, Rosemarie. *Celtic Oracles*. New York: Harmony Books, 1998.

Arden, Harvey. *Dreamkeepers: A Spirit Journey into Aboriginal Australia*. New York: HarperCollins, 1994.

Armstrong, Karen. *A History of God*. New York: Alfred A. Knopf, 1993.

Aveni, Anthony. *Behind the Crystal Ball*. New York: Times Books, 1996.

Begley, Sharon. "How to Build a Baby's Brain." *Newsweek*. Spring/Summer 1997, pp. 28–32.

Berman, Dennis. "Late-Blooming Scholars." *Businessweek*. 20 July 1998, p. 106.

Bierhorst, John., editor. *Myths and Tales of the American Indian*. New York: Indian Head Books, 1992.

Born, Margot. *Seven Ways to Look at a Dream*. Washington, D.C.: Starrhill Press, 1991.

Bosnak, Robert. *Tracks in the Wilderness of Dreaming*. New York: Delacorte Press, 1996.

Brennan, Richard P. *Dictionary of Scientific Literacy*. New York: John Wiley and Sons, Inc., 1992.

Buhlman, William. *Adventures Beyond the Body*. New York: HarperCollins, 1996.

Cameron, Julia. *The Vein of Gold*. New York: A Jeremy P. Tarcher/Putnam Book, 1996.

Cameron, Julia, with Mark Bryan. *The Artist's Way*. New York: A Jeremy P. Tarcher/Putnam Book, 1992.

Cameron, Norman, and Joseph F. Rychlak. *Personality Development and Psychopathology: A Dynamic Approach, Second Edition*. Boston: Houghton Mifflin Company, 1985.

Campbell, Joseph, with Bill Moyers. *The Power of Myth*. New York: Doubleday, 1988.

Carroll, Lewis. *Alice's Adventures in Wonderland and Through the Looking Glass*. John Tenniel, editor. New York: William Morrow, 1993.

Carskadon, Mary A., editor. *Encyclopedia of Sleep and Dreaming*. New York: Simon & Schuster Macmillan, 1995.

Chopra, Deepak, M.D. *Restful Sleep: The Complete Mind/Body Program for Overcoming Insomnia*. New York: Three Rivers Press, 1994.

Coleridge, Samuel Taylor. *Poems by Coleridge*. New York: Alfred A. Knopf, 1997.

Cowley, Geoffrey. "The Language Explosion." *Newsweek*. Spring/Summer 1997, pp. 16–22.

Crisp, Tony. *Dream Dictionary: An A to Z Guide to Understanding Your Unconscious Mind*. New York: Wings Books, 1990.

Dee, Nerys. *The Dreamer's Workbook: A Complete Guide to Interpreting and Understanding Dreams*. New York: Sterling Publishing Co. Inc., 1990.

Delaney, Gayle. *All About Dreams*. New York: HarperCollins, 1998.

———. *In Your Dreams*. New York: HarperCollins, 1997.

———. *Living Your Dreams*. New York: HarperCollins, 1996.

D'Millio, John, and Estelle B. Freeman. *Intimate Matters: A History of Sexuality in America*. New York: Harper & Row, 1988.

Epel, Naomi. *Writer's Dreaming*. New York: Carol Southern Books, 1993.

Erikson, Erik H. *Identity and the Life Cycle*. New York: W.W. Norton & Company, 1980.

Faraday, Ann. *The Dream Game.* New York: Harper & Row, 1990. First published by AFAR, 1974.

Ferber, Richard, M.D. *Solve Your Child's Sleep Problems.* New York: Fireside, 1986.

Freud, Sigmund. *Introductory Lectures on Psychoanalysis.* Edited by James Strachey. New York: W.W. Norton & Company, 1966.

Gill, Sam D. *Native American Traditions.* Belmont: Wadsworth, 1983.

Goldstein, Eda G. *Ego Psychology and Social Work Practice.* New York: The Free Press, 1984.

Goodison, Lucy. *The Dreams of Women: Exploring and Interpreting Women's Dreams.* New York: Berkley Books, 1997.

Gordon, David. "Preventing a Hard Day's Night." *Newsweek.* Spring/Summer 1997, pp. 56–57.

Harary, Keith, Ph.D. and Pamela Weintraub. *Lucid Dreams in 30 Days: The Creative Sleep Program.* New York: St. Martin's Griffin, 1999.

Inlander, Charles B., and Cynthia K. Moran. *67 Ways to Good Sleep.* New York: Ballantine, 1995.

Jung, Carl G. *Memories, Dreams, Reflections.* Recorded and edited by Aniela Jaffe. New York: Vintage Books, 1990.

Kamm, Jane A. "Grief and Therapy: Two Processes in Interaction." *Psychotherapy and the Grieving Patient.* Edited by E. Mark Stern. New York: Harrington Park Press, 1985.

Kübler-Ross, Elisabeth. *On Death and Dying.* New York: Macmillan, 1969.

LaBerge, Stephen. *Lucid Dreaming: The Power of Being Awake in Your Dreams.* New York: Ballantine Books, 1985.

LaBerge, Stephen, and Howard Rheingold. *Exploring the World of Lucid Dreaming.* New York: Ballantine Books, 1990.

Lansky, Vicki. "Bedtime Routines." *ParenTalk Newsletter, The Parenting Resource Center on the Web.* Last modified Oct. 24, 1995.

Lerner, Gerda. *The Creation of Feminist Consciousness.* New York: Oxford University Press, 1993.

Lewis, James R. *The Dream Encyclopedia.* Detroit: Visible Ink Press, 1995.

Linn, Denise. *The Hidden Power of Dreams.* New York: Ballantine, 1988.

Lundstrum, Meg, and Amy Barrett. "First Steps to a Second Career." *Businessweek.* 20 July, 1998, p. 108.

McNamee, Mike. "The Glory Days Aren't Over Yet." *Businessweek.* 20 July 1998, p. 104.

———. "Where Silver-Haired Surfers Browse." *Businessweek.* 20 July 1998, pp. 94–95.

Mellick, Jill. *The Natural Artistry of Dreams.* Berkeley: Conari Press, 1996.

Michaels, Stase. *The Bedside Guide to Dreams.* New York: Fawcett Crest, 1995.

Miller, Gustavus Hindman. *10,000 Dreams Interpreted.* New York: Rand McNally & Company, 28th printing, 1997.

Moody, Raymond, with Paul Perry. *Reunions: Visionary Encounters with Departed Loved Ones.* New York: Times Books, 1996.

Mosby's Medical, Nursing & Allied Health Dictionary, Fourth Edition. St. Louis: Mosby-Year Book, Inc., 1994.

Moyers, Bill. *The Language of Life: A Festival of Poets.* New York: Doubleday, 1995.

Murdock, Maureen. *The Heroine's Journey: Women's Quest for Wholeness.* Boston: Shambala Publications, 1990.

Natterson, Joseph M., editor. *The Dream in Clinical Practice.* New York: Jason Aronson, 1980.

Parker, Julia and Derek. *The Secret World of Your Dreams.* New York: Perigee Books, 1990.

Phillips, Will. *Every Dreamer's Handbook: A Step-by-Step Guide to Understanding and Benefiting from Your Dreams.* New York: Kensington Publishing Corp., 1994.

"Poet Essayist Paz Dies: Had a Huge Influence on Mexican Literature." *The Arizona Daily Star* (Tucson). 21 April 1998, p. 6, section A.

Policoff, Stephen Phillip. *The Dreamer's Companion: A Young Person's Guide to Understanding Dreams and Using Them Creatively.* Chicago: Chicago Review Press, 1997.

Powell, Arthur Edward. *The Astral Body and Other Astral Phenomena.* Wheaton, IL: The Theosophical Publishing House, 1987.

Prospero's Library. *The Book of Dream Symbols.* London: Duncan Baird Publishers, 1994.

Rhine, Joseph Banks, Ph.D. *Extrasensory Perception (1934).* Kila, MT: Kessinger Publishing, 2003.

Rycroft, Charles. *The Innocence of Dreams.* Northvale: Jason Aronson, 1996. First published 1979.

Sacks, Oliver. *Awakenings.* New York: HarperPerennial, 1990.

Sarton, May. *From May Sarton's Well: Writings of May Sarton*. Selection and photographs by Edith Royce Schade. Watsonville, CA: Papier-Mâché Press, 1994.

Sheehy, Gail. *Passages: Predictable Crises of Adult Life*. New York: Bantam Books, 1977.

————. *The Silent Passage*. Revised and updated. New York: Pocket Books, 1995.

Slouka, Mark. "Hitler's Couch: When history makes an unexpected entrance." *Harper's Magazine*. April 1998, pp. 51–57.

Siegel, Alan B., Ph.D. *Dreams That Can Change Your Life*. New York: Berkeley, 1996.

Styron, William. *Darkness Visible*. New York: Vintage Books, 1990.

Taylor, Jeremy. *Where People Fly and Water Runs Uphill*. New York: Warner Books, Inc., 1992.

Thorpy, Michael J., M.D., and Jan Yager, Ph.D. *The Encyclopedia of Sleep and Sleep Disorders, Second Edition*. New York: Facts On File, Inc., 2001.

Tonay, Veronica. *The Creative Dreamer: Using Your Dreams to Unlock Your Creativity*. Berkeley: Celestial Arts, 1995.

————. *The Creative Dreamer's Journal and Workbook*. Berkeley: Celestial Arts, 1997.

The Treasury of American Poetry: A Collection of the Best Loved Poems by American Poets. Edited by Nancy Sullivan. New York: Barnes & Noble, 1978.

Ullman, Montague, M.D., and Stanley Krippler, Ph.D., with Alan Vaughan. *Dream Telepathy*. Charlottesville, VA: Hampton Roads Publishing Company, 2003.

Van de Castle, Robert L., Ph.D. *Our Dreaming Mind*. New York: Ballantine Books, 1994.

Viorst, Judith. *Necessary Losses: The Loves, Illusions, Dependencies and Impossible Expectations That All of Us Have to Give Up in Order to Grow*. New York: Simon & Schuster, 1986.

Wadeson, Harriet. *Art Psychotherapy*. New York: John Wiley and Sons, Inc., 1980.

Walker, Barbara G. *The Woman's Dictionary of Symbols and Sacred Objects*. San Francisco: Harper & Row, 1988.

Webster's II New Riverside Dictionary. Boston: The Riverside Publishing Company, 1988.

Winnicott, D. W. *Psychoanalytic Explorations*. Cambridge: Harvard University Press, 1989.

Index

T